Searching for Spirituality in Higher Education

PETER LANG
New York • Washington, D.C./Baltimore • Bern
Frankfurt am Main • Berlin • Brussels • Vienna • Oxford

Searching for Spirituality in Higher Education

Edited by
Bruce W. Speck & Sherry L. Hoppe

PETER LANG
New York • Washington, D.C./Baltimore • Bern
Frankfurt am Main • Berlin • Brussels • Vienna • Oxford

Library of Congress Cataloging-in-Publication Data

Searching for spirituality in higher education /
edited by Bruce W. Speck, Sherry L. Hoppe.
p. cm.
Includes bibliographical references and index.
1. Universities and colleges—Religion. 2. Spirituality—
Study and teaching (Higher).
I. Speck, Bruce W. II. Hoppe, Sherry L. (Sherry Lee).
LC383.S42   378'.01—dc22   2006101467
ISBN 978-0-8204-8159-3

Bibliographic information published by **Die Deutsche Bibliothek**.
Die Deutsche Bibliothek lists this publication in the "Deutsche
Nationalbibliografie"; detailed bibliographic data is available
on the Internet at http://dnb.ddb.de/.

Cover design by Lisa Barfield

The paper in this book meets the guidelines for permanence and durability
of the Committee on Production Guidelines for Book Longevity
of the Council of Library Resources.

© 2007 Peter Lang Publishing, Inc., New York
29 Broadway, 18th floor, New York, NY 10006
www.peterlang.com

All rights reserved.
Reprint or reproduction, even partially, in all forms such as microfilm,
xerography, microfiche, microcard, and offset strictly prohibited.

Printed in the United States of America

CONTENTS

Introduction   ix

Part One: Theory   1

1. *Spirituality in Higher Education: A Literature Review*   3
   Bruce W. Speck

2. *The Relationship between Religion and Spirituality*   35
   Christina Murphy

3. *Spirituality and Higher Education Law*   53
   John Wesley Lowery

4. *Biological Basis of Spirituality*   69
   Dixie Dennis

5. *Spirituality, the Professorate, and the Curriculum*   85
   Al DeCiccio

6. *Spirituality and Student Development*   97
   Deborah M. Cady

7. *Spirituality and Higher Education Leadership*   111
   Sherry L. Hoppe

8. *Moral Conversation: A Theoretical Framework for Talking about Spirituality on College Campuses*   137
   Robert J. Nash and DeMethra LaSha Bradley

Part Two: Practice in the Disciplines   155

9. *Art, Spirituality, and Teaching*   157
   Laurel Campbell

10. *When Religious Beliefs Conflict with Assigned Readings in Literature*   167
William Jenkins

11. *Spirituality and the Discipline of History*   175
Rick Ostrander

12. *Recognizing Plurality, Promoting Civility: Religious Pluralism in the Political Science Classroom*   183
Paul Brink

13. *Integrating Psychology and Christianity*   191
Bryce E. Fox

14. *Science and Spirituality*   201
David K. Scott

15. *Religion and Spirituality in the Practice of Health Care*   213
Allen Pelletier

16. *The Strident Duet*   221
Moses L. Pava

17. *Integrating Spirituality in Education Courses*   227
Larry D. Burton and Constance C. Nwosu

Part Three: Practice in Student Affairs   237

18. *Campus Ministries*   239
Keith Garner

19. *Practice in Student Affairs: Counseling*   249
Elliott Ingersoll and Karsten Siebert

20. *Spirituality and Leadership Development in Student Affairs*   259
Diane Berty

21. *Fostering Student Spiritual Development through Selected Student Affairs Practices* 267
    David M. Eberhardt and Jon C. Dalton

Part Four: Directions for Future Research   277

22. *Spirituality in Higher Education: Directions for Future Research* 279
    Bruce W. Speck and Sherry L. Hoppe

Contributors   289

Index   295

INTRODUCTION

Bruce W. Speck
Sherry L. Hoppe

In 2003, we approached an editor about an idea we had for editing a collection of essays on spirituality in higher education. We had begun to see more and more literature on spirituality in higher education, and we thought it would be a topic that would attract attention. The editor's response to our proposal serves to represent a dominant view of our topic. He advised us to seek out a publisher of theological works, an appropriate venue for our topic in his professional judgment. Frankly, we were a bit startled by his response. We could demonstrate that literature on our topic was being published in academic journals and books that were not tethered to specific venues devoted to theology. We didn't argue, but we did persevere, and found in Marilla Svinicki an editor who was warm to our project. The fruit of our collaboration with Marilla was *Spirituality in Higher Education* (2005), a volume in New Directions for Teaching and Learning published by Jossey-Bass.

The publication of that volume did not satiate our appetite concerning our topic, and we began to envision another volume that would take a much more comprehensive view of spirituality in higher education. We knew that Peter Lang had already published volumes on spirituality in higher education, so when we approached Lang, we were delighted to find yet another editor, Heidi Burns, who did not relegate spirituality to theological journals and books.

We use the term *relegate* because the sad fact is that within the academy, some consider spirituality to be outside the domain of academic scholarship, except when that scholarship can be tethered to theological education of some sort. We think such a position is based on perceptions about spirituality and higher education that are difficult to defend, especially considering the number of authors in this volume who attempt to make clear distinctions between spirituality and religion. Nevertheless, we acknowledge how firmly such a view is entrenched in the academy, as witnessed by an article in *The Chronicle of Higher Education* ominously entitled "Reason, Unfettered by Faith." The author of that article states, "…reason must be unfettered by faith if we are to truly educate our children and our students, and if we as a society are to overcome violence committed in the name of religion" (Krauss 2007, B20).

The assumptions behind such an assertion are both enormous and insidious, especially linking faith to violence, as though "reasonable" people, i.e., people who assiduously avoid the corrosive influence of religious faith, never commit violence. Indeed, to unfetter reason from faith, an undertaking with highly dubious validity that various distinguished scientists in the past would have thought impossible, is to unleash the Gulag, the "scientific" medical tests conducted at Tuskegee and Auschwitz, and other social "experiments" that equal the horrors created by people claiming that religious faith motivates them to kill, maim, rape, and plunder. But Krauss is undeterred in his narrow perception of reason, particularly as it relates to higher education. He boldly affirms, "To equate reason with faith at an institution that defines itself in terms of the former rather than the latter does a disservice to its goals" (B20). Krauss's position might be easier to dissect if his definition of faith was clear, but a reader is left to speculate whether Krauss is referring to spirituality or religion or some combination of the two. Unfortunately, even if one assumes religion is his target, Krauss lumps all religions into his negative harangue.

Justifiably, responses to the Krauss diatribe were severe. For example, McGaughey (2007) criticizes Krauss's understanding of reason and faith as "pre-Copernican" (B17), a cutting accusation given that Krauss is a professor of physics and astronomy. Gruenwald (2007), making the assumption that Krauss is narrowly focusing "faith" on religion, echoes that accusation when he says, "Oddly, Krauss melds a 19th-century, positivist, reductionist conception of science with a 20th-century disdain for religious faith....However, the basic flaw in Krauss's argument is the assumption that reason and science are always rational, whereas faith and religion are always irrational. This is simply not so....Reason, uninformed by morality and faith, can be just as irrational as religious faith unaided by reason" (B17). Donohue (2007) agrees, noting, "...when reason is pursued and faith ignored, the consequences are disastrous. Millions of people were killed in the last century alone by totalitarian despots who hated religion" (B17). In addition, Groothuis (2007) faults Krauss for failing to interact with arguments that pose serious questions to his assertions. "Instead," Groothuis notes, "he simply claims that religious beliefs must emanate from bad sources. Now who is being unreasonable?" (B17).

We suspect Krauss would counter that anything not measuring up to his notion of rationality wouldn't be worth the effort of response, yet another indication of a closed system of thought that clearly borders on narrow mindedness masquerading as intellectual high ground. Our suspicion about Krauss's response gains credence when the only affirmative response to Krauss's article bluntly states, "Belief carries no weight in science....Religion is good for keeping humanity in line ('the opium of the masses')" (Friedberg 2007, B17). The author of that remarkable piece of reasoned discourse, also a scientist, does criticize Krauss, but his criticism is that Krauss didn't go far enough; Krauss should have insisted that "Reason fettered by faith is not reason" (B17). Mock (2007), however, does not take kindly to Krauss's thinking, saying, "I was surprised to learn that reason was the goal of the university. I had thought the goal was truth.... If reason is all the university is about, surely creative, empathetic, or intuitional disciplines like the arts and literature are distractions and should be marginalized" (B17–B18). One of the rather startling implications of Krauss's argument, the lone goal of elevating reason to the pinnacle of mission statements, would be cutting art, music, literature, and a variety of other disciplines from higher education.

To be fair to Krauss, we acknowledge that he does tip his hat every so slightly to religion but clearly does not see that religion, or perhaps even spirituality, has much use in the university as an academic subject that can advance the project reason is pursuing. It appears to us that some academics—among them a number of scientists—have such an animus toward religion that they find it difficult to even engage in civil discourse about religion. Krauss's discourse, for example, is a thinly viewed attempt to throw a bone to the pathetic old dog praying in the doghouse while totally ignoring the broader view of spirituality, choosing instead to amalgamate all faiths with the stroke of his black pen. We do not know what the editor who rejected our idea about a book on spirituality believed about spirituality, but he, too, did not see spirituality as a topic that was of interest to mainstream academics. He may have been spot on if he had folks like Krauss in mind. One spirit abroad concerning religion or spirituality in the academy has no stomach for *any* academic discourse on things spiritual, unless that discourse is relegated to theological journals, books, blogs, and other forums explicitly designated as limited to things religious or spiritual. Such relegation, of course, is dismissive.

But religion and spirituality aren't easily dismissed. A steady flow of academic works, including studies about spirituality in the academy (Astin and Astin 1999), continue to surface, even supported by respectable sponsors, such as the Lilly Foundation. In fact, Langdon (2007) reviews *Train Your Mind, Change Your Brain*, published in 2007, noting, "The book challenges the scientific belief that our physical brain controls our mental health, not vice versa" (36). Langdon cites the Center for Spirituality and Mind at the University of Pennsylvania, formed in 2006 "to combine the brainpower of neurologists, psychologists, anthropologists, and other scholars who want to investigate the connection between belief and the brain" (36). For the Center, meditation is a legitimate subject of study regarding brain activity. Candidly, though, what the

Center is investigating is only new in the sense that the academic disciplines engaged in the interdisciplinary quest for answers to questions about the relationship between belief and how people function is a new alliance of scholars. A broad view of history would find laughable the premise that an educated person can live only on the bread of philosophical materialism.

Our point, however, is not that spirituality or religion is good. Historically, religion has been both an ally of social good and an enemy of human progress, while spirituality has been more consistently and positively focused on the search for meaning. Our point is that religion has been such a staple of human existence that to attempt to eliminate it from the academy in any meaningful way is to commit intellectual lobotomy. Likewise, the quest for truth has been and continues to be one of the hallmarks of liberal education. To make religion—and even the broader notion of spirituality—the foil for reason is intellectually dishonest, as though we can deify reason on the altar of our meager knowledge. Moreover, the more expansive nature of spirituality, part of man's perpetual search for "being," seeks rather than defies reason.

Nothing we've said, however, makes the study of religion or spirituality easy. As this volume attests, issues related to spirituality are complex, and, undoubtedly to the smug delight of the rationalists, messy. Even after thoroughly reading this volume, which seriously attempts to address a variety of issues, one could legitimately ask, "So what exactly is spirituality?" The answer to that query depends on who's defining the term, which is not particularly reassuring to academics seeking some sense of stability in their understanding of the universe. Unfortunately, a mantra in the literature on spirituality in higher education—reinforced by the most of the chapters in this volume—is that spirituality is not religion, but surely, such a position is fraught with difficulties that may be insuperable, allowing the possibility of a narcissism that challenges any authority other than its own, thus unwittingly permitting anarchy.

Our claim, then, in recommending this volume to interested readers is modest. We have sought to provide informed perspectives on the theory and praxis of spirituality in higher education. Those perspectives, however, are not unified by one theory of spirituality or by common practice. As editors, we did not impose definitional restrictions on how authors would approach their topics. Instead, this volume seeks to provide multiple perspectives on issues that we think are germane to serious dialogue about spirituality in higher education. Those perspectives emanate from both theory and real-life applications. This volume in no way pretends to be the definitive work on our topic, and, in fact, we hope academics will respond to the ideas in this work by producing other scholarship to shed more light on the topics addressed here.

As editors, we have many debts to acknowledge regarding the production of *Searching for Spirituality in Higher Education*. Clearly, we are indebted to the authors who wrote chapters for this book. We thank them for working with us and allowing us to work with them to produce what we believe is a useful work of scholarship in toto. All of us who have written chapters for this volume are indebted to the thinking of others, particularly those we cited throughout in our References. We stand on the shoulders of those who have had the perspicuity to allocate that precious resource of time to inform us about spirituality. As editors, we give obeisance to Carol Clark, Executive Assistant to the President at Austin Peay State University. Carol wrote the textbook on the organization of virtually any task, and her assistance has been invaluable at every stage of the preparation of the manuscript for publication. We are particularly grateful to our spouses, Carmen Speck and Bob Hoppe, for nurturing us intellectually, emotionally, and spiritually during our long lives together. For their unfailing support of our labors not only on this volume but day in and day out, we gratefully acknowledge soul mates who continue to show us what genuine human kindness looks like.

References

Astin, A. W., and H. S. Astin. 1999. *Meaning and spirituality in the lives of college faculty: A study of values, authenticity, and stress*. Los Angeles: Higher Education Research Institute.

Donohue, W. A. 2007. Opinion letter in response to Faith or reason: Odd couple or natural allies? *Chronicle of Higher Education* 53(24): B17.

Hoppe, S. L., and B. W. Speck, eds. 2005. *Spirituality in higher education*. New Directions for Teaching and Learning, no. 104. San Francisco: Jossey-Bass.

Friedberg, F. 2007. Opinion letter in response to Faith or reason: Odd couple or natural allies? *Chronicle of Higher Education* 53(24): B17.

Groothuis, D. 2007. Opinion letter in response to Faith or reason: Odd couple or natural allies? *Chronicle of Higher Education* 53(24): B17.

Gruenwald, O. 2007. Opinion letter in response to Faith or reason: Odd couple or natural allies? *Chronicle of Higher Education* 53(24): B17.

Krauss, L. M. 2007. Reason, unfettered by faith. *Chronicle of Higher Education* 53(19): B20.

Langdon, L. 2007. Mind control. *World* 22(5): 36.

McGaughey, D. 2007. Opinion letter in response to Faith or reason: Odd couple or natural allies? *Chronicle of Higher Education* 53(24): B17.

Mock, R. 2007. Opinion letter in response to Faith or reason: Odd couple or natural allies? *Chronicle of Higher Education* 53(24): B17–B18.

PART ONE

Theory

CHAPTER 1

Spirituality in Higher Education: A Literature Review

Bruce W. Speck

Spirituality is not a new topic for investigation in the academy. When Plato taught in the Groves of Academe, he raised questions about what constitutes ultimate reality (philosophically called ontology/metaphysics, the study of being). So profound has Plato's influence been that Alfred North Whitehead (1979, 39) noted, "All Western thought is but a footnote to Plato." Whether Whitehead has overstated the case can be argued, but that he has made an insightful observation concerning the breadth and depth of thinking in which Plato engaged across a wide spectrum of philosophical issues is indisputable, including seminal ideas related to "spirituality." When viewed as an ontological/metaphysical concern, spirituality is a very old topic that academicians have been discussing for a very long time.

So why is spirituality seen as a "new" concern in the academy, an emerging field of inquiry? Why is it that in the last twenty or so years a spate of literature about spirituality in the academy has been increasingly produced? To answer those questions, I have consulted the literature on spirituality in higher education (predominantly in the United States), and my purpose in this chapter is to cite that literature to explain why spirituality has become a renewed topic of interest to academicians. Based on the literature, I have divided my task into four parts. First, I discuss the current production of literature on spirituality as a counter-movement against a way of thinking about what constitutes ultimate reality or being, generally referred to as a positivist epistemology. Second, I explain that the literature on spirituality is a reflection of the concerns of the larger societal order in the United States. Third, I show that the literature on spirituality in those academic fields that prepare students for a profession is dominated by a focus on practical issues. Fourth, in conclusion, I discuss three criticisms of spirituality that I believe need to be addressed if spirituality is to appeal to a wider academic audience.

Spirituality as a Counter-Movement

To trace the arguments from Plato to the present regarding the shifting sands of metaphysical insights that have influenced the current renewed interest in spirituality in the academy is outside the purview of this chapter. However, Bradshaw (1994) provides a succinct summary of major philosophical shifts that have shaped discussions about being, and a standard work that reviews the history of philosophical thought is Copleston's multivolume classic (1977). Most of the writers about religion and spirituality in the academy, however, trace the current academic renascence in interest about religion and spirituality to a shift in thinking during the Enlightenment that began to minimize and discredit religion and anything pertaining to a supernatural realm. Current academic attempts to reestablish the viability of religion and spirituality are essentially a counter-movement to the Enlightenment program that has become the reigning paradigm in much of the academy. So what happened in the Enlightenment that caused a shift in the time-honored study of religion as a genuine academic field of inquiry?

The Enlightenment program aimed to limit knowledge to what could be ascertained via the scientific method. This approach to epistemology is variously referred to as empiricism, positivism, naturalism, or objectivism. Purportedly, such an approach is objective in that it relies on reason and eliminates subjectivity, focusing on what can be measured quantifiably in the natural or seen world. In referring to such an epistemology, Fahlberg and Fahlberg (1991) speak "of an overriding emphasis on the sensate realm—the turf of the five senses..." (273) that either minimizes anything that cannot be apprehended by the senses and studied scientifically or discards it altogether. As Rocheleau (2004) notes, "Values, holds positivism, cannot be reflected upon rationally but are arbitrary matters of subjective or cultural choice. Genuine knowledge, then, must involve empirically or logically testable theories characteristic of science and math. Students can study—in humanities and social sciences—what people have held to be valuable, but educators and students have no defensible basis for making judgments of value" (10).

Because the positivist approach limited what counted as real knowledge, the problem of accounting for whatever passed for metaphysical knowledge could be handled in one of two ways. First, anything that could not be measured via the scientific process could be private, unverifiable knowledge, such as the values Rocheleau cites. A person could believe in a supernatural realm, but that had nothing to do with real knowledge gained through scientific investigation. Thus, what one knows can be divided into the public and personal realms, resulting in objective and subjective "truths," creating a secular-sacred dichotomy. Scientists can believe in God, for instance, but that belief (which does not count as "real" scientific knowledge) should have no influence on their work in the laboratory. Second, a positivist could claim that the first possibility is impossible. Sagan, for example, takes the position that the cosmos, the natural world, is all that exists (1980). If the natural world is all that exists, period, then any belief in anything existing outside the natural world is a fool's approach to epistemology. The first approach is an attempt to leave some (albeit small and cramped) space for the supernatural, however it is defined; the second approach dismisses any such compromise as anti-intellectual—and dangerous.

Of course, the Enlightenment ideal did not immediately capture the imagination of all intellectuals, but it raised questions about the viability of religion and the supernatural that many found hard to address intellectually. Scientific evidence, after all, carries a great deal of weight because it claims to provide the unvarnished truth about whatever it investigates. Indeed, scientists, because of their ability to find cures to diseases, explain complex phenomena using sophisticated statistical analysis, and speak authoritatively about a variety of public policy issues, have become respected public intellectuals. In short, those who ply the scientific method certainly seem to produce better living through chemistry, so their method of achieving those results appears to be worthy of veneration. Religion, on the other hand, at least among the intelligentsia, was seen as a destructive force in the world, primarily, they believed, because it was based on superstition, ignorance, and fear, all of which militated against the vigorous objective approach they advocated. Thus, when scientists either dismiss the supernatural as unworthy of scientific investigation or assign it to a realm of personal preference, over time, they set a standard for what is worthy of academic respectability.

Today, the academy is the heir of the Enlightenment belief in the superiority of the scientific method as the tool for creating knowledge. This is especially true in the sciences, even the social sciences, because the prestige associated with scientific advances is widely revered not only by the very people who have achieved prestige through their scientific achievements but also by those who benefit from the fruits of scientific enquiry. (If the hunger for external funding to support scientific research is any indication of the driving force science has become in the economic realities of the modern academy, positivism is alive, well, and thriving.) Indeed, those who have proved the virtue of positivism by their scholarly endeavors (then translated their discoveries into products for the general welfare of society) hold the entry key for those who aspire to achieve permanent membership in the academic club through the door of tenure. That a positivist epistemology has become the reigning paradigm in the academy is not an overstatement, but it is not the whole story either.

Positivism has not gone unchallenged in the academy. In fact, scholars have historically questioned the assumptions of a positivist epistemology, and some scholars are persuaded that those challenges were delivered with cannonade that continues to reverberate. In particular, I will focus on two philosophical movements that stormed the barricades of positivism: pragmatism and postmodernism. A brief review of these two movements helps to further explain the theoretical genesis of current academic discussions about the reemergence of spirituality and why it is a counter-movement to a positivist epistemology.

Pragmatism

The word *pragmatism*, like most words that try to summarize a variety of viewpoints, cannot be construed to refer to a monolithic philosophy. However, as a philosophy, pragmatism, which hinges on the necessity of understanding knowledge as inherently personal, does offer an unfavorable critique of positivism. Unlike the positivists, the pragmatists did not believe that knowledge was something external to the individual that could be studied objectively. In fact, knowledge could not be the product of the seemingly sterile approach positivism required because knowledge is inherently subjective. However, like the positivists, the pragmatists did not necessarily believe in a transcendent realm outside of nature. Thus, the shift from the objective to the subjective entailed a shift in epistemology that allowed for real knowledge not dependent on a supernatural realm.

Frankenberry (1996) provides a helpful summary of what she terms pragmatic naturalism, a worldview that can be associated with the works of C. S. Peirce, William James, John Dewey, George Santayana, George Herbert Mead, and Alfred North Whitehead. "For these thinkers," Frankenberry observes, "despite their significant differences, the critique of supernaturalism was accompanied by a shift of focus to the transcendent qualities of immanent relationships in this world. No longer pointing vertically to infinite, absolute Being, transcendence came to signify the horizontal process of temporal movement toward an open-ended future state" (104). The shift in thinking allows metaphysical terms to become markers for non-transcendent actualities and possibilities. Thus, a person can experience some sense of, say, community here and now, or some sense of freedom, but community and freedom are ideals that can never be completely realized. They can always be improved, and they are not absolute because they depend on creative human thinking to shape them. Because such creativity cannot be adjudicated by any absolute standards—there are none—"perfection" in the social order is always an ideal in the making. As Frankenberry notes, "so too the mode of American spirituality depicted here valued possibility, temporality, and contingency in a universe still 'in the making'" (104). In other words, "Spiritual life in the secular world consists in the progressive integration of ever more complex feelings, thoughts, and habits by which one reacts to an ever larger portion of the world and relates oneself to the whole of reality" (105).

Some have argued that civil religion is a manifestation of the displacement of transcendence to terra firma. Bellah (1967) is the originator of the concept of civil religion, and he says, "civil religion at its best is a genuine apprehension of universal and transcendent religious reality as seen in or, one could almost say, as revealed through the experience of the American people" (12). The inherent ambiguity in Bellah's assessment can be seen when he notes, "This religion—there seems to be no other word for it—while not antithetical to and indeed sharing much in common with Christianity, was neither sectarian nor in any specific sense Christian" (8). In other words, civil religion is somehow grounded in religious ideals, specifically Christian ideals, but is tied to those ideals in such a way that when it calls upon religious language to frame the American experience religious language is identified with the American republic. Or as Lovin (1986) notes, "Religious language is a pervasive feature of our public life, but a canny observer soon notes that it is usually a language of legitimation, not a language of persuasion…religious language enters public speech when the speaker has some confidence that the audience already agrees" (132).

It appears, then, that religious symbols are transferred to the social order while still maintaining some status as religious symbols. Civil religion, as a scholarly topic, has a long and contentious history (Handy 1980; Mathisen 1989; Richey and Jones 1974), but for our purposes, whether Bellah's formulation of civil religion is entirely accurate is not at issue. What is important is his observation that American presidents have consistently appealed to God, not Christ, in their public addresses, and their appeal to God is linked to the purpose of the nation as a moral enterprise. As Miller (1990) asserts, "To a quite unusual degree…the founding of the United States was a moral project, a venture in bringing into being a worthy answer to the ancient problem of living together in an organized society" (30). Indeed, Miller rejects the notion "that insists upon religion as the necessary foundation of America's republican institutions" (35) because Enlightenment ideals, as represented by Thomas Jefferson, had a significant influence on American republicanism. Miller notes,

> …when the modern day heirs of the Enlightenment (if such they be) who occupy many of the seats of power and influence and scholarship and intellectual leadership in twentieth-century America, reject or more often just assume away any serious role of religious belief in the formation of the United States—that needs to be qualified.…Whereas later believers look aback at the founding through the screen of the evangelical revivals and of their own sympathies to find more piety than there was in early America, the cultured among the despisers look back through the screen of their unbelief to find only Thomas Jefferson and Tom Paine and more unabashed secularism than there really was.
>
> The successive waves of American intelligentsia keep expecting religion to have vanished; or they write as though it has already done so, and then are continually surprised that it has not.…They write whole histories of American life and spirit that skimp the religious element in the imagination of the American people; they say, about religious affirmations, "nobody believes that anymore." One is reminded of the statement that Yogi Berra is said to have made about a well-known restaurant: "Nobody goes there anymore. It's too crowded." (36–37)

Miller quite correctly notes that religion is endemic to American life, including American political thought, but he also affirms the Enlightenment perspective that has existed alongside religion in America's history. The coexistence of both a religious impulse and a positivist impulse certainly fits with Bellah's notion of a civil religion that allows for religious language borrowed heavily from the Judeo-Christian tradition that nonetheless transfers the ideals of that tradition to the seen world. One reason for this transference is that, absent a supernatural realm and given the diversity of a world that no longer believes in a positivist epistemology, the polis must represent plural perspectives. Thus, pluralism becomes a primary concern when unity is the longed-for possibility, and unity is a longed-for possibility, which includes the freedom guaranteed by genuine peace, if the political order is to promote human potentiality. Such pluralism is even more critical when spirituality (now dissociated from religion at least in some cases) is taken seriously. Civil religion then becomes the quest for community, and education, as Dewey noted, becomes a primary means for teaching students how to be good citizens, "under God," as the Pledge would have it. But, as Marty (1974) points out, "there has been considerable talk about transcendence which may or may not go on 'under God.' New models are being sought. The Marxians, Sartreans, Marcuseans join spokesmen of Eastern and African religions to speak of transcendence without deity, or at least without seeing deity integral to the process. This is transcendence 'from below,' as it were, what philosopher Ernst Bloch calls 'transcending without transcendence'" (150).

A critical point in understanding spirituality in higher education is to recognize that what the pragmatists have allowed is language such as "transcending without transcendence" so that terms generally associated with metaphysics that have historically pointed to a reality beyond what is seen are permissible when used to point to symbolic realities in the here and now. Thus, civil religion becomes a compromise that seeks to evoke religious imagery in the service of political unity. Even though the religious imagery is unabashedly borrowed from the Judeo-Christian tradition, it is only used in a generic sense so that the Judeo-Christian tradition is not privileged. God becomes a term that can be defined broadly to include personal concepts of God or god. I am not saying that the pragmatists advocated civil religion. To do so would be to impose on them a concept that Bellah articulated. However, the argument can be made that what the pragmatists advocated can be legitimately linked to civil religion because the pragmatists helped lay the groundwork for a spirituality that could be discussed in numinous terms but that referred to the here and now. In addition, any idea of truth as a settled concern was abandoned because the potentiality of spirituality was all that could be advertised in good faith. The goal was to make the world the place it ought to be by teaching students to understand their own spirituality (i.e., potential as community builders) so that they could become good citizens in helping to build the ideal community. I have taken time to discuss the political implications of pragmatism and civil religion because one of the outcomes of a renewed interest in spirituality is a renewed interest in community that can be traced to the growing body of literature about service-learning (Bischetti 2001; Koth 2003; Speck 2001, 2004). Service-learning has various political-social motivations that attempt to address problems related to fractured community (Speck and Hoppe 2004), a concern shared with those who champion spirituality.

Postmodernism

In addition to pragmatists, postmodernists assaulted the barricades of positivism. Postmodernists agreed with many of the fundamental tenets of the pragmatists, and in their own way have helped shape current discussions about spirituality in higher education. (*Postmodernism*, too, should not be treated as a monolithic term, and in what I say about postmodernism, I am using generalization at the expense of specificity.) Yes, the postmodernists agreed with the pragmatists, truth is contingent, so it can change as the search for truth progresses. Yes, any talk about a supernatural realm was useless because the focus should be on a critique of society. And because postmodernism opened the door to widespread skepticism about the viability of any "grand narratives," overarching stories that ultimately explained reality, traditional religion, based on narratives that purport to explain reality, was eyed with skepticism. Clearly, epistemology was not an objective enterprise.

But postmodernists disagree with the pragmatists on a critical point. While the pragmatists put a great deal of stock into community building as the goal of human development, postmodernists took the viewpoint that social structures—prisons, families, churches, governments, social clubs—existed to restrain and limit people so that individuals serve the interests of those in charge of the structures. The abuse of power to create and maintain inherently destructive sociological structures became the centerpiece of "deconstructing" (literally, destroying) any notion that, for example, colonialism in any way could be conceived as "helping" native peoples. Those in power impose their wishes upon the powerless, not only engineering social results but interpreting them to justify a social-political-theological framework that oppresses. For postmodernists, virtually every action, every motivation is suspect, and because of its dedication to the "deconstruction" of every motivation, to demonstrating that oppression was the underlying character of motivations, postmodernism has been seen as a grand form of relativism heavily influenced by nihilism. After all, if every motivation is suspect, why should anyone believe that the postmodernists should not be suspect in their motivations to uncover oppressive power structures? Are postmodernists not merely grabbing power by showing that their view is the one to which we should subscribe? How can they maintain a purity that they say cannot exist when knowledge is indubitably influenced by race, gender, and socio-political influences that ultimately cannot be disentangled from the way we produce knowledge? The postmodern focus on power can be seen in what has been called critical pedagogy. "In critical pedagogy, the focus of education should be on learning about the functioning of power, and the teaching method itself should attempt to unmask and disperse power" (Rocheleau 2004, 16).

The problem of deconstructing the deconstructions of the postmodernists does not go unrecognized, even among them, and they address the problem, in part, by using language that turns in upon itself, so that hyphenated words become double entendres, such as dis-ease. That postmodernists can laugh at themselves (one would think with some despair) does not mean that the general notion of subjectivity the postmodernists espouse is taken to be comic by people who may not even know that postmodernism is an intellectual movement. Like many philosophical movements, postmodernism has spread its tenets through literature, art, and film, thus influencing the public even when the public probably could not articulate postmodern precepts clearly. In the academy, postmodernism's influence has served to open the door for even more subjectivity than the pragmatists allowed, and, hence, for a corrective to a positivist epistemology.

This all-too-brief history of how the academy got from the Enlightenment goal of objectivity in epistemology to the pragmatist and postmodernist goal of subjectivity in epistemology helps to explain why spirituality in the academy today is a counter-movement to a positivist epistemology. Various writers say as much. Chickering (2003), for example, criticizes "unleavened doses of objectivity and empirical rationality" (41) in the academy. In fact, "Our overwhelming valuation of rational empiricism—a conception of the truth as objective and external—and of knowledge as a commodity delegitimizes active public discussions of purpose and meaning, authenticity and identity, or spirituality and spiritual growth" (44). Palmer (2003) agrees, noting that "the bright light of science has been almost exclusively focused on 'objective realities' such as technique, curricula, and cash, rather than on soulful factors such as relational trust" (385). In fact, Palmer (1987) calls objectivism in higher education a "seemingly bloodless epistemology" (22). Elsewhere, Palmer (1997) lays bare his soul when he talks about the relationship of his educational experience with clinical depression. "It was a depression partly due to my schooling, partly due to the way I was formed in the educational systems of this country to live out of the top inch and half of the human self, to live only with cognitive rationality and with the powers of the intellect, out of touch with anything that lay below that top inch and a half: body, intuition, feeling, emotion, relationship" (9). Glazer (1999) agrees when he affirms that a feeling of disconnection "is born in our schools: in the way we are taught to perceive, understand, and interact with the world" (3).

For both Chickering and Palmer and others (Coburn 2005) the academy's debt to Enlightenment epistemology is too onerous to bear, and they are sure that a return to community and all that the word community entails is the appropriate goal for higher education. But community must be couched in paradoxical terms. As Palmer says, "'To have a good conversation about the reform of higher education, we need to break out of the conventional logic of 'either/or' and learn to think and talk in terms of paradox. Just as our epistemology has wanted to make the subjective and the objective into an either/or, our normal discourse treats personal and professional as mutually exclusive. But since life is not so neatly compartmentalized, our discourse is meaningless unless it embraces these complementary opposites'" (Edgerton 1992, 5). Dialectic becomes the means of achieving a holistic view of education, but dialectic does not lead to closure; it maintains a tension while attempting to understand more about the tension so that a new tension can be achieved, hopefully a higher-level tension. As Gummer (2005) notes, "Understanding is a dialogical process of questioning oneself and the other that is guided by the (endless) search for truth" (47). The goal is not truth with a capital T. The goal is greater awareness and understanding. Truth with a capital T was the goal of the Enlightenment program, but such a goal, according to pragmatists and postmodernists is unattainable.

Chickering and Palmer are not alone in their sharp criticism of an academy that has forsaken ways of knowing that are not grounded in a positivist epistemology. Other scholars complain about the barricades that still exist in the academy as an ominous warning not to transgress the secular-sacred dichotomy (Bennett 1998, 2003). The voices of such scholars are swelling, and although positivism is alive and quite well in the academy, spirituality, as a field of study emerging from the shadow of an epistemology that disavowed anything that smacked of the supernatural, has become a counter-movement, and as I now hope to show, a counter-movement that reflects the larger societal order in the United States.

Spirituality as a Reflection of American Society

The view that dismisses spirituality/religion as topics outside the purview of legitimate academic inquiry is, at best, parochial, given the wider world beyond the halls of ivy. As Nash (1999) notes, "even though the existence of God cannot be scientifically or logically demonstrated, millions of people still choose to live their lives as though it can be, and life is often made better for them, and others, as a result" (2). In fact, contrary to the academic stereotype that insists anyone who believes in God and subscribes to religious tenets is a ninny, historically, many noted intellectuals have identified themselves as "believers." The self-assurance of those who dismiss the rich history of the world that is woof and warp with the history of religion certainly smacks of an anti-intellectual posture. However, if history begins with the Enlightenment, little wonder that whatever transpired before the dawn of intellectual history in the Age of Reason is of little moment. Indeed, what is of moment can be interpreted as valuable only in that it heralds the dawn of Reason. But such a view is woefully inadequate. Again, Nash (1999) goes to the crux of the matter in saying, "Religion is such a fundamental part of human existence that students simply cannot understand the history or politics of most societies, including the United States, without a serious examination of religion's central role in producing both good and evil throughout the world during the last several millennia" (4). The positivist epistemology, in dismissing religion or any form of supernaturalism from the stage of intellectual inquiry, jettisoned something that most people believe to have substance.

The importance of spirituality/religion to the masses is particularly obvious in the United States. As various authors have pointed out, by all accounts, Americans are self-proclaimed religionists (Nord 1995; Nash 1999; Fox 2004), and the overwhelming percentage of Americans polled profess to believe in God, an afterlife, and, even that Jesus is God. As Cimino and Lattin (1998) note, "Americans believe in God. Around 95 percent of us, the pollsters say, believe in God or a universal life spirit. Those numbers have changed very little over the past fifty years" (1).

The grip of positivism on the academy is particularly surprising because higher education in America, as American institutions in general, has historically been deeply influenced by Judeo-Christian religion. Institutions such as Harvard, Yale, Princeton, and Duke, now considered leaders in a broadly liberal approach to life that has little room for the traditional Judeo-Christian tenets of truth, were founded with the express intention of promulgating the Christian faith in large part by preparing ministers to serve congregations of believers (Marsden 1992b, 1994). It would be incorrect to assume that the founding principles animating the development of many American colleges and universities were uniformly held by all who participated in the endeavors to create a Christian higher education. Marsden's assertion, "Even at its most religious the United States has in many ways been a very secular place" (2000, 10), is in accord with the historical fact that in America, Protestant theology (generally indebted to a Reformed tradition) coexisted with Enlightenment thought. Marsden's well-documented claim is not surprising when one considers that the Judeo-Christian faith comes in a large variety of packages, some of which make clear distinctions between the sacred and secular (Niebuhr 1951), thus creating what many times becomes an untenable tension that fractures on the sacred side of the tug of war, accounting for a rhetoric of religion wed to the practice of secularism. In fact, various forms of heterodoxy are part and parcel of the history of the development of religious doctrine because the task of interpreting the texts of a religion's traditions is a multifaceted and contentious labor attended not merely with the quest for truth but also the goal of arriving at the truth. And once one arrives at the truth, once one constructs a worldview that accounts for the totality of life, even though some sticky questions remain elusive of answers, the propagation of the truth, the faith, becomes a matter of teaching by word and deed, which some might call indoctrination. Thus, a primary concern of religion, as traditionally understood, is to enable people to convert to the truth and then live as converts. When the Judeo-Christian faith was assumed to be the gold standard for moral and intellectual integrity, institutions of higher education, even public institutions, did not question that assumption vigorously.

Just as a footnote to this point, I am told that at the public university where I work, only 50 years ago the president asked all perspective faculty where they went to church. As the head of a "secular" institution of higher education, the president obviously saw some need to query prospective professorial candidates about their religious affiliation. After all, they would be teaching students, influencing them, and most of the students who were being influenced were locals. Part of the reason for the president's query may have been the close ties between town and gown in a small, conservative Southern town. He probably had the boldness to ask about a prospective faculty member's religion because such a question would obviously be on the minds of the general population. Christianity, it was assumed, was a common thread that ran though people's lives, and questions about one's faith were unquestionably acceptable during the interview phase of the professorial hiring process.

The outward and explicit dominance of the Judeo-Christian faith is not characteristic of the academy today, and, in fact, laws prohibit asking questions about religious affiliation during the hiring process for public servants. Clearly, the common wisdom today is that such questions have no bearing upon professorial work; thus, they have no place in the hiring process. The rise of positivism helps explain the dramatic reversal in what counts concerning academic credentials, including personal character, vis-à-vis religious affiliation and thus helps explain "the remarkable revolution from a little over a century ago, when Christianity was a leading force in higher education, to today, when at most it is tolerated as a peripheral enterprise and often is simply excluded" (Marsden and Longfield 1992, v).

One could legitimately ask whether the academy is simply fulfilling its proper function by shining a bright light on the culture and questioning popular values, even religious values. Is it not the case that a primary function of the academy is to enjoin students in a vigorous and thorough evaluation of their often parochial, inchoate ideas, including their religious concerns? Can anyone, except perhaps those in private religious institutions of higher education, seriously hold to the premise that religion, so pervasive in American culture, should not be scrutinized by the intellectual powers resident in the academy, and if religion is found wanting, so be it?

Certainly, a proper function of the secular academy is to lay hold of the universe (hence the University) and examine it in minute detail. But that function does not begin with a tight definition of the universe that excludes what continues to be of vital concern to most people, a concern that has historically been part and parcel of higher education. It is one thing to take a genuine "objective" view of knowledge and another thing to *ipso facto* determine what counts as real knowledge. Gummer (2005) states the case this way, "I am questioning those secularists who (implicitly or explicitly) claim to have determined the truth *prior* to inquiry and dialogue—secularists who set their own truth claims against those of religious traditions and thus become precisely what they oppose" (46). The only "reasonable" response to such a criticism is that the intelligentsia has corporately studied all issues sufficiently to come to the conclusion that religion/spirituality is not a valid academic enterprise. Such a response, though, fails to account for the long history of religious education in the United States (not to mention the world) and thus limits the rich history of ideas infused with religious concepts. What is worse, such a response fails to attend to the intellectual concerns students bring to the classroom, and thus fails to address legitimate *intellectual* issues students should have an opportunity to address as they study the universe. In short, those who hold to a positivist epistemology and are unwilling to allow for the legitimacy of other epistemological approaches are not representative of American culture. In fact, one can honestly wonder whether such denizens of the academy represent the spirit of intellectual enquiry that is part and parcel of intellectual life or, rather, are examples of a byroad representing a downward path leading away from genuine intellectual life.

Spirituality Dominated by a Focus on Practical Issues

Because religion/spirituality is deeply embedded in American culture, it simply will not go away, even though significant segments of the academy have jettisoned religion/spirituality from the curriculum. The persistence of religion/spirituality in affairs in the wider world outside the ivy halls helps explain why applied disciplines within the academy—the health sciences, counseling, business—have been emboldened to publish books and articles about religion/spirituality. Those who prepare students to address religious/spirituality needs they will face as practitioners have led the way in building the literature about spirituality in higher education. The focus on helping students to prepare for life outside of academe is also a prime motivator for professionals in student affairs who see their task as providing students with a holistic education that has practical application not only while students are citizens of the university community but also as they take more and more responsibility as citizens of various other communities (Butler 1989; Fried 1997; Fried and Associates 1995; Jablonski 2001; Love and Talbot 1999; Martin 2001; Moran 2003; Raper 2001). Logically, the literature on spirituality in higher education also has influenced concerns about community and character development, notably through the service-learning movement. One cannot read the literature on service-learning without encountering time and again references to Dewey. As a representative of pragmatism, Dewey has profoundly influenced educational theory in schools and colleges of education and is the patron saint of various forms of constructivism that provide a theoretical foundation for nurturing social engagement and reform of society. Thus, spirituality/religion, even when seen through the prism of constructivism, is preeminently the study of an epistemology that seeks to change the world by acknowledging the legitimacy of personal wholeness and promoting the active engagement of students in social reforms that honor community building.

In this section, I will review literature pertaining to applied disciplines that have explored spirituality, generally with a view to preparing students to become effective when dealing with issues related to spirituality in the workplace. I have chosen the applied disciplines because they represent a significant portion of the literature on spirituality in higher education.

Spirituality in Applied Disciplines

A significant portion of the literature on spirituality in higher education is derived from the health sciences, primarily nursing. A primary concern of the literature on spirituality in health care is not whether spirituality is a legitimate concern but how the concern can be addressed. It would be a mistake to assume that the focus on what works in nursing to promote the spiritual dimension of health care disallows either empirical research or theoretical observations about spirituality. In fact, among those who write about spirituality in nursing, a sizable number apply scientific methodologies to answer questions about nurses' attitudes about spirituality (Cornette 1997; Harrison and Burnard 1993; Highfield and Cason 1983; Narayanasamy 1993; Pullen, Tuck, and Mix 1996; Ross 1994; Sodestrom and Martinson 1987; Soeken and Carson 1986; Taylor, Highfield, and Amenta 1994; Tuck, Pullen, and Lynn 1997), about measuring spiritual well-being (Peterman, Fitchett, Brady, Hernandez, and Cella 2002) and daily spiritual experience (Underwood and Teresi 2002). Indeed, Soeken (1989) provides a programmatic approach for conducting research in spirituality in nursing.

In addition to studies based on scientific methodologies, the literature on spirituality in nursing also includes sources that address ways to approach spirituality in particular health-care situations, including oncology patients (Grantsrom 1985), aging patients (Carr 1993; Heriot 1992; Narayanasamy 1998); chronically-ill patients (Soeken and Carson 1987), and dying patients (Conrad 1985; Froggatt 1997; O'Brien 1982; Taylor and Amenta 1994). Sellers and Haag (1998) also discuss spiritual interventions basing their research on practicing nurses, and Burnard (1987) addresses responses to spiritual distress in patients. Stoll (1979) provides questions nurses can ask patients to ascertain a patient's spiritual history. Again, the focus is on how to effectively promote spirituality in health care, not whether spirituality should be promoted. The focus on practicing nurses fits well with the desire to determine what role spirituality plays in nursing care as it is provided by practitioners.

Studies of spirituality in nursing also include curricular concern. For example, Lemmer (2002) conducted a survey of how spirituality is being taught in baccalaureate nursing programs. Others also address curricular issues, including how to teach spirituality in nursing (Banks 1980; Boutell and Bozett 1990; Bradshaw 1997; Brittain and Boozer 1987; Bush 1999; Forshee, Wiebe, Siegel, Ayers, and Bacon 1984; Gallia 1996; Ross 1996). Greenstreet (1999) reviewed the literature about teaching spirituality in nursing, and various scholars have conducted literature reviews of spirituality (Bensley 1991; Burkhardt 1989; Emblen 1992; Meraviglia 1999; McSherry and Draper 1998; Dyson, Cobb, and Forman 1997). Literature that provides a theoretical basis for spirituality in nursing education by describing models, explaining the historical context of nursing practice, and in general demonstrating why spirituality is appropriate in nursing education are also represented (Carson 1989; Carson and Gerardi 1985; Cobb and Robshaw 1998; Fish and Shelly 1978; Fulton 1996; Golberg 1998; Halstead and Mickley 1997; McGilloway and Myco 1985; McSherry and Draper 1997; Mayer 1992; Narayanasamy 1999; Oldnall 1996; Pelletier and McCall 2005; Pesut 2002; Piles 1986; Ross 1995; Walter 1997).

Two threads run throughout the literature on nursing. The first thread is that spirituality is a given, both in patients and in nurses. As Hurley (1999) states, "Spiritual care, in fact, becomes a necessity for the patient and the nurse" (8). Hurley's perspective is representative of the literature and is buttressed by a repudiation of positivism, the perspective spawned by the Enlightenment that limits health care to a medical model disavowing any notion of a nonmaterial component of human life (Burnard 1987; Dossey and Dossey 1998). In fact, Swaffield (1988) notes that nursing's roots can be traced to Florence Nightingale, who recognized that nursing care included a spiritual dimension. Widerquist (1992) avers that Nightingale, a woman who called upon God for strength to do her work, bequeathed to nurses a "vision of secular nursing carried out by women of calling and character" (54). Indeed, Nightingale was driven "by the need to achieve the perfection her spirituality relentlessly demanded" (54). The union of religious calling with secular nursing is a theme that resonated in the literature on spirituality in higher education, and in some ways hearkens to the pragmatists' quest to see the transcendent in the non-transcendent, even to identify the two. In other words, nursing is an ideal discipline for the study and promotion of spirituality because it has a history founded on religious impulses, including the initial establishment of nursing programs in church-related hospitals, and nurses cannot profitably avoid the spiritual dimension of health care because a person is more than his or her physical being (Clark, Cross, Deane, and Lowry 1991; Lane 1987). However, Simsen (1988) argues, "There is little consideration in our nursing education of spiritual issues" (31), a lament heard throughout the literature.

The second thread that runs throughout the literature on nursing is the Protean definition of spirituality. Cornette (1997) voices a typical judgment when she says, "'Spirituality' is a vague and elusive notion" (6). In fact, the instability of a definition of spirituality allows a multitude of definitions that can be decoupled from religion to allow for a person's individual notions of spirituality. Thus, atheists and agnostics can be said to have spiritual needs, but not as framed by traditional religious precepts (Burnard 1988; Myco 1985). That nurses and patients can be spiritual without being religious is a pervasive theme in the literature en masse on spirituality in higher education, and a definitional approach that allows for diversity of meaning is in accord with the spirit of American thinking that prizes individualism. I will address the definitional issue later.

Perhaps unremarkably, the literature on health care barely breathes a mention of physicians and spirituality. Buckle (1993) may have pinpointed the reason such is the case when she says, "Nurses, because of the nature of their work, have the ability to incorporate the spiritual and the mystical into their everyday life. Who but a nurse has access to the most powerful experiences of mankind—birth and death—on a daily basis, as well as the ability to communicate. Most doctors are recognized as being nervous of involvement and 'poking around in a patient's psyche' (Strong, 1977)" (744). "Being nervous of involvement" certainly echoes an Enlightenment ideal of objectivity squeamish about human concerns that cannot be measured scientifically.

In addition to the literature on nursing, literature on counseling addresses issues related to spirituality in higher education. Like nursing, counseling is a professional program, so it could be expected that the literature on spirituality in counseling also employed the perspective of how counselors might address clients' spiritual needs. Indeed, such is the case, and just as the nursing literature used scientific methodologies to examine religion/spirituality, so the literature on counseling includes empirical studies of religion/spirituality as they are related to personal well-being (Bufford, Paloutzian, and Ellison 1991; Ingersoll 1998; Paloutzian and Ellison 1982), coping (Pargament 1999a; Pargament, Koenig, and Perez 2000), loneliness (Fischer and Phillips 1982), and alcohol use (Johnson, Kristeller, and Sheets 2004). Researchers have also sought to measure mystical experiences (Hood 1975), personal spiritual development (Hamilton and Jackson 1998), and religion as quest (Batson and Schoenrade 1991a, 1991b). MacDonald (2000) found that religion and spirituality are distinct constructs. Slater, Hall, and Edwards (2001) also investigated various instruments used to measure religion and spirituality and found that more work needs to be done to create better instruments.

As with nursing, literature on spirituality in counseling addresses conceptual concerns, such as defining spirituality vis-à-vis religion (Pargament 1999b; Zinnbauer, Pargament, and Scott 1999), defining religiousness (Pargament 2002; Pargament, Sullivan, Balzer, Haitsma, and Raymark 1995), and defining spirituality (Elkins, Hedstrom, Hughes, Leaf, and Saunders 1988; Hinterkopf 1997). Other scholars provide a variety of psychological perspectives on religion/spirituality in counseling (Burke and Miranti 1995; Kelly 1995; Plante and Sherman 2001). The pedagogical elements of spirituality in counseling education are also addressed (Burke, Hackney, Hudson, Miranti, Watts, and Epp 1999; Fukuyama and Sevig 1997; Hinterkopf 1994; Kelly 1994; Matthews 1998; Pate and High 1995; Sansone, Khatain, and Rodenhauser 1990; Souza 2002).

Like the literature on spirituality in nursing, the literature on spirituality in counseling assumes that religion/spirituality is an appropriate topic for practitioners and students to study because in dealing with human needs, counselors will be required to consider the religious/spiritual dimension of human nature. This is Christopher's (1996) point when he asserts that counseling is inherently engaged in promoting a moral vision, and Christopher repudiates Enlightenment ideals when he says, "The significance of the term *moral vision* is that it is a way of talking about human reality that moves away from the modern Western predilection to sharply distinguish fact and value" (18). The sharp distinction between fact and value is a positivist construct that, according to Christopher, has no legitimate place in counseling.

The importance of a moral vision in counseling is reinforced by Worthington and Scott (1983) who found that Christian counselors and secular counselors chose different treatment goals: "Counselors in secular settings tend not to define problems in spiritual terms and tend not to set goals concerning clients' spiritual lives for potentially religious clients as often as counselors in Christian settings" (326). Indeed, Worthington and Scott say that some evidence suggests "secular counselors might not like religious clients as much as nonreligious clients" (326). Bergin (1980) is quite pointed when he says, "Religion is at the fringe of clinical psychology when it should be at the center. Value questions pervade the field, but discussion of them is dominated by viewpoints that are alien to the religious subcultures of most of the people whose behavior we try to explain and influence" (103).

What Bergin noted over 25 years ago is reinforced by Richmond (2004) when he responds to an issue of the *American Psychologist* devoted to spirituality, religion, and health: "I was surprised, shocked might be a better word, when I read in the January 2003 issue of the *American Psychologist* that the area of spirituality, religion, and health is seen as an emerging field....The truth is that many people in the respective fields of mental health counseling, pastoral counseling, and counseling psychology have been researching and publishing in this area consistently since the 1970s" (52). What's at issue here?

As Zinnbauer, Pargament, and Scott (1999) note, religion and spirituality are defined in a variety of ways, so the terms do not provide definitional stability. Although many people have been conducting research on spirituality in counseling, as Richmond avers, that research is fragmentary because it has not yielded a body of literature with consistent results. What has happened in counseling, as in other academic disciplines producing practitioners, is that spirituality is seen as a new field of study because it has been disaggregated from religion and even put in opposition to religion (Pargament 1999a). Religion can then become demonized as hostile to human potential because it cannot allow for sufficient pluralism to embrace everyone. Recall that religion has traditionally been engaged in the work of converting people to a particular viewpoint, generally in opposition to the convert's previous worldview. Spirituality, however, is defined by personal preferences, and personal preferences are not imposed by counselors but evoked so that the client can come to a better understanding of his or her worldview or spirituality. And while this approach seems to suggest a value-free method to counseling, such is not the case. Counseling, as Christopher affirmed, has a moral vision, and counselors who don't share the moral vision of their religious clients, as Worthington and Scott noted, feel less comfortable working with those clients. As a counselor believes so he or she counsels, and as teachers in higher education believe so they impart a moral vision to their students of what constitutes effective counseling. It appears that the production of literature on religion/spirituality in counseling has not had a demonstrable effect on the field because the emergence of literature about spirituality in counseling is hailed by many as a new area of study.

The last discipline that produces practitioners and is significantly represented in the literature on spirituality is business. Because Chapter 16 is devoted to spirituality in business, I will limit my review of the literature. I purposely have not consulted the large body of literature that addresses spirituality in the workplace, but Butts (1999) provides an overview of that literature. Although the literature on spirituality in the workplace takes varied perspectives, it is not too simplistic to note that conceptually the focus is pragmatic with a heavy dose of techniques drawn from disparate religious/spiritual traditions. For example, Biberman and Whitty (1999), writing as the guest editors of a special issue of the *Journal of Organizational Change Management*, applaud a new paradigm in business organizational processes that promotes higher consciousness (170). In introducing an article by Cavanagh, Biberman and Whitty say Cavanagh

> argues convincingly that spirituality is a vital asset to individuals, organizations and society. Simply put, it helps people treat themselves and others properly. That, Cavanagh argues, is why more managers and firms are encouraging spirituality in the workplace. Cavanagh offers a strong case for bridging current ethical concerns in the here and now world of business to the higher aspirations of the best in world religion and spirituality. His agenda for business schools includes service learning, justice, spirituality and faith. He observes that religiously-oriented universities may provide a model for integrating spirituality and service into their mission. In this essay the reader can see the interrelationship of spirituality and religion as it plays itself out in work and higher education. (171–172)

Note that Biberman and Whitty ground their argument for workplace spirituality in an ethic of proper human treatment derived from an eclectic approach to religion-spirituality.

What Cavanagh (1999) says in the article is that spirituality is difficult to define, a theme that runs throughout all the literature on spirituality in higher education. Nevertheless, after discussing various views of spirituality,

Cavanagh says, "In conclusion, the spirituality in business movement helps the business person to become more centered on the important things in life: God, people, family, and a physical world that can be passed on to our children. It enables the business person to gain a better understanding of God and other people in our world" (193). Cavanagh's use of the word *God* carries with it some ambiguity. He attempts, it appears, to give Christianity a prominent place in business spirituality, but he also wants room for the New Age Movement, so Cavanagh explains points of agreement between the two: "Both find society in crisis. Both have a new enthusiasm for God and prayer. And both find traditional churches deficient" (192). To suggest that the New Age Movement and Evangelical Christianity both "have a new enthusiasm for God and prayer" is to suggest that they share the same concept of God and prayer, but such a statement is highly contestable. Nevertheless, Cavanagh's argument itself is an example of a pragmatic approach to success in business that includes personal fulfillment and personal profit, at the expense, one might say, of the integrity of particular religious/spiritual perspectives. Cavanagh does provide pedagogical advice for business schools regarding spirituality, and notes that religiously-oriented universities can "take a leadership role in helping all universities to integrate spirituality, religion and religious values into their education" (198). Again, Cavanagh introduces ambiguity by making religiously-oriented universities models for all universities regarding the implementation of pedagogical initiatives that promote spirituality. How that could happen is left an open question.

Pedagogically, Naughton and Bausch (1996) agree with Cavanagh by outlining a theoretical approach for Catholic institutions of higher education to promote particular ethical values in management education. Whether such an approach can be implemented successfully is, again, an open question, and given Benne's (2003) viewpoint on the capitulation of Lutheran quietism as a reforming force in Lutheran education, the question of reform, even in religiously-oriented schools, is suspect. Note, the question is not the maintenance of the historically-informed mission of religiously-oriented schools but the reform of those schools so that the historically-informed mission is reinstituted; thus reform, not maintenance, is at issue, so the reform of secular higher education may or may not be a genuine hope for those who seek such reform via spirituality. Interestingly, the focus of a pedagogy of spirituality is management/leadership courses (Barnett, Krell, and Sendry 2000; Bento 2000; Daniels, Franz, and Wong 2000; Harlos 2000; Haroutiounian et al. 2000), and two themes that are hospitable to the literature on spirituality in higher education are articulated in the literature on spirituality in the business classroom.

First, "spirituality is the experience of the transcendent, or the quality of transcendence, something that welcomes, but does not require, religious beliefs" (Bento 2000, 653). Spirituality is uncoupled from religion—or, more precisely, *can* be uncoupled. This uncoupling allows for the focus on the individual. "The spiritual imperative," as Barnett, Krell and Sendry (2000) affirm, "is that management education must engage students in self-discovery about the inner energies of the soul, their connections to personal and professional development, and their contributions to social and economic evolution" (563). Second, "The idea of a reality beyond the five senses is something that has been of increasing interest to management scholars and educators" (Daniels, Franz, and Wong 2000, 542). In fact, Daniels, Franz, and Wong develop a model that frames worldviews in terms of a metaphysical dimension and an epistemological dimension. The metaphysical or transcendent part of the model "acknowledges a dimension of reality outside the closed system of physical cause and effect" (542). Thus, positivism is nudged aside to make room for spirituality. As in the other literature in nursing and counseling, spirituality is seen instrumentally because it can benefit the individual in ways that benefit the social order. Spirituality, as it was for the pragmatists, is preeminently a practical concern focused on the here and now, even when appeals are made to Judeo-Christian values.

Conclusion

I have intentionally been selective in my review of the literature on spirituality in higher education. However, the themes that I have cited are not liable to significant revision given literature I have not cited. In closing, I summarize the major tenets of spirituality as seen in the literature and briefly cite three concerns that Hoppe and I will discuss in Chapter 22 on future research concerning spirituality in higher education.

In sum, then, spirituality is seen as antithetical to religion, even though room is left open for religion as long as spirituality does not have to be dependent on it. Religion denotes a set of precepts that must be affirmed; spirituality, on the other hand, does not carry the doctrinal baggage characteristic of religion and allows flexibility because nobody has to believe in a prescribed set of precepts. Thus, spirituality has no commonly accepted definition and has been defined in a variety of ways, often at odds with one another

(Speck 2005). As a term, spirituality allows for great definitional flexibility and can be considered common ground, so that even atheists can become engaged in conversations about their spirituality (Bagwell 2003; Nash 2003). In fact, everyone is on a personal quest, and nobody can really say with absolute certainty that one quest is superior to another. The definitional flexibility of spirituality can be explained by its epistemology, which is contingent personal knowledge that must remain open to possible radical revision as the world unfolds, a philosophical position that can be traced to pragmatism and reinforced by postmodernism. Indeed, according to this view of epistemology, individuals make their own meaning, a proposition affirmed by Dewey and enshrined in the various forms of constructivism widely promulgated in schools and colleges of education throughout the United States.

Given that sketch of spirituality, I see three legitimate criticisms that could be raised. First, because spirituality tends to focus on individual spirituality, especially when decoupled from religion, the problem of community will have to be addressed. How can individual spirituality, which depends on personal preferences, give rise to any legitimate notion of community? Second, the problem of individual spirituality vis-à-vis community cohesion raises a further question about the nature of tolerance. If pluralism is the ideal, how can individual spirituality be the norm when community is the embodiment of pluralism at work? And ethically what is the community's tolerance level for those who hold to truth with a capital T, for those who do not subscribe to the relativism required for individual spirituality to function? Third, what is the proper relationship between spirituality and political activity? To suggest that spirituality is apolitical is to disregard the premise of transcending without transcendence, which is foundational to pragmatism. Without a real metaphysical realm over and above the seen world, transcendence must be vested in the cosmos, and the political implications of vesting transcendence in the cosmos are vital because this life becomes highly prized as the *telos* of human aspirations. For example, even literature about contemplation invests the ordinary with sacredness (Brown 1999; Gravos 2005; Mayes 1998), and logically leads to behaviors that cannot be extricated from living in community. However, social-political motivations linked with spirituality to address community concerns cannot be assumed to automatically translate into a great social good. Such motivations will have to be open to criticism and revision, and such criticism should include questions about the viability of spirituality. But those questions could easily be frustrated by the lack of definitional stability in the word *spirituality*, and so we come full circle to the concern of basing spirituality on individual preference. The literature on spirituality in higher education opens the door to complex questions about the relationships among individualism, community, political-social activism, and metaphysics. And, of course, the complex questions raised by those interactions lead to queries about how to incorporate spirituality into higher education. The authors in this volume provide various answers to those questions.

References

Bagwell, T. 2003. Defining spirituality in public higher education: A response to R. J. Nash from a spiritually engaged atheist. *Religion & Education* 30(2):23–44.

Banks, R. 1980. Health and the spiritual dimension: Relationships and implications for professional preparation programs. *The Journal of School Health* 50:195–202.

Barnett, C. K., T. C. Krell, and J. Sendry. 2000. Learning to learn about spirituality: A categorical approach to introducing the topic into management courses. *Journal of Management Education* 24(5):562–579.

Batson, C. D., and P. A. Schoenrade. 1991a. Measuring religion as quest: 1) validity concerns. *Journal for the Scientific Study of Religion* 30(4):416–429.

———. 1991b. Measuring religion as quest: 2) reliability concerns. *Journal for the Scientific Study of Religion* 30(4):430–447.

Bellah, R. N. 1967. Civil religion in America. *Daedalus* 96:1–21.

Benne, R. 2003. Lutheran quietism in higher education. http://www.luc.edu/projectfaculty/publications.html (accessed September 22, 2004).

Bennett, J. B. 1998. *Collegial professionalism: The academy, individualism, and the common good*. Phoenix, AZ: American Council on Education and The Oryx Press.

———. 2003. *Academic life: Hospitality, ethics, and spirituality*. Boston, MA: Anker.

Bensley, R. J. 1991. Defining spiritual health: A review of the literature. *Journal of Health Education* 22(5):287–290.

Bento, R. F. 2000. The little inn at the crossroads: A spiritual approach to the design of a leadership course. *Journal of Management Education* 24(5):650–661.

Bergin, A. E. 1980. Psychotherapy and religious values. *Journal of Consulting and Clinical Psychology* 48(1):95–105.

Biberman, J., and M. Whitty. 1999. Editorial. *Journal of Organizational Change Management* 12(3):170–174.

Bischetti, D. 2001. Service, spirituality, and social change. In *Developing non-hierarchical leadership on campus: Case studies and best practices in higher education*, ed. C. L. Outcalt, S. K. Faris, and K. N. McMahon, 129–138. Westport, CT: Greenwood Press.

Boutell, K. A., and F. W. Bozett. 1990. Nurses' assessment of patients' spirituality: Continuing education implications. *The Journal of Continuing Education in Nursing* 21(4):172–176.

Bradshaw, A. 1994. *Lighting the lamp: The spiritual dimension of nursing care*. Middlesex, England: Scutari Press.

———. 1997. Teaching spiritual care to nurses: An alternative approach. *International Journal of Palliative Nursing* 3(1):51–57.

Brittain, J. N., and J. Boozer. 1987. Spiritual care: Integration into a collegiate nursing curriculum. *Journal of Nursing Education* 28(4):155–160.

Brown, R. C. 1999. The teacher as contemplative observer. *Educational Leadership* 56(4):70–73.

Buckle, J. 1993. When is holism not complementary? *British Journal of Nursing* 2(15):744–745.

Bufford, R. K., R. F. Paloutzian, and C. W. Ellison. 1991. Norms for the spiritual well-being scale. *Journal of Psychology and Theology* 19(1):56–70.

Burke, M. T., H. Hackney, P. Hudson, J. Miranti, G. A. Watts, and L. Epp. 1999. Spirituality, religion, and CACREP curriculum standards. *Journal of Counseling & Development* 17:251–257.

Burke, M. T., and J. G. Miranti, eds. 1995. *Counseling: The spiritual dimension*. Alexandria, VA: American Counseling Association.

Burkhardt, M. A. 1989. Spirituality: An analysis of the concept. *Holistic Nursing Practice* 3(3):69–77.

Burnard, P. 1987. Spiritual distress and the nursing response: Theoretical considerations and counseling skills. *Journal of Advanced Nursing* 12:377–382.

———. 1988. The spiritual needs of atheists and agnostics. *The Professional Nurse* December:130–132.

Bush, T. 1999. Journaling and the teaching of spirituality. *Nurse Education Today* 19:20–28.

Butler, J. 1989. *Religion on campus*. New Directions for Student Services, no. 46. San Francisco: Jossey-Bass.

Butts, D. 1999. Spirituality at work: An overview. *Journal of Organizational Change Management* 12(4):328–331.

Carr, K. K. 1993. Integration of spirituality of aging into a nursing curriculum. *Gerontology & Geriatrics Education* 13(3):33–46.

Carson, V. B. 1989. *Spiritual dimensions of nursing practice*. Philadelphia, PA: W. B. Saunders.

Carson, V., and R. Gerardi. 1985. Spirituality for credit: Finding a place in the secular curriculum. *Journal of Christian Nursing* 2(3):28–30.

Cavanagh, G. F. 1999. Spirituality for managers: Context and critique. *Journal of Organizational Change Management* 121(3):186–199.

Chickering, A. W. 2003. Reclaiming our soul: Democracy and higher education. *Change* 35(1):39–44.

Christopher, J. C. 1996. Counseling's inescapable moral visions. *Journal of Counseling & Development* 75:17–25.

Cimino, R., and D. Lattin. 1998. *Shopping for faith: American religion in the new millennium*. San Francisco: Jossey–Bass.

Clark, C. C., J. R. Cross, D. M. Deane, and L. W. Lowry. 1991. Spirituality: Integral to quality care. *Holistic Nursing Practice* 5(3):67–76.

Cobb, M., and V. Robshaw, eds. 1998. *The spiritual challenge of health care.* Edinburgh, Scotland: Churchill Livingston.

Coburn, T. B. 2005. Secularism and spirituality in today's academy: A heuristic model. *Liberal Education* 91(3):58–61.

Conrad, N. L. 1985. Spiritual support for the dying. *Nursing Clinics of North America* 20(2):415–422.

Copleston, F. 1977. *A history of philosophy.* 9 vols. New York: Doubleday.

Cornette, K. 1997. For whenever I am weak, I am strong… *International Journal of Palliative Nursing* 3(1):6–13.

Daniels, D., R. S. Franz, and K. Wong. 2000. A classroom with a worldview: Making spiritual assumptions explicit in management education. *Journal of Management Education* 24(5):540–561.

Dossey, B. M., and L. Dossey. 1998. Attending to holistic care. *American Journal of Nursing* 98(8):35–38.

Dyson, J., M. Cobb, and D. Forman. 1997. The meaning of spirituality: A literature review. *Journal of Advanced Nursing* 26:1183–1188.

Edgerton, R. 1992. Community and commitment in higher education: An interview with Parker J. Palmer. *American Association for Higher Education Bulletin* 45(1):3–7.

Elkins, D. N., L. J. Hedstrom, L. L. Hughes, J. A. Leaf, and C. Saunders. 1988. Toward a humanistic-phenomenological spirituality: Definition, description, and measurement. *Journal of Humanistic Psychology* 28(4):5–18.

Emblen, J. D. 1992. Religion and spirituality defined according to current use in nursing literature. *Journal of Professional Nursing* 8(1):41–47.

Fahlberg, L. A., and L. A. Fahlberg. 1991. Exploring spirituality and consciousness with an expanded science: Beyond the ego with empiricism, phenomenology, and contemplation. *American Journal of Health Promotion* 5(4):273–281.

Fischer, C. S., and S. L. Phillips. 1982. Who is alone? Social characteristics of people with small networks. In *Loneliness: A source book of current theory, research and therapy,* ed. L. A. Peplau and D. Perlman, 21–39. New York: John Wiley & Sons.

Fish, S., and J. A. Shelly. 1978. *Spiritual care: The nurse's role.* Downers Grove, IL: InterVarsity Press.

Forshee, T., S. Wiebe, M. A. Siegel, A. B. Ayers, and J. M. Bacon. 1984. How we teach spiritual care: Faculty confront the issues. *Journal of Christian Nursing* 1(3):20–23.

Fox, R. W. 2004. America's national obsession. *Chronicle of Higher Education* 20 February, B7–B10.

Frankenberry, N. 1996. The American experience. In *Spirituality and the secular quest,* ed. P. H. Van Ness, 102–126. New York: Crossroad.

Fried, J. 1997. Changing ethical frameworks for a multicultural world. In *Ethics for today's campus: New perspectives on education, student development, and institutional management.* New Directions for Student Services, no. 77, ed. J. Fried, 5–22. San Francisco: Jossey-Bass.

Fried, J., and Associates, eds. 1995. *Shifting paradigms in student affairs: Culture, context, teaching, and learning.* Alexandria, VA: American College Personnel Association.

Froggatt, K. 1997. Signposts on the journey: The place of ritual in spiritual care. *International Journal of Palliative Nursing* 3(1):42–46.

Fukuyama, M. A., and T. Sevig. 1997. Spiritual issues in counseling: A new course. *Counselor Education & Supervision* 36(3):233–244.

Fulton, R. A. B. 1996. Spirituality and nursing education. In *Review of research in nursing education*, ed. K. R. Stevens, 127–147. New York: National League for Nursing.

Gallia, K. S. 1996. Teaching spiritual care: Beyond content. *Nursing Connections* 9(3):29–35.

Glazer, S. 1999. Introduction. In *The heart of learning: Spirituality in education*, ed. S. Glazer, 1–5. New York: Jeremy P. Tarcher/Putnam.

Golberg, B. 1998. Connection: An exploration of spirituality in nursing care. *Journal of Advanced Nursing* 27:836–842.

Granstrom, S. L. 1985. Spiritual nursing care for oncology patients. *Topics in Clinical Nursing* 7(1):39–45.

Gravois, J. 2005. Meditate on it. *Chronicle of Higher Education* 52(9):A10-A12.

Greenstreet, W. M. 1999. Teaching spirituality in nursing: A literature review. *Nurse Education Today* 19:649–658.

Gummer, N. 2005. A profound unknowing: The challenge of religion in the liberal education of world citizens. *Liberal Ed.* 91(2):44–49.

Halstead, M. T., and J. R. Mickley. 1997. Attempting to fathom the unfathomable: Descriptive views of spirituality. *Seminars in Oncology Nursing* 13(4):225–230.

Hamilton, D. M., and M. H. Jackson. 1998. Spiritual development: Paths and processes. *Journal of Instructional Psychology* 25(4):262–270.

Handy, R. T. 1980. A decisive truth in the civil religion debate. *Theology Today* 37(3): 342-350.

Harlos, K. P. 2000. Toward a spiritual pedagogy: Meaning, practice, and applications in management education. *Journal of Management Education* 24(5):612–627.

Haroutiounian, A., S. Ghavam, S. J. Gomez, E. Ivshin, S. Phelan, B. Freshman, M. Griffin, and C. Lindsay. 2000. Learning and being: Outcomes of a class on spirituality at work. *Journal of Management Education* 24(5):662–681.

Harrison, J., and P. Burnard. 1993. *Spirituality and nursing practice*. Aldershot, England: Avebury.

Heriot, C. S. 1992. Spirituality and aging. *Holistic Nursing Practice* 7(1):22–31.

Highfield, M. F., and C. Cason. 1983. Spiritual needs of patients: Are they recognized? *Cancer Nursing* June 6(3):187–192.

Hinterkopf, E. 1994. Integrating spiritual experiences in counseling. *Counseling & Values* 38(3):165–176.

———. 1997. Defining the spiritual experience. *Texas Counseling Association Journal* 25(2):75–82.

Hood, R. W., Jr. 1975. The construction and preliminary validation of a measure of reported mystical experience. *Journal for the Scientific Study of Religion* 14:29–41.

Hoth, W. 2004. Local teaching: The spirit of place. In *Spirituality, action, and pedagogy: Teaching from the heart*, ed. D. Denton and W. Ashton, 89–96. New York: Peter Lang.

Hurley, J. E. 1999. Breaking the spiritual care barrier. *Journal of Christian Nursing* 16(3):8–13.

Ingersoll, R. E. 1998. Refining dimensions of spiritual wellness: A cross-traditional approach. *Counseling & Values* 42(3):156–166.

Jablonski, M. A., ed. 2001. *The implications of student spirituality for student affairs practice.* New Directions for Student Services, no. 95. San Francisco: Jossey-Bass.

Johnson, T. J., J. Kristeller, and V. L. Sheets. 2004. Religiousness and spirituality in college students: Separate dimensions with unique and common correlates. http://www.collegevalues.org/pdf (accessed September 20, 2004).

Kelly, E. W., Jr. 1994. The role of religion and spirituality in counselor education: A national survey. *Counselor Education & Supervision* 33(4):227–238.

———. 1995. *Spirituality and religion in counseling and psychotherapy: Diversity in theory and practice.* Alexandria, VA: American Counseling Association.

Koth, K. 2003. Deepening the commitment to serve: Spiritual reflection in service-learning. *About Campus* 7(6):2–7.

Lane, J. A. 1987. The care of the human spirit. *Journal of Professional Nursing* 3(6):332–337.

Lemmer, C. 2002. Teaching the spiritual dimension of nursing care: A survey of U.S. baccalaureate nursing programs. *Journal of Nursing Education* 41(11):482–490.

Love, P., and D. Talbot. 1999. Defining spirituality development: A missing consideration for student affairs. *NASPA Journal* 37(1):361–375.

Lovin, R. W. 1986. Social contract or a public covenant? In *Religion and American public life: Interpretations and explorations*, ed. R. W. Lovin, 132–145. New York: Paulist Press.

MacDonald, D. A. 2000. Spirituality: Description, measurement, and relation to the five factor model of personality. *Journal of Personality* 68(1):153–197.

Marsden, G. M. 1992a. Introduction. In *The secularization of the academy*, ed. G. M. Marsden and B. J. Longfield, 3–7. New York: Oxford University Press.

———. 1992b. The soul of the American university: A historical overview. In *The secularization of the academy*, ed. G. M. Marsden and B. J. Longfield, 9-45. New York: Oxford University Press.

———. 1994. *The soul of the American university: From Protestant establishment to established nonbelief.* New York: Oxford University Press.

———. 2000. *Religion and American culture.* San Diego, CA: Harcourt Brace Jovanovich.

Marsden, G. M., and B. J. Longfield. 1992. Preface. In *The secularization of the academy*, ed. G. M. Marsden and B. J. Longfield, v-vi. New York: Oxford University Press.

Martin, P. E. 2001. Approaches to conflict from spiritual and religious perspectives: Lessons from student affairs. In *Transforming campus life: Reflections on spirituality and religious pluralism*, ed. V. W. Miller and M. M. Ryan, 245–260. Vol. 1, Studies in Education and Spirituality. New York: Peter Lang.

Marty, M. E. 1974. Two kinds of two kinds of civil religion. In *American civil religion*, ed. R. E. Richey, 139–157. New York: Harper and Row.

Mathisen, J. A. 1989. Twenty years after Bellah: Whatever happened to American civil religion? *Sociological Analysis* 50(2):129–146.

Matthews, C. O. 1998. Integrating the spiritual dimension into traditional counselor education programs. *Counseling & Values* 43(1):3–19.

Mayer, J. 1992. Wholly responsible for a part, or partly responsible for a whole?: The concept of spiritual care in nursing. *Second Opinion* 17(3):26–56.

Mayes, C. 1998. The use of contemplative practices in teacher education. *Encounter: Educating for Meaning and Social Justice* 11(3):17–31.

McGilloway, O., and F. Myco, eds. 1985. *Nursing and spiritual care*. London: Harper and Row.

McSherry, W., and P. Draper. 1997. The spiritual dimension: Why the absence within nursing curricula? *Nurse Education Today* 17:413–417.

———. 1998. The debates emerging from the literature surrounding the concept of spirituality as applied to nursing. *Journal of Advanced Nursing* 27:683–691.

Meraviglia, M. G. 1999. Critical analysis of spirituality and its empirical indicators. *Journal of Holistic Nursing* 17(1):18–33.

Miller, W. L. 1990. The moral project of the American founders. In *Articles of faith, articles of peace: The religious liberty clauses and the American public philosophy*, ed. J. D. Hunter and O. Guinness, 17–39. Washington, DC: The Brookings Institute.

Moran, C. D. 2003. Spirituality and religion: Through the eyes of the "hidden educators." *Religion & Education* 30(1):40–58.

Myco, F. 1985. The non-believer in the health care situation. In *Nursing and spiritual care*, ed. O. McGilloway and F. Myco, 36–52. London: Harper and Row.

Narayanasamy, A. 1993. Nurses' awareness and educational preparation in meeting their patients' spiritual needs. *Nurse Education Today* 13(3):196–201.

———. 1998. Religious and spiritual needs of older people. In *Promoting positive practice in nursing older people*, ed. S. Pickering and J. Thompson, 128–151. London: Bailliere Tindall.

———. 1999. ASSET: A model for actioning spirituality and spiritual care education and training in nursing. *Nurse Education Today* 19:274–285.

Nash, R. J. 1999. *Faith, hype, and clarity: Teaching about religion in American schools and colleges*. New York: Teachers College Press.

———. 2003. Inviting atheists to the table: A modest proposal for higher education. *Religion & Education* 30(1):1–23.

Naughton, M. J., and T. A. Bausch. 1996. The integrity of a Catholic management education. *California Management Review* 38(4):118–140.

Niebuhr, H. R. 1951. *Christ and culture*. New York: Harper & Row.

Nord, W. A. 1995. *Religion and American education: Rethinking a national dilemma*. Chapel Hill, NC: The University of North Carolina Press.

O'Brien, M. E. 1982. Religious faith and adjustment to long-term hemodialysis. *Journal of Religion and Health* 21(1):68–80.

Oldnall, A. 1996. A critical analysis of nursing: Meeting the spiritual needs of patients. *Journal of Advanced Nursing* 23:138–144.

Palmer, P. 1987. Community, conflict, and ways of knowing: Ways to deepen our educational agenda. *Change* 19(5):20–25.

———. 1997. The grace of great things: Reclaiming the sacred in knowing, teaching, and learning. *Holistic Education Review* 10(3):8–16.

---. 2003. Teaching with heart and soul: Reflections on spirituality in teacher education. *Journal of Teacher Education* 54(5):376–385.

Paloutzian, R. F., and C. W. Ellison. 1982. Loneliness, spiritual well-being and the quality of life. In *Loneliness: A sourcebook of current theory, research and therapy*, ed. L. A. Peplau and D. Perlman, 224–237. New York: John Wiley & Sons.

Pargament, K. I. 1999a. Religious/spiritual coping. In *Multidimensional measurement of religiousness/spirituality for use in health research: A report of the Fetzer Institute/National Institute on Aging Working Group*, 43–56. Kalamazoo, MI: John E. Fetzer Institute.

---. 1999b. The psychology of religion *and* spirituality?: Yes and no. *The International Journal for the Psychology of Religion* 9(1):3–16.

---. 2002. The bitter and the sweet: An evaluation of the costs and benefits of religiousness. *Psychological Inquiry* 13(3):168-181.

Pargament, K. I., H. G. Koenig, and L. M. Perez. 2000. The many methods of religious coping: Development and initial validation of the RCOPE. *Journal of Clinical Psychology* 56(4):519–543.

Pargament, K. I., M. S. Sullivan, W. K. Balzer, K. S. Van Haitsma, and P. H. Raymark. 1995. The many meanings of religiousness: A policy-capturing approach. *Journal of Personality* 63(4):953–983.

Pate, R. H., Jr., and J. H. High. 1995. The importance of client religious beliefs and practices in the education of counselors in CACREP-accredited programs. *Counseling & Values* 40(1):2–5.

Pelletier, A. J., and J. W. McCall. 2005. A modular curriculum for integrating spirituality and health care. In *Spirituality in higher education*, ed. S. L. Hoppe and B. W. Speck, 51–58. New Directions for Teaching and Learning, no. 104. San Francisco: Jossey-Bass.

Pesut, B. 2002. The development of nursing students' spirituality and spiritual care-giving. *Nurse Education Today* 22:128–135.

Peterman, A. H., G. Fitchett, M. J. Brady, L. Hernandez, and D. Cella. 2002. Measuring spiritual well-being in people with cancer: The functional assessment of chronic illness therapy—spiritual well-being scale (FACIT-Sp). *Annals of Behavioral Medicine* 24(1):49–58.

Pickering, S., and J. Thompson, ed. 1998. *Promoting positive practice in nursing older people*. London: Bailliere Tindall.

Piles, C. L. 1986. Putting spiritual care into the curriculum. *Journal of Christian Nursing* 6(3):18–21.

Plante, T. G., and A. C. Sherman, eds. 2001. *Faith and health: Psychological perspectives*. New York: The Guilford Press.

Pullen, L., I. Tuck, and K. Mix. 1996. Mental health nurses' spiritual perspectives. *Journal of Holistic Nursing* 14(2):85–97.

Raper, J. 2001. "Losing our religion": Are students struggling in silence? In *Transforming campus life: Reflections on spirituality and religious pluralism*, ed. V. W. Miller and M. M. Ryan, 13–32. Vol. 1, Studies in Education and Spirituality. New York: Peter Lang.

Richmond, L. J. 2004. Religion, spirituality, and health: A topic not so new. *American Psychologist* 59(1):52.

Richey, R. E., and D. G. Jones, eds. 1974. *American civil religion*. New York: Harper & Row.

Rocheleau, J. 2004. Theoretical roots of service-learning: Progressive education and the development of citizenship. In *Service-learning: History, theory, and issues*, ed. B. W. Speck and S. L. Hoppe, 3–21. Westport, CT: Praeger.

Ross, L. 1994. Spiritual care: The nurse's role. *Nursing Standard* 8(29):33–37.

———. 1995. The spiritual dimension: Its importance to patients' health, well-being and quality of life and its implications for nursing practice. *International Journal of Nursing Studies* 32(5):457–468.

———. 1996. Teaching spiritual care to nurses. *Nurse Education Today* 16:38–43.

Sagan, C. 1980. *Cosmos*. New York: Random House.

Sansone, R. A., K. Khatain, and P. Rodenhauser. 1990. The role of religion in psychiatric education: A national survey. *Academic Psychiatry* 14:34–38.

Sellers, S. C., and B. A. Haag. 1998. Spiritual nursing interventions. *Journal of Holistic Nursing* 16(3):338–354.

Simsen, B. 1988. Nursing the spirit. *Nursing Times* 84(37):31–32.

Slater, W., T. W. Hall, and K. J. Edwards. 2001. Measuring religion and spirituality: Where are we and where are we going? *Journal of Psychology and Theology* 29(1):4–21.

Sodestrom, K. E., and I. M. Martinson. 1987. Patients' spiritual coping strategies: A study of nurse and patient perspectives. *Oncology Nursing Forum* 14(2):41–46.

Soeken, K. L. 1989. Perspectives on research in the spiritual dimension of nursing care. In *Spiritual dimensions of nursing practice*, ed. V. B. Carson, 354-378. Philadelphia, PA: W. B. Saunders.

Soeken, K. L., and V. J. Carson. 1986. Study measures nurses' attitudes about providing spiritual care. *Health Progress* 67(3):52–55.

———. 1987. Responding to the spiritual needs of the chronically ill. *Nursing Clinics of North America* 22(3):603–611.

Souza, K. Z. 2002. Spirituality in counseling: What do counseling students think about it? *Counseling and Values* 46:213–217.

Speck, B. W. 2001. Why service-learning? In *Developing and implementing service-learning programs*, ed. M. Canada and B. W. Speck, 3–13. New Directions for Higher Education, no. 114. San Francisco: Jossey-Bass.

———. 2004. Selected sources on service-learning. In *Service-learning: History, theory, and issues*, ed. B. W. Speck and S. L. Hoppe, 179–202. Westport, CT: Praeger.

———. 2005. What is spirituality? *In Spirituality in higher education*, ed. S. L. Hoppe and B. W. Speck, 3–13. New Directions for Teaching and Learning, no. 104. San Francisco: Jossey-Bass.

Speck, B. W., and S. L. Hoppe. 2004. Introduction. *In Service-learning: History, theory, and issues*, ed. B. W. Speck and S. L. Hoppe, vii–xi. Westport, CT: Praeger.

Stoll, R. I. 1979. Guidelines for spiritual assessment. *American Journal of Nursing* 79(9):1574–1577.

Swaffield, L. 1988. Religious roots. *Nursing Times* 84(37):28–29.

Taylor, E. J., and M. Amenta. 1994. Midwifery to the soul while the body dies: Spiritual care among hospice nurses. *The American Journal of Hospice & Palliative Care* 11(6):28–35.

Taylor, E. J., M. Highfield, and M. Amenta. 1994. Attitudes and beliefs regarding spiritual care: A survey of cancer nurses. *Cancer Nursing* 17(6):479–487.

Tuck, I., L. Pullen, and C. Lynn. 1997. Spiritual interventions provided by mental health nurses. *Western Journal of Nursing Research* 19(3):351–364.

Underwood, L. G., and J. A. Teresi. 2002. The daily spiritual experience scale: Development, theoretical description, reliability, exploratory factor analysis, and preliminary construct validity using health-related data. *Annals of Behavioral Medicine* 24(1):22–33.

Walter, T. 1997. The ideology and organization of spiritual care: Three approaches. *Palliative Medicine* 11:21–30.

Whitehead, A. N. 1979. *Process and reality*. NewYork: The Free Press.

Widerquist, J. G. 1992. The spirituality of Florence Nightingale. *Nursing Research* 41(1):49–55.

Worthington, E. L., and G. G. Scott. 1983. Goal selection for counseling with potentially religious clients by professional and student counselors in explicitly Christian or secular settings. *Journal of Psychology and Theology* 11(4):318–329.

Zinnbauer, B. J., K. I. Pargament, and A. B. Scott. 1999. The emerging meanings of religiousness and spirituality: Problems and prospects. *Journal of Personality* 67(6):889–919.

CHAPTER 2

The Relationship between Religion and Spirituality

Christina Murphy

Introduction

In *The Eden Express*, an autobiographical novel by Mark Vonnegut (1976), a running joke occurs about how Vonnegut chose his major in college. Originally, he had planned to be a psychology major, but he soon switched to being a religion major as religion was psychology without the rats. This distinction, albeit a humorous one, provides insight into the various ways that religion and spirituality are distinguished. Often the issue consists of what can be added to spirituality to make it more akin to religion, or what can be removed from religion to make it more akin to spirituality. While this is a limited form of approaching a major philosophical and ideological issue, it is often the manner of reasoning used in considering what the relationship may be between religion and spirituality and in deciding on how to demarcate or eliminate the differences between these two modes of knowing and being in the world.

As with all logical arguments or investigations into meaning, the issue of how one defines religion or spirituality greatly influences the nature of the insights to be revealed. Traditionally, spirituality is defined as all matters related to the spirit, and views of what constitutes the spirit also vary. Religion is generally understood as a set of beliefs focusing upon the nature of a higher power or divine being and what conduct is required of the individual in relation to that supernatural entity. A set of codified ideas usually understood as dogma and generally some sacred text are also key components of religion while spirituality may require neither component. In the more restrictive sense, religion is often understood as organized religion, and, as such, takes on cultural, social, economic, and even legal implications that spirituality commonly does not. Religion and religious institutions, too, are seen as playing a greater role in world history than does spirituality, which often is viewed as a more contemporary phenomenon (Noss 2002). However, if spirituality is viewed as the search for holistic awareness of the supernatural, spirituality may be a component of many of the world's religions and also share in their extensive histories (Noss 2002). Then again, there are social theorists who envision the contrast between spirituality and religion as the rise of new religious organizations (Perrin and Mauss 1991) and the decline of old ones (Hoge and Roozen 1979)—a reality that R. Stephen Warner (1993) considers to be a "new paradigm" for understanding emerging cultural changes with regard to religious or spiritual systems (1080).

Conceptual Frameworks

The picture of what may or may not distinguish spirituality from religion is so unclear that it has led theorists to declare that the distinctions are "fuzzy" concepts (Zinnbauer et al. 1997). The concepts are so "fuzzy," in fact, that social scientists seeking to define these concepts, determine how participants experience them, or understand how these concepts may vary by demographics, socio-economic status, and psychosocial variables, generally find themselves unable to reach consensus (Zinnbauer et al. 1997). Interestingly, some theorists find the "fuzziness" a benefit in that it attests to the complexity of human experience in confronting the ultimate questions of existence (Dein 2005), whereas other theorists find the "fuzziness" to be chaotic and indicative of the disadvantages of non-rational, metaphysical thinking (Spilka and McIntosh 1997).

Adding to the philosophical turbulence is that issues of how to define religion or spirituality have shifted within each historical era. Even concepts of what mode of inquiry should be used to examine this question have changed over time. At one point in the ancient world, this question was a matter of metaphysics to be explored within the realm of subjective experience. While, certainly, the core elements of subjectivity and the personal validation of experience in both religion and spirituality remained as constants for a number of eras, theorists contend that a significant transformation occurred with the rise of secularism and the accompanying disillusionment with societal institutions (Boyer 2002). However, even as theorists note the rise of a heightened subjectivity and an intense secularism as the primary components of contemporary definitions of religion and spirituality, and even as theorists grapple with the implications of these new conceptual frameworks, a common unifying principle still remains; i.e., that religion and spirituality both embody states of consciousness far different from those of ordinary experience.

And therein lies an important distinction in terms of the implications of our ability to experience qualitatively different levels of perception and awareness. In large measure, these are issues associated with the question of what constitutes authoritative self-knowledge or an epistemic awareness of intentional states not based upon what is commonly understood to be "evidence." That is—as many empirical philosophers have claimed—consciousness of one's own thinking processes and the ideas and beliefs that emerge as a result cannot be validated or invalidated by the accepted concepts of what constitutes evidence (Davidson 1987; Dennett 1987). Consequently, as Heidegger, Nietzsche, Kierkegaard, and many other modern and postmodern philosophers have stated, there is no epistemology for authoritative self-knowledge beyond the self and what the self knows—or thinks it knows (Hardy 1999; Westphal 2004). This is a paradox, indeed—if not a philosophical conundrum. One way this paradox is stated ironically is in terms of Descartes' famous dictum: "I think; therefore I am" which, if truly taken to its most logical conclusion, would be stated as: "I think; therefore I think I am." The potential humor of this contra-statement is of significance in attempting to determine the relationship (or lack thereof) between religion and spirituality. What some see as a strength within both concepts, others see as an irresolvable conflux of contradictory ideas and impulses that negate any discernible meaning.

One fable associated with this issue is the story of the "infinite turtles." The story, as it is related in the opening paragraph of Stephen W. Hawking's *A Brief History of Time,* goes as follows:

> A well-known scientist (some say it was Bertrand Russell) once gave a public lecture on astronomy. He described how the earth orbits around the sun and how the sun, in turn, orbits around the center of a vast collection of stars called our galaxy. At the end of the lecture a little old lady at the back of the room got up and said: "What you have told us is rubbish. The world is really a flat plate supported on the back of a giant tortoise." The scientist gave a superior smile before replying, "What is the tortoise standing on?" "You're very clever, young man, very clever," said the old lady. "But it's turtles all the way down!" (1998, 2)

While different ideas of how to interpret the implications of this story of "turtles all the way down" abound, of importance to our discussion is the idea of infinite regression within philosophical assumptions—whether those assumptions focus upon cosmology (as with "infinite turtles"), authentic self-knowledge (as with Descartes), or distinctions between religion and spirituality. The pursuit of certain knowledge or "truth"—which often is the impetus for religion and spirituality—rests upon justifications that, in turn, rest upon justifications that must justify their means of justification through an infinite regression of "justifications all the way down." To abandon this infinite regression is to enter into the realm of probabilities or conclusions based upon what is generally deemed common sense reasoning. It remains to be seen if common sense reasoning can ever provide certain knowledge or "truth." It seems to be a shared component of both religion and spirituality that common sense reasoning is not the mode of consciousness that leads to experiencing or understanding the supernatural. Instead, significantly different modes of consciousness are required that exceed or eliminate common sense reasoning based upon concepts of possibility or plausibility (Plantinga 1990).

Knowledge Domains and Knowledge Claims

Interestingly, the same questions and epistemological dilemmas seem to arise with concepts of transcendent knowledge, which is the type of knowledge identified with and claimed by both religion and spirituality. This mode of understanding claims that what is known is known through the self, and the justification or "proof" is provided by non-rational means. The non-rational means may be the revelation of spiritual truths by a supernatural being or through intensely subjective and self-validating states of higher consciousness. Definitions of these states of higher consciousness vary, too, as one might expect, given their highly personal nature and non-rational core. Generally, they are described as states of unitive or holistic consciousness that can embody transcendent experiences, mystical experiences, or cosmic consciousness (Wuthnow 1978). They are also sometimes described as peak-experiences, a concept that comes from psychologist Abraham Maslow (1964). As the founder of humanistic psychology, Maslow believed that peak-experiences are moments of intense awareness that fill the individual with awe and wonder and provide a momentary but exceedingly powerful sense of the ultimate essence of all things. However, all is not quite as simple or clear as Maslow and other advocates of unitive consciousness contend. John Rowan, for example, states that in such highly charged states, both emotionally and psychologically, "the possibilities for deception and self-deception are also much greater" (1983, 17).

While the contemporary trend is to be cautious about—if not dismissive of—justifications for knowledge based upon infinite regressions, or "turtles all the way down," at least one prominent philosopher regards a chain of justifications that may go on forever as a perfectly acceptable characteristic of knowledge. Peter D. Klein (1971) considers such infinitism a branch of propositional knowledge and certainly no less valid or invalid in its claims than are foundationalism, coherentism, or skepticism. All provide theories about how beliefs can be justified, and all may be as invalid or as valid as any aspect of epistemology. All of these philosophies are based upon the idea that any proposition that cannot be justified by some means internal or external to the proposition itself is not knowledge. It is, instead, mere belief or simple relativism and, as such, will lead us into either the lived realities of Maslow or the deceptions and self-deceptions of Rowan.

Whether we examine knowledge from the perspective (or belief set) of foundationalism and assert there are foundational truths that are self-justifying or self-evident; whether we contend that a coherent system of beliefs that is internally consistent and logical is a sufficient justification for knowledge; or whether we pursue skepticism and contend that all knowledge is uncertain, we must still base our thought systems, presuppositions, and conclusions upon infinitism. We must do so because we must either allow premises and justifications to pursue and build upon each other in a never-ending sequence, or we must decide where and how to break the sequence. If we do break the sequence, we must justify that break on the basis of other justifications that will continue on in a potentially infinite sequence of concepts and justifications for concepts—which will bring us back to infinitism, albeit by a different route. So says Klein (1971), and his contentions are relevant to considering whether religion and spirituality are interchangeable terms, polar opposites, or subsets of each other within some grand metaphysical Venn diagram.

Of course, making the case for any of these three positions about the relationship between religion and spirituality depends upon the philosophical lens and the historical moment by which these positions are understood. Part of the complexity involved in deciphering these terms resides in distinguishing the locus of religious or spiritual reality. For some, the simplest line of demarcation is between the "internal" and the "external" in that spirituality is an "internal" experience while religion is an "external" experience. One can see here, too, the inherent assumption that religion is primarily known and experienced as a cultural and social construct with institutional warrants and standing—a status that is seldom identified with spirituality (Noss 2002).

Most interpretations of the concept of religion tend to focus upon organized religion, and so the distinction between organized religion as a societal institution, versus spirituality as a conceptual understanding or popular social movement largely independent of institutional structures, is a common distinction that continues throughout numerous discussions of these constructs. However, for whatever value may be found in the simple dichotomy of "internal" and "external" loci, some theorists do contend that spirituality resides within the individual and is primarily an act of intentionality, whereas religion requires the "external" constructs of a socially recognized and socially constructed faith that is based upon a creed or dogma. Also, religion generally involves a text regarded to be true (and often divinely inspired) that is delivered by a prophet or a divine being and that requires believers to comply with external codes of conduct (Roof 2001). Spirituality, on the other hand, does not require these components, and, in fact, some individuals are drawn to spirituality precisely for that reason (Holloway 2003).

Often such "internal" and "external" distinctions between spirituality and religion can generate the sense that spirituality is a falling away from religion. In other words, the desire to experience and relate to the supernatural realm remains as a part of spirituality, even if (or after) the traditional components and requirements of religion have no relevance or meaning to the individual. Thus, spirituality is sometimes viewed as a type of religion *manqué* or a lesser dimension of religious experience. The opposite can often be the case, too, in that those who were once religious (in the sense of following a particular creed and code of conduct) may look upon spirituality as a higher plane of awareness now freed from the constraints of a restrictive and limited way of interpreting and experiencing existence. In the first construct, a "spiritual" person is viewed as lost or misguided; in the second construct, a "religious" person is viewed as unable or unwilling to experience a freer engagement with life and with the divine. In other words, a "religious" person is viewed as lost or misguided.

Lest we feel stymied by this contrast in the way that "spiritual" and "religious" people may view each other and thus qualitatively distinguish between their experiences, perhaps a better approach is to move from epistemology, in which the certainty of knowledge is the goal. Perhaps our inquiries might be best served by examining religion and spirituality within axiology, or the study of the nature of values and value judgments. If we do so, we find a number of fields that focus upon concepts of meaning versus concepts of knowledge. Scientific psychology, for example, focuses upon mental phenomena and the relationship between mental acts and the external world. In contrast to physical phenomena, mental phenomena (mental acts) are intentionally directed toward an object, and that intentionality is often the distinguishing characteristic of what creates positive or negative feelings toward an object (McAlisdair 1976). From that premise, it is an easy transition to the philosophy of phenomenology and the sense that perception and introspection are related—if not identical modes—of consciousness and knowledge (Cronbach 1957).

If the relationship between religion and spirituality is examined in this context, the most significant emphasis would be upon the motivations and the values that structure intentionally directed behavior. Phrased differently, the issue would be: what motivates a person to be religious or spiritual and what motivates a social system to value religious or spiritual behavior? A related question would be: is there a qualitative difference in the experience of religious or spiritual consciousness? The answers to these questions are likely to reside in intentionality; i.e., the object toward which the mental phenomena of consciousness are directed (Mandler 2004). In this regard, religion is sometimes defined as an intentional focus on redemption or salvation, variously defined, while the intentional object of consciousness for spirituality is enlightenment, also variously defined (Watts and Williams 1995).

Intentionality and Knowledge: Contemporary Views

Locating religious or spiritual impulses or desires in the mental operations and phenomena of consciousness has led to new explorations of consciousness within the field of neurobiology. This new sub-field of exploration is being called the "cognitive neuroscience of religion" (Monastersky 2006, A14). While it is still cutting edge and controversial to identify religion with neuroscience, part of the impetus resides with the contemporary questioning of a centuries-old edict that scientific knowledge must operate independently of human values.

To some extent, this approach via neuroscience is a highly technological exploration of dualism or the mind/body problem of whether there can be consciousness independent of the physical body—more specifically, of the brain itself. For some researchers and theorists, the answer is that mental states (or consciousness itself) are independent of or superior to the physical brain. Thus, they reflect a transcendent experience of awareness or "beingness" that is an expression of a universal, cosmic life force. For others, there is no distinction between mental states (or consciousness) and the operations of the physical brain. Or phrased differently, "your joys and your sorrows, your memories and your ambitions, your sense of personal identity and free will, are in fact no more than the behavior of a vast assembly of nerve cells and their associated molecules" (Monastersky 2006, A17). So to argue that consciousness occurs independently of the brain or somehow transcends its physical functions is more an expression of wishful thinking than of a scientific reality. And those who do adhere to a materialistic view of the brain and consciousness as identical point to something as major as traumatic brain injuries or something as minor as metabolic changes in brain chemistry as proof of how a person's perceptions, emotions, sense of identity, and sense of well-being are rooted in the functionings of the organic brain. It is the brain that determines consciousness, and, for these individuals, no mental acts or states can ever occur independently of the brain.

Significantly, this argument about consciousness may well provide insights into differences in the intentional constructs and outcomes of religion and spirituality. For example, if there is an evidentiary basis—or a strong personal inclination—to believe that consciousness itself is a form of transcendent awareness, the willingness to accept a peak-experience of higher consciousness as the ultimate human goal will not likely be present. Whatever experience of higher consciousness that would satisfy the person who is seeking enlightenment would be unlikely to satisfy the person who is seeking transcendence itself—especially if ultimate transcendence is the capacity to have consciousness exist beyond the ephemeral physical realm and extend into an eternal supernatural realm. Neither would a momentary peak-experience of unitive, holistic consciousness that reveals a glimpse of the supernatural be likely to satisfy the person who is seeking through belief to find salvation or redemption. Obviously, the desired outcomes, internal motivations, and epistemological focus are inherently different and, as such, account for substantially different behaviors and social norms.

Social psychologists may see these distinctions as cultural in nature since there is no question that ideas of religion and spirituality—as well as of transcendent experiences—differ among cultures. For contemporary American society, though, spirituality has become identified with "interconnectedness" and so, consequently, spirituality can be perceived as a way of "being in the world" (Dein 2005, 526). An even more succinct way to state this idea is the famous dictum of Baba Ram Dass: "Be here now" (1971). While "interconnectedness" as a way of "being in the world" and as a means to "be here now" may seem too elusive or ethereal to provide much actual guidance for existence, philosopher Robert C. Solomon says that "our very being in the world" is a form of "basic trust" that is "an essential ingredient of spirituality" (2002, 45). If so, then the "basic trust" of spirituality may be more akin, or less akin, to the "faith" of religion. Once again, we return to our two starting points—whether what is added to spirituality makes religion, or what is subtracted from religion makes spirituality. To a certain extent, these two starting points also embody our additional questions of whether religion and spirituality are identical, opposite, or inter-connected concepts and experiences.

Disciplinary Interpretations

If we once again focus on modes of inquiry (which higher education tends to associate with academic disciplines), we could explore our questions about the relationship between religion and spirituality by examining how this issue affects the academic enterprise and also how the academic enterprise affects those who personally identify with religion or spirituality. Certainly, there is evidence that some in higher education use the terms interchangeably. One example is an article in the May 26, 2006, edition of *The Chronicle of Higher Education* titled "Religion on the Brain" that uses the terms "religion" and "spirituality" indistinguishably throughout to identify and discuss "the ethereal world of the spirit" (Monastersky 2006, A15). Brian J. Zinnbauer et al. (1997) make a similar point in support of the "fuzzy" amalgamation of ideas created by those writing on religion or spirituality in that theorists tend to use these terms "interchangeably" and "inconsistently" and to do so even after, in some instances, they have claimed distinguishing or isolating characteristics for one or the other concept (550). Zinnbauer et al. (1997) also comment upon the consequences of this lack of conceptual clarity for academic investigations:

> While this diversity of opinion regarding religiousness and spirituality may enrich our understanding of the constructs, the inconsistency in the definitions can also have some negative implications for social scientific research. First, without a clearer conception of what the terms mean, it is difficult to know what researchers and participants attribute to these terms. Second, a lack of consistency in defining the terms impairs communication within the social scientific study of religion and across other disciplines interested in the two concepts. Third, without common defi-

nitions within social scientific research it becomes difficult to draw general conclusions from various studies. (550)

In support of this argument, Kenneth I. Pargament (1997) contends that social scientists have traditionally addressed these inconsistencies by distinguishing between substantive or functional approaches. Substantive approaches look at the beliefs, emotions, and actions that individuals bring to their understandings of the supernatural realm, while functional approaches examine the purposes that such beliefs serve in the individual's life, especially in response to the most significant and complex issues of existence such as the meaning of life, death, suffering, good and evil, injustice, and ultimate purpose.

In academics, it is not surprising that differences between substantive and functional approaches may indicate different disciplinary emphases. A focus on the impact of beliefs upon the individual may fall within the domain of disciplines such as philosophy, psychology, and counseling that focus upon an individual's search for identity, purpose, and meaning as well as perhaps the most elusive of concepts—personal happiness or fulfillment. Functional approaches, on the other hand, would focus on how religion and spirituality function as social systems and thus would be of interest to such disciplines as anthropology, sociology, economics, political science, and history that tend to place primary emphasis upon group interactions within society and culture. This distinction between substantive and functional approaches in various disciplines is, of course, painted with broad strokes because nearly all disciplines contain both micro and macro focuses that examine the individual and/or society. Of greater significance, though, than how tightly the demarcating lines are drawn between a focus on the individual or on society is the issue of conceptualization; i.e., how the definitional questions surrounding religion and spirituality are drawn into larger questions. For higher education, the larger questions may also have implications for the contours and the crossroads of specific disciplines and also the methods by which disciplines investigate key questions and conduct their research.

Cultural Validation and Social Capital

What is also worthy of note in this regard is that some theorists see within functional approaches a leveraging point for distinguishing between religion and spirituality in terms of social capital, which is a concept that emerged primarily from sociology and political science to describe the benefits that accrue to individuals as the result of their membership in community networks (Coleman 1990). Ram A. Cnaan, Stephanie C. Boddie, and Gaynor I. Yancey (2003) believe that differences exist between the types of social capital generated by the role religion plays in contemporary society and the role that spirituality plays. They note, too, that religious life is often carried out through congregations and that America is rather distinctive in the way that congregations play a significant and often defining role in communities and thus contribute to the creation of social capital. While certainly community life and congregations can be components of spirituality and are not the exclusive domain of religion, generally there is less of a focus upon group and community in spirituality than there is in religion. In large measure, this is a historical and cultural function in that spirituality is often perceived and enacted as an individual experience and not as a communal one, and it is also often identified with a rejection of established social institutions, especially those associated with organized religion.

James S. Coleman (1990) recognizes the difference in power, historical longevity, and socio-cultural impact between religion and spirituality and the various aspects of social capital. However, unlike Cnaan, Boddie, and Yancey (2003), Coleman does believe that a framework of social trust exists within all social groupings, facilitating work and cooperation for mutual benefit. In this regard, he sees social capital as a set of "moral resources" that lead to increased cooperation among individuals of similar outlooks, attitudes, and dispositions (302–304). Thus, he contends that within both religion and spirituality there lies the activating principle that social capital makes "possible the achievement of certain ends that would not be attainable in its absence" (302).

We can also find within Coleman's theories particular unifying principles suggesting that, even though religion and spirituality may diverge in beliefs, actions, and definitions, they are also unified in the social trust that is essential to all interpersonal relationships. Consequently, a meaningful and motivating sense of purpose emerges from these relationships because there is a modification of self-interest that encourages the individual to look beyond the self to larger ideas, principles, responsibilities, and actions (Coleman 1990; 1988). Whether this modification is in terms of community and congregation or a more generalized sense that there is something spiritual or life-affirming beyond the self to which the self should show allegiance and fidelity, the principle is still a unifying one and may perhaps serve as a connection between religion and spirituality.

In a similar vein, sociologist Mark A. Granovetter (1973) contends that "weak ties" among social groups in American culture can create overlaps of ideas and impulses among people, many of whom can hold multiple memberships and identities within several social groups. In essence, "multiple layers of religious identity imply fluidity in religious organizational boundaries" (Ammerman 1997, 207). Individuals within several groups, or at the periphery of related groups, are often able to move among the groups and provide an intellectual equivalent to cross-pollination as the bearers of new ideas and information. Thus, the capacity for the overlapping of related social groups to share similar ideas and connections may lead to intellectual and experiential transactions (both societal and interpersonal) that reshape the social capital associated with religion and spirituality. Essentially, there may be the possibility for individuals holding memberships within multiple groups, or for social groups that are ideationally related, to reshape religious and spiritual understandings and thus further blur or clarify the distinctions between religion and spirituality—depending upon how one evaluates the outcomes of those interactions. They may, in the words of Zinnbauer et al. (1997), either further "fuzzy" or "unfuzzy" the philosophical complexities of each domain of understanding and experience. Nancy T. Ammerman (1997) provides another way to conceptualize this process:

> If persons are defined by an ever-changing and multifaceted set of interactions, they bring that multidimensionality to the organizations they inhabit, as well. The culture of a given organization is constantly reshaped by the changing array of persons in it, each bringing a complicated history of practices into the mix. In addition, the organization's "structure" must be seen to include both its own programs and governance and its network of connections. It is a space in which certain actions are made possible, a space with connections to other spaces inhabited by related persons and actions. Religious organizations are as much a more-or-less portable collection of skills and resources as a location on a theological map. (208)

One outgrowth of this interconnectedness is that cultural change is both unifying and diversifying, a principle that, as social theorists tell us, all of human history demonstrates (Martin 1978; Berger 1996). No doubt, as history and theory also both attest, a tendency often occurs to place in opposition perspectives that are actually complementary realities—such as freedom and responsibility, independence and relatedness, or objectivity and subjectivity.

Conclusion

Human experience is such that we understand, interpret, and act within a spectrum of possibilities rather than within the confines of strict and unbridgeable polarities. Thus, any discussion of the relationship between religion and spirituality must consider the spectrum of possibilities rather than the reductive arguments that would separate complex human experiences and beliefs into simple binary choices or outcomes. In fact, any analysis of conscious experience cannot so easily polarize subjective and objective mental acts from each other as social scientists might prefer or hope to discover. Equally valid is the idea that the finite may or may not yield insights into the infinite, and yet conscious experiences of the finite and the infinite may tell a different story to the person whose subjective sense of self is shaped by the experience. The fact is that there is an intrinsic, essentialist experience to consciousness, and many aspects may well be irreducible by nature. Only to the observer are there two sides of the coin, whereas, to the coin itself, there is only the reality of oneness.

This conceptual attempt to separate qualities of being from essences is similar, in scientific parlance, to an individual's experience of a primary color like red that is an irreducible reality and cannot be analyzed into constituent parts. In technical terms, the red is a quale—or a property (such as redness) considered apart from things having the property. Intellectually, we can imagine red as a reality, but our experience of it is through the entities that manifest redness. Thus, it is conceivable that those who seek an experience of the sacred may encounter Descartes' famous dictum in another way whether they pursue the sacred through religion or spirituality. They may realize that immediate experience, in some form, might be all that exists because the spectrum of experience as a totality may well be itself a quale. In other words, immediate experience may be the unity of the coin versus the two sides of the coin, in the same way that distinguishing the experience of the sacred in either religion or spirituality may be more a judgment call of the observer than an inherent quality of the essence of the experience.

Applying these metaphors of quale and coin to a consideration of the relationship between religion and spirituality may prove as insightful or as specious as endeavoring to understand intuition and intellect as polarities, for surely in this, as in all things, there are crossroads where paths meet and diverge. In this regard, religion and spirituality are united in essence even if deemed distinct or different by the judgment of observers. There is a quality to the experience of the sacred or divine that is essential and non-translatable into causal intuitions or rationalist categories based upon what/where/who/how/why questions (Warner 1993; Güzeldere 1995).

Accepting this premise would seem to suggest that knowledge can be discovered through individual experience independent of social structures. However, there is one epistemological caveat to accepting this premise entirely. As Harry M. Collins (1993) points out, knowledge is always encultured knowledge—meaning that the experience of knowledge (or the knowledge of a particular experience) is always socially instantiated. Consciousness itself is largely (if not fully) shaped by the language structures of a given culture. There is an encultured element to language and thus to thought, and if thought and consciousness are one ("I think; therefore I am") or if thought is a function of consciousness (I think; therefore, I think I am), both realities reflect the cultural basis of knowledge. Many theorists have upheld this view of the enculturation of language and its relationship to consciousness, perhaps chief among them is the noted philosopher Ludwig Wittgenstein (1953).

In turn, the idea that knowledge is encultured means that human experience, including that of the sacred, cannot be understood apart from culture and language. This concept leads us once more to the "fuzziness" associated with defining the types of knowledge that derive from religious and spiritual understandings. In order to "unfuzzy" some of the confusion associated with these terms, Zinnbauer et al. (1997) examined participants' understanding of what religion and/or spirituality meant to them. In this domain, they found some significant distinctions:

> ...spirituality was most often described in personal or experiential terms, such as belief in God or a higher power, or having a relationship with God or a higher power. Definitions of religiousness included both personal beliefs and practices such as church membership, church attendance, and commitment to the belief system of a church or organized religion. (561)

However, they go on to conclude that "although religiousness and spirituality appear to describe different concepts, they were not fully independent" in large measure due to the fact that "religiousness and spirituality did not significantly differ in the nature of the sacred" (561).

If so, the conclusion of Ralph W. Hood et al. (1996) that no single perspective on religion or spirituality dominates postmodern culture but, instead, multiple perspectives exist simultaneously, is as valid as the varied and enormous range of subjective experiences possible to individuals. In addition, contrasting these terms and the realities they represent as good-bad or superior-inferior dichotomies only adds to the confusion and diminishes our capacity to understand these concepts and their significant personal and societal outcomes. For Ammerman (1997), such an integrative approach would require "nothing less than the decentering of modernism as our primary interpretive frame" largely because:

> Modern frames assumed functional differentiation, individualism, and rationalism as "the way things are." Modern frames looked for bureaucratically organized institutions with clear lists of members and tasks. Modern frames looked for a clear line between rational, this-worldly, action and action guided by any other form of wisdom. Modern frames looked for the individualized "meaning system" that would be carved out of differentiation and pluralism. I hesitate to invoke the word postmodern, given all its baggage, but it seems to me a useful concept here. The root of our problems with the either/or concepts with which we work is that we now live in a both/and world. (212)

Instead of either/or concepts that may no longer fit a both/and world, what seems an appropriate means of resolution and insight is to consider both religion and spirituality as dimensions of holistic awareness (Roberts 2003). In doing so, we may avoid running the risk of limiting personal understanding and the social scientific study of the relationship between religion and spirituality to "narrow religion" and "fuzzy spirituality" (Zinnbauer et al. 1997, 563).

References

Ammerman, N. T. 1997. Organized religion in a voluntaristic society. *Sociology of Religion* 58:203–215.

Berger, P. L. 1996. Secularism in retreat. *National Interest* 46:3–12.

Boyer, P. 2002. *Religion explained: The evolutionary origins of religious thought.* New York: Basic Books.

Cnaan, R. A., S. C. Boddie, and G. I. Yancey. 2003. Bowling alone but serving together: The congregational norm of community involvement. In *Religion as social capital: Producing the common good*, ed. C. Smidt. Waco, TX: Baylor University Press.

Coleman, J. S. 1988. Social capital in the creation of human capital. *American Journal of Sociology Supplement* 94:S95–S120.

———. 1990. *Foundations of social theory*. Cambridge, MA: Harvard University Press.

Collins, H. M. 1993. The structure of knowledge. *Social Research* 60:95–116.

Cronbach, L. J. 1957. The two disciplines of scientific psychology. *American Psychologist* 12: 671–684.

Dass, B. R. 1971. *Be here now*. New York: Three Rivers Press.

Davidson, D. 1987. Knowing one's own mind. *Proceedings and Addresses of the American Philosophical Association* 60:441–58.

Dein, S. 2005. Spirituality, psychiatry and participation: A cultural analysis. *Transcultural Psychiatry* 42(4):526–544.

Dennett, D. C. 1987. *The intentional stance*. Cambridge, MA: MIT Press.

Granovetter, M. S. 1973. The strength of weak ties. *American Journal of Sociology* 78:1360–1380.

Güzeldere, G. 1995. Problems of consciousness: A perspective on contemporary issues, current debates. *Journal of Consciousness Studies* 2:112–143.

Hardy, L. 1999. Postmodernism as a kind of modernism: Nietzsche's critique of knowledge. In *Postmodern philosophy and Christian thought*, ed. M. Westphal. Bloomington: Indiana University Press.

Hawking, S. W. 1998. *A brief history of time: From the big bang to black holes*. New York: Bantam Books.

Hoge, D. R., and D. A. Roozen, eds. 1979. *Understanding church growth and decline, 1950–1978*. New York: Pilgrim Press.

Holloway, R. 2003. *Doubts and loves: What is left of Christianity*. Edinburgh, Scotland: Canongate Books.

Hood, R. W., B. Spilka, B. Hunsberger, and R. Gorusch. 1996. *The psychology of religion: An empirical approach*. New York: Guilford Press.

Klein, P. D. 1971. A proposed definition of propositional knowledge. *Journal of Philosophy* 67:471–482.

Mandler, J. Matter. 2004. *The foundations of mind: Origins of conceptual thought*. New York: Oxford University Press.

Martin, D. 1978. *A general theory of secularization*. Oxford: Blackwell.

Maslow, A. 1964. *Religions, values and peak-experiences*. New York: Penguin Books.

McAlisdair, L. L. 1976. *The philosophy of Franz Brentano*. London: Duckworth.

Monastersky, R. 2006. Religion on the brain. *The Chronicle of Higher Education* 52(38): A14–A19.

Noss, D. S. 2002. *A history of the world's religions*. Englewood Cliffs, NJ: Prentice Hall.

Pargament, K. I. 1997. *The psychology of religion and coping*. New York: Guilford Press.

Perrin, R. D., and A. L. Mauss. 1991. Saints and seekers: Sources of recruitment to the Vineyard Christian Fellowship. *Review of Religious Research* 33:97–111.

Plantinga, A. 1990. Justification in the twentieth century. *Philosophy and Phenomenological Research* 50:45–71.

Roberts, K. A. 2003. *Religion in sociological perspective.* Belmont, CA: Wadsworth Publishing.

Roof, W. C. 2001. *Spiritual marketplace: Baby boomers and the remaking of American religion.* Princeton, NJ: Princeton University Press.

Rowan, J. 1983. The real self and mystical experiences. *Journal of Humanistic Psychology* 23: 8–27.

Solomon, R. C. 2002. *Spirituality for the skeptic: The thoughtful love of life.* New York: Oxford University Press.

Spilka, B., and D. N. McIntosh. 1997. *The psychology of religion: Theoretical approaches.* Boulder, CO: Westview Press.

Vonnegut, M. 1976. *The Eden express.* New York: Bantam Books.

Warner, R. S. 1993. Work in progress toward a new paradigm for the sociological study of religion in the United States. *The American Journal of Sociology* 98(5):1044–1093.

Watts, F. N., and M. Williams. 1995. *The psychology of religious knowing.* London: Geoffrey Chapman Publishers.

Westphal, M. 2004. *Transcendence and self-transcendence: On God and the soul.* Bloomington: Indiana University Press.

Wittgenstein, L. 1953. *Philosophical investigations.* Oxford: Blackwell.

Wuthnow, R. 1978. Peak experiences: Some empirical tests. *Journal of Humanistic Psychology* 18:59–75.

Zinnbauer, B. J., K. I. Pargament, B. Cole, M. S. Rye, E. M. Butter, T. G. Belavich, K. M. Hipp, A. B. Scott, and J. L. Kadar. 1997. Religion and spirituality: Unfuzzying the fuzzy. *Journal for the Scientific Study of Religion* 4:549–564.

CHAPTER 3

Spirituality and Higher Education Law

John Wesley Lowery

With a renewed interest in the role of spirituality in higher education, many colleges and universities (especially public ones) are seeking to understand and resolve the complex legal issues that arise in addressing spirituality and religion in and outside of the classroom. Robert O'Neil (1997), former president of the University of Virginia, warns, "Religious expression on the public campus has been persistently troublesome and may become more so" (xv). Clark (2001) notes that much of the hesitation to address spirituality on campus may be because we are "unaware of or confused about the legal issues involved in religion and spirituality on the college campus" (38). This confusion stems largely from two conflicting clauses of the First Amendment that address religious issues: the Establishment Clause and the Free Exercise Clause. Kaplin and Lee (1995) describe the requirements under the Establishment Clause for public institutions of higher education:

> Under the Establishment Clause of the First Amendment, public institutions must maintain a neutral stance regarding religious beliefs and activities; they must, in other words, maintain religious neutrality. Public institutions cannot favor or support one religion over another, and they cannot favor or support religion over nonreligion. (56)

However, institutions of higher education also run the risk of violating the constitutional demands of the First Amendment by favoring or supporting nonreligion over religion (Lowery 2004).

General Principles

To place spirituality in higher education today in its proper context, it is vital to consider the Constitution's protection of the free exercise of religion and prohibition against the establishment of religion by the government as set forth in the First Amendment (Lowery 2000, 2004). The courts have been forced to seek a balance between these two competing fundamental rights in deciding cases involving education. In *Lemon v. Kurtzman* (1971) and *Tilton v. Richardson* (1971), the Supreme Court of the United States established its three-part test for determining whether a government activity violates First Amendment's establishment of religion clause. In *Lemon*, the Court concluded an official state religion does not need to create bylaws or policies to violate the First Amendment stating, "A given law might not establish a state religion, but nevertheless be one 'respecting' that end in the sense of being a step that could lead to such establishment, and hence offend the First Amendment" (403 U.S. at 611). Drawing upon earlier decisions in this area, the Supreme Court in *Lemon* set forth its new three-part test: "First, the statute must have a secular legislative purpose; second, its principal or primary effect must be one that neither advances nor inhibits religion; finally, the statute must not foster 'an excessive government entanglement with religion'" [citations omitted] (403 U.S. at 612–613).

Kaplin and Lee (1995) acknowledge that while the first part of the *Lemon* (1971) test is relatively easy to understand, "the other two prongs (effect and entanglement) have been both very important and very difficult to apply in particular cases" (59). Chief Justice Burger noted in his *Tilton* (1971) ruling, "Candor compels the acknowledgment that we can only dimly perceive the boundaries of permissible government activity in this sensitive area of constitutional adjudication" (403 U.S. at 678). The courts continue to seek to establish these boundaries more than three decades later (McCarthy 2001).

The majority of cases in which the U.S. Supreme Court has addressed the free exercise of religion in the context of education originated in a K-12 setting. However, many of these decisions have significant importance in the context of higher education as well. In *West Virginia v. Barnette* (1943), the Supreme Court ruled a West Virginia policy requiring students to salute the American flag, which violated Jehovah's Witnesses' religious beliefs, to be unconstitutional. Justice Jackson opined,

> If there is any fixed star in our constitutional constellation, it is that no official, high or petty, can prescribe what will be orthodox, in politics, nationalism, religion, or other matters of opinion or force citizens to confess by word or act their faith therein. (319 U.S. at 642)

In *Employment Division v. Smith* (1990), the Supreme Court refined its test articulated in *Sherbert v. Verner* (1963) and *Wisconsin v. Yoder* (1972) for determining if a government regulation related to religious practice violated the Free Exercise of Religion clause of the First Amendment. The Court allowed "a neutral, generally applicable regulatory law that compelled activity forbidden by an individual's religion" (494 U.S. at 880).

The U.S. Supreme Court's most recent effort at balancing these two competing clauses of the First Amendment involving higher education was *Locke v. Davey* (2004). The Court upheld a Washington State scholarship program, the Promise Scholarship, which prohibited students pursuing a degree in theology from receiving the scholarship. Joshua Davey had received a Promise Scholarship from the State of Washington. However, he learned he could not use the scholarship if he pursued his desired degree in pastoral ministries at Northwest College. The Promise Scholarship would allow Davey to attend a religious college such as Northwest College to major in a subject other than theology. He sued, claiming that the restrictions upon the Promise Scholarship violated the Free Exercise and Establishment Clauses. The late Chief Justice Rehnquist writing for the majority concluded, "The State's interest in not funding the pursuit of devotional degrees is substantial and the exclusion of such funding places a relatively minor burden on Promise Scholars. If any room exists between the two Religion Clauses, it must be here" (540 U.S. at 1315). The fact that the Promise Scholarship allowed Davey to attend the institution, but not major in pastoral studies, was evidence of a lack of "the hostility toward religion" (540 U.S. at 1314). Only Justices Scalia and Thomas dissented in this case.

Spirituality in the Classroom

In recent years, legal disputes have arisen on public college campuses resulting from conflicts between students' religious beliefs and academic requirements or activities of the institution. These cases illustrate the legal issues that may arise from both students' and faculty members' religious beliefs in the classroom.

In *Axson-Flynn v. Johnson* (2004), the Court of Appeals for the Tenth Circuit considered the case of Christina Axson-Flynn, a devout Mormon and a student in the University of Utah's Actor Training Program (ATP). During her first semester in the program, she refused to take God's name in vain or curse during classroom acting exercises because such actions violated her strong religious beliefs. Christina was told by the ATP faculty to "'get over' her refusal to use those words, saying that not using the words would stunt her growth as an actor" (356 F.3d at 1280). Christina decided to withdraw from the ATP program after her second semester believing that eventually she would be forced to leave the program by the ATP faculty for her refusal to use profane language. She brought suit under 42 U.S.C. § 1983 in federal district court against the University. Her suit was dismissed by the district court, and she appealed the decision to the Court of Appeals for the Tenth Circuit. She claimed that forcing her to use this profane language under the penalty of a reduced grade or eventual removal from the Actor Training Program violated her rights under the First Amendment to both Freedom of Speech and Free Exercise of Religion. The court observed in analyzing her free speech claims:

> That schools must be empowered at times to restrict the speech of their students for pedagogical purposes is not a controversial proposition. By no means is such power limited to the very basic level of a teacher's ability to penalize a student for disruptive classroom behavior. (356 F. 3d at 1291)

The court distinguished between Christina's claims and the compelled speech cases addressed by the Supreme Court, such as *West Virginia v. Barnette* (1943). In a similar case, *Settle v. Dickson County Sch. Bd.* (1995), the U.S. Court of Appeals for the Sixth Circuit upheld the right of a ninth-grade teacher to prohibit a student from writing her research paper on Jesus Christ because of the educational goals of the assignment. The court distinguished between students' free speech claims arising out of class assignments from those outside of the classroom noting,

> Where learning is the focus, as in the classroom, student speech may be even more circumscribed than in the school newspaper or other open forum. So long as the teacher limits speech or grades speech in the classroom in the name of learning and not as a pretext for punishing the student for her race, gender, economic class, religion or political persuasion, the federal courts should not interfere. (53 F. 3d at 156)

However, the Tenth Circuit also considered whether the requirement that Christina use words which she considered to violate her Mormon beliefs was a result of an educational goal or pedagogical concern or instead simply an excuse to punish her for her religious beliefs. The court did not resolve this issue, but instead remanded the case for further consideration on this issue and the issue of her Free Exercise claims. The district court was also instructed to place greater emphasis on her free speech claims. Brown (2002) notes that in recent years plaintiffs in cases involving both Freedom of Speech and Free Exercise of Religion claims have found the greater success through Freedom of Speech Claims. French (2002) advises students, "Religious individuals and groups can *enhance* the level of constitutional protection by combining their First Amendment *free exercise* rights with other constitutional rights—such as *freedom of speech* and *freedom of association*" (12).

After the Court of Appeals for the Tenth Circuit ruled in this case, the University of Utah settled Axson-Flynn's case under which the university agreed to appoint a committee to develop a policy on religious accommodation. In 2005, the University of Utah officially adopted the resulting accommodations policy which creates a formal system for students to request accommodations when the content of the course violates their "sincerely held core beliefs." However, the policy does not require faculty to grant accommodations when "the subject course requirement has a reasonable relationship to the legitimate pedagogical goal."

Another case which garnered considerable public attention involved the University of North Carolina at Chapel Hill's decision to use Michael Sells's *Approaching the Qur'An: The Early Revelations* (1999) as part of the university's summer orientation reading program in 2002 (*Yacovelli v. Moeser* 2004). Several groups attempted to block the reading program claiming the program violated the Establishment Clause of the First Amendment, but the federal district court and the Court of Appeals for the Fourth Circuit refused to grant a preliminary injunction to these external groups. A group of students at UNC continued this case claiming the program violated their rights under the Free Exercise Clause of the First Amendment because they would be forced to read about a religion other than their own. The district court soundly rejected the students' claim for several key reasons: first, UNC had a clearly established policy which allowed any student to refrain from reading the book and the students presented no factual evidence that reading the book in question would limit the Free Exercise of their religious beliefs. Furthermore, the district court also noted that the book was not a religious reading, but rather should be characterized as an academic discussion of a religious work. In granting summary judgment for the university, the district court concluded:

> UNC implemented a program asking students to discuss a religion thrust into recent controversy, and to do so from an academic perspective. Part of the purpose of this program was to introduce students to the type of higher-level thinking that is required in a university setting. Students who were not members of the Islamic faith,

> probably the great majority of students, were neither asked nor forced to give up their own beliefs or to compromise their own beliefs in order to discuss the patterns, language, history, and cultural significance of the Qu'ran. (324 F. Supp. 2d at 764)

Taken together, these cases demonstrate that religion and spirituality are clearly a topic which is not out of bounds in public higher education (*Yacovelli v. Moeser*), but public institutions must also give some consideration to students' Free Speech and Free Exercise rights (*Axson-Flynn v. Johnson* 2004). Provided that the content is reasonably related to educational goals and not a pretext for religious discrimination, the courts are most likely to side with colleges and universities.

In considering the issue of faculty speech in the classroom, issues of academic freedom also come into play. The leading case on this intersection of religion and academic freedom is *Bishop v. Aronov* (1991). Professor Bishop taught courses in exercise physiology and would occasionally mention his religious beliefs in the classroom, a practice about which some students complained. Bishop was ordered by the university to discontinue this practice at which time he brought suit against the university claiming that this action was a violation of his academic freedom. The U.S. Court of Appeals for the Eleventh Circuit ruled for the institution concluding "the university's authority in matters of course content as superior to that of the professor" (Kaplin and Lee 1995, 310). However, several commentators have suggested the court may not have been sensitive enough to Bishop's academic freedom claims (Kaplin and Lee 1995; O'Neil 1997). Justice Alito, while serving on the U.S. Court of Appeals for the 3rd Circuit, wrote for the majority in *Edwards v. California University of Pennsylvania* (1998) reaching a similar conclusion. Justice Alito wrote, "Professor Edwards does not have a First Amendment right to choose classroom materials and subjects in contravention of the University's dictates" (156 F. 3d at 493).

More recently, James Tuttle, an adjunct professor of philosophy at Lakeland Community College, sued the institution claiming he was being punished for discussing his religious beliefs in the classroom (Evelyn 2004). While this case has not been tried, it does clearly indicate these issues are far from resolved. Furthermore, the courses which Tuttle taught, philosophy and religion, have direct bearing on his claim. O'Neil (1997) noted that the relevancy of the professor's religious beliefs to the course subject must be considered when determining the impact of academic freedom on the matter.

Spirituality Outside the Classroom

Colleges and universities must also carefully consider the legal implications of addressing issues related to spirituality and religion outside of the classroom. Controversies most often arise in the context of student-initiated religious expression. One area in which these issues most often arise are related to the relationship with student religious groups. Often this confusion stems from an overemphasis of the Establishment Clause of the First Amendment without fully considering the Free Speech and Free Exercise Clauses. Summarizing the rights of students in this area, Kaplin and Lee (1995) conclude that students have "A general right to organize; to be officially recognized whenever the school has a policy of recognizing student groups; and to use meeting rooms, bulletin boards, and similar facilities open to student groups" (516).

In *Healy v. James* (1972), the United States Supreme Court ruled President James of Central Connecticut State College had violated the First Amendment by refusing to approve a student group's request for recognition. The students sought to form a student organization to serve as a local chapter of the Students for a Democratic Society (SDS). The Court concluded this decision was based largely upon the president's disagreement with SDS' philosophy. In describing association rights, the Court observed:

> While the freedom of association is not explicitly set out in the [First] Amendment, it has long been held to be implicit in the freedom of speech, assembly, and petition. There can be no doubt that denial of official recognition, without justification, to college organizations burdens or abridges that associational right. (408 U.S. at 181)

The Court acknowledged this was not absolute, however. In three specific situations a public college or university would be justified in its refusal to recognize a student organization:

1. The group has a known "affiliation with an organization possessing unlawful aims and goals, and a specific intent to further those illegal goals." (408 U.S. at 186)
2. The group poses a "substantial threat of material disruption through its conduct." (408 U.S. at 189)
3. The group refuses to comply with "reasonable school rules governing conduct." (408 U.S. at 191)

The U.S. Court of Appeals for the First Circuit specifically addressed the issues involving recognition of student religious organizations in *Aman v. Handler* (1981). In this case, the University of New Hampshire refused to recognize a campus chapter of the Collegiate Association for Research of Principles (CARP). The university based its decision on the organization alleged ties with Reverend Sun Myung Moon and the Unification Church. While the university attempted to justify its decision through exemption articulated in *Healy*, the court ruled the university had not provided sufficient justification under the *Healy* standard, which places the burden for justifying non-recognition on the institution.

Beyond the initial recognition of student religious organizations, colleges and universities must also consider issues related to space and funding for student religious organizations. In *Widmar v. Vincent* (1981), the Supreme Court ruled that once a public institution allows student groups access to university facilities, a student religious organization could not be denied access to the same facilities for religious services. Justice Powell noted, "Having created a forum generally open to student groups, the University seeks to enforce a content-based exclusion of religious speech. Its exclusionary policy violates the fundamental principle that a state regulation of speech should be content-neutral" (454 U.S. at 277). Kaplin and Lee (1997) warned that this ruling did not allow public institutions to create facilities specifically for religious groups.

The Supreme Court expanded its *Widmar* (1981) decision to apply to the distribution of mandatory student activity fees in *Rosenberger v. Rector and Visitors of Univ. of Va.* (1995). Justice Kennedy opined that the University of Virginia had created a "metaphysical" (515 U.S. at 830) forum by funding student organizations to which the same principles expressed in *Widmar* could be applied. Once the university began to pay for the printing of student publications, the institution could not refuse to pay for the printing of *Wide Awake*, a student Christian publication, because of the religious viewpoint it expressed. Justice Kennedy wrote in his opinion,

> By the very terms of the SAF prohibition, the University does not exclude religion as a subject matter but selects for disfavored treatment those student journalistic efforts with religious editorial viewpoints. Religion may be a vast area of inquiry, but it also provides, as it did here, a specific premise, a perspective, a standpoint from which a variety of subjects may be discussed and considered. The prohibited perspective, not the general subject matter, resulted in the refusal to make third-party

payments, for the subjects discussed were otherwise within the approved category of publications. (831)

The Supreme Court turned specifically to the question of the constitutionality of mandatory student activity fees in *Board of Regents of Univ. of Wis. System v. Southworth* (2000). Again writing for the majority, Justice Kennedy concluded, "The First Amendment permits a public university to charge its students an activity fee used to fund a program to facilitate extracurricular student speech if the program [by which funds are allocated] is viewpoint neutral" (529 U.S. at 251).

Taken as a whole, these Supreme Court cases clearly illustrate that public colleges and universities cannot exclude student religious speech or organizations from settings, or "forums" in the language of the Court, to which other student speech or organizations are granted access. In these circumstances, the courts, following Supreme Court precedent, will emphasize students' Free Speech and Free Exercise rights over institutional concerns regarding the Establishment of Religion.

Several issues have arisen on college campuses in recent years that the courts have not yet resolved. Legal disputes have arisen on a number of campuses related to the recognition of student organizations by public colleges and universities. These disputes have involved the denial of recognition to student groups, most commonly student religious groups, which have refused to comply with one of more provisions of the institution's non-discrimination policy. The student religious groups have argued that forcing the organizations to accept as members or leaders gay, lesbian, bisexual, and transgendered students, or other students who, in the group's view, do not share their religious beliefs would interfere with the members' free exercise of their religious beliefs. The institutions, however, have typically responded that they have a legal obligation to prevent this type of discrimination. These conflicts have arisen at the University of Minnesota, University of North Carolina at Chapel Hill, Ohio State, Penn State, Purdue University, and Rutgers University, among others ("Alliance Defense Fund Champions" 2004; Bartlett 2004; French 2004; Lukianoff 2004; "Ohio State Throws" 2004; "Penn State Gives" 2004; "Penn State Weasels" 2004; "Univ. of North Carolina Refuses" 2004). Most recently, the United States Court of Appeals for the Seventh Circuit issued a preliminary injunction ordering the Southern Illinois University School of Law to recognize the Christian Legal Society while the group's lawsuit moved forward. To succeed in its request for a preliminary injunction, the Christian Legal Society needed to convince the court it was reasonably likely to succeed on the merits of its lawsuit. Judge Sykes concluded,

> First, it is not clear CLS actually violated any SIU policy, which was the justification offered for revoking its recognized student organization status. Second, CLS has shown a likelihood that SIU impermissibly infringed on CLS's right of expressive association. Finally, CLS has shown a likelihood that SIU violated CLS's free speech rights by ejecting it from a speech forum in which it had a right to remain. (*Christian Legal v. Walker*, 2006)

Although only a preliminary injunction, the court's decision offered a clear indication that judges looked favorable on the Society's claim.

Ultimately, this question must be evaluated in light of the Supreme Court's rulings in *Roberts v. United States Jaycees* (1984), *Board of Directors of Rotary Int'l v. Rotary Club of Duarte* (1987), and *Boy Scouts of America v. Dale* (2000). While it seems far less likely that these groups would meet standards set by the Court for intimate association, there can be little doubt that student religious groups are engaged in expressive association. The very purpose of these groups is to further the members' individual and collective expression of their religious beliefs. Many institutions of higher education require that student organizations not discriminate in membership on the basis of religion, and a growing number of institutions also prohibit recognized student groups from discriminating on the basis of sexual orientation. In either case, student religious groups could very effectively argue that compliance with these prohibitions against discrimination in membership would infringe upon a religious group's "freedom of expressive association if the presence of that person affects in a significant way the group's ability to advocate public or private viewpoints" (*Boy Scouts of America v. Dale*, 648). Such a claim would apply to both general membership and eligibility to hold leadership positions within the organization. As Chief Justice Rehnquist noted, the Court would give deference to the group's belief regarding the impact of the forced inclusion of other members. While it may well be a number of years before the Supreme Court ultimately answers this question, the Court's precedents in this area clearly suggest the Court will ultimately side with the student groups in most cases. More recently the Supreme Court discussed these concepts in a higher education case, *Rumsfeld v. Forum for Academic & Institutional Rights, Inc.* (2006), although the Supreme Court refused to overturn the Solomon Amendment as the members of the Forum for Academic & Institutional Rights. While rejecting the application of *Dale*, *Roberts*, and *Duarte*, the Court clearly indicated continuing significance of these cases.

During the 2005–2006 academic year, the University of Wisconsin-Eau Claire was embroiled in a controversy that would ultimately involve the entire University of Wisconsin system. The University of Wisconsin-Eau Claire sent letters to resident assistants ordering them to stop holding voluntary Bible studies in their residence hall rooms. After attempting to negotiate a compromise, the RAs sought assistance from the Foundation for Individual Rights in Education (FIRE), which ultimately intervened publicly after the group's own efforts at private resolution were unsuccessful. With considerable press attention to the case, the University of Wisconsin Board of Regents sought a system-wide review of the policy ("Religious Liberty," 2006). In March 2006, the Board of Regents adopted a new policy governing resident assistants' use of their rooms for private meetings:

> RAs may participate in, organize, and lead any meetings or other activities, within their rooms, floors or residence halls, or anywhere else on campus, to the same extent as other students. However, they may not use their positions to pressure, coerce, or inappropriately influence student residents to attend or participate. ("Taxpayer's Protection Amendment" 2006)

Ultimately, the University of Wisconsin concluded that a public institution of higher education could not simply exclude religion from possible topics of discussions, without violating the First Amendment.

Prayer at Graduation and Other Public Events

One of the most visible and perplexing aspects of religion on public college campuses involves prayers or invocations at graduation and other public events on campus. Part of this confusion stems from the Supreme Court's own limited rulings in this area. The Supreme Court has consistently ruled that prayers at public events, such as graduation or football games, were unconstitutional in the context of K–12 public education, even when led by students (*Engel v. Vitale*, 1962; *Lee v. Weisman*, 1992; *Santa Fe Independent School District v. Doe*, 2000; *School Dist. of Abington Township v. Schempp*, 1963; *Wallace v. Jaffree*, 1985). In its school prayer cases, the Supreme Court has stressed the coercive nature of prayer in public school context even while acknowledging that participation in some events was not purely mandatory. In *Lee*, the Court warned "the Constitution guarantees that government may not coerce anyone to support or participate in religion or its exercise" (505 U.S. 587).

The Supreme Court has not, however, heard a case involving prayer of this type in public higher education. Generally, the federal appellate courts have distinguished between higher education and K–12 setting and reached a different conclusion than the one suggested by the Supreme Court's K–12 rulings. In both *Tanford v. Brand* (1997) and *Chaudhuri v. Tennessee* (1997), the U.S. Courts of Appeals for the Seventh and Sixth Circuits, respectively, upheld as constitutional religious invocations at the graduations of Indiana University and Tennessee State University. One of the most important factors in each court's analysis was the absence of the coercive environment described by the Supreme Court in its rulings. In *Chaudhuri*, the court also stressed the absence of any likely influence of prayers upon the college graduates, unlike the impressionable nature of school-aged students at the heart of the Supreme Court's cases. The one exception to this trend is the U.S. Court of Appeals for the Fourth Circuit's ruling in *Mellen v. Bunting* (2003). The court ruled that General Bunting, then Superintendent of Virginia Military Institution (VMI), had violated the Constitution in reinstating the tradition of supper prayer in 1995. The implications of *Mellen* are significantly limited by the unique environment at VMI, which the court described as highly coercive. Such conditions are unlikely to be found at other non-military public institutions. The Commonwealth of Virginia appealed the case to the United States Supreme Court which declined to grant certiorari. In an unusual move, two justices wrote opposing opinions regarding their views on whether the Court should hear the case (Klein 2004). Justice Scalia, joined by the late Chief Justice Rehnquist, argued that the Court should have taken up the case because of the "weighty questions" (541 U.S. at 1022) involved and his concerns regarding application of the Court's rulings from K–12 education to colleges and universities.

Conclusion

With the renewed interest in both spirituality in higher education and traditional religious expression in American society and on campus, it is vital that faculty and administrators understand the potential legal implications of their choices in these areas. As this chapter has sought to resolve, these are not questions which lend themselves to simplistic answers. Institutions must be mindful of two seemingly conflicting obligations: to respect students' right to the free exercise of their religious beliefs coupled with free speech rights, and to avoid violating the Establishment Clause by unconstitutionally favoring religion.

References

Accommodations policy. 2005. University of Utah. http://www.admin.utah.edu/facdev/accommodations-policy.pdf (accessed January 7, 2006).

Alliance Defense Fund champions free speech at three university campuses. 2004. Alliance Defense Fund. http://www.alliancedefensefund.org/story/?id=435 (accessed October 12, 2004).

Aman v. Handler, 653F.2d 41 (1st Cir. 1981).

Axson-Flynn v. Johnson, 356 F.3d 1277 (10th Cir, 2004).

Bartlett, T. 2004. Christian fraternity sues U. of North Carolina over Chapel Hill's refusal to recognize it. *Chronicle of Higher Education*, 10 September, A35.

Bishop v. Aronov 926 F.2d 1066 (11th Cir. 1991).

Board of Directors of Rotary Int'l v. Rotary Club of Duarte, 481 U.S. 537 (1987).

Board of Regents of Univ. of Wis. System v. Southworth, 529 U.S. 217 (2000).

Boy Scouts of America v. Dale, 530 U.S. 640 (2000).

Brown, S. P. 2002. *Trumping religion: The new Christian right, the free speech clause, and the courts*. Tuscaloosa: The University of Alabama Press.

Chaudhuri v. Tennessee, 130 F.3d 232 (6th Cir. 1997), cert. denied, 523 U.S. 1024 (1998).

Christian Legal v. Walker, 453 F.3d 853 (7th Cir. 2006).

Clark, R. T. 2001. The law and spirituality: How the law supports and limits the expression of spirituality on the college campus. In *The Implications of Student Spirituality for Student Affairs Practice: New Directions for Student Services*, no. 95, ed. M. A. Jablonski, 37–46. San Francisco: Jossey-Bass.

Edwards v. California University of Pennsylvania, 156 F.3d 488 (3d. Cir.1998), cert. denied 525 U.S. 1143 (1999).

Employment Div., Dept. of Human Resources of Ore. v. Smith, 494 U.S. 872 (1990).

Engel v. Vitale, 370 U.S. 421 (1962).

Evelyn, J. 2004. Saying he was punished for revealing his faith, adjunct sues Ohio college. *Chronicle of Higher Education*, 16 July, A13.

French, D. A. 2002. FIRE's guide to religious liberty on campus. Philadelphia: Foundation for Individual Rights in Education.

———. 2004. FIRE's letter to Ohio State. http://www.thefire.org/pdfs/Ohio_State_french_to_holbrook_082004.pdf (accessed September 20, 2004).

Healy v. James, 408 U.S. 169 (1972).

Kaplin, W. A., and B. A. Lee. 1995. *The law of higher education* 3d ed. San Francisco: Jossey-Bass.

———. 1997. *A legal guide for student affairs professionals.* San Francisco: Jossey-Bass.
Klein, A. 2004. Supreme Court declines to hear Virginia Military Institute's prayer case. *Chronicle of Higher Education,* 7 May, A40.
Lee v. Weisman, 505 U.S. 577 (1992).
Lemon v. Kurtzman, 403 U.S. 602 (1971).
Locke v. Davey 540 U.S. 712 (2004).
Lowery, J. W. 2000. Walking the halls of ivy with Christ: The classroom and residential experiences of undergraduate evangelical students. Unpublished doctoral dissertation, Bowling Green State University, Bowling Green, Ohio.
———. 2004. Understanding the legal protections and limitations upon religion and spiritual expression on campus. *College Student Affairs Journal* 23: 146–157.
Lukianoff, G. 2004. Victory for religious freedom at Purdue. http://www.thefire.org/issue.php?doc=purdue_stewart_victory_051904.htm (accessed September 20, 2004).
McCarthy, M. 2001. Preserving the establishment clause: One step forward and two steps back. *Brigham Young University Education and Law Journal* 2001(2): 271–298.
Mellen v. Bunting, 327 F.3d 355 (4th Cir. 2003), cert. denied, 541 U.S. 1019 (2004).
Ohio State University throws in the towel, agrees to change non-discrimination policy. 2004. http://www.alliancedefensefund.org/story/?id=509 (accessed October 12, 2004).
O'Neil, R. M. 1997. *Free speech in the college community.* Bloomington: Indiana University Press.
Penn State gives in: Christian student club gets approval. 2004. http://www.alliancedefensefund.org/story/?id=449 (accessed October 12, 2004).
Penn State weasels out. 2004. http://www.alliancedefensefund.org/story/?id=516# (accessed October 12, 2004).
Religious liberty vindicated across University of Wisconsin System. 2006. http://www.thefire.org/index.php/article/6899.html (accessed March 15, 2006).
Roberts v. United States Jaycees, 468 U.S. 609 (1984).
Rosenberger v. Rector and Visitors of Univ. of Va., 515 U.S. 819 (1995).
Rumsfeld v. Forum for Academic & Institutional Rights, Inc., 126 S. Ct. 1297 (2006).
Santa Fe Independent School Dist. v. Doe, 530 U.S. 290 (2000).
School Dist. of Abington Township v. Schempp, 374 U.S. 203 (1963).
Sells, M. A. 1999. *Approaching the Qur'An: The early revelations.* Ashland, OR: White Cloud Press.
Settle v. Dickson County Sch. Bd., 53 F3d 152 (6th Cir. 1995).
Sherbert v. Verner, 374 U.S. 398 (1963).
Tanford v. Brand, 104 F.3d 982 (7th Cir. 1997), cert. denied, 522 U.S. 814 (1997).
Taxpayer's Protection Amendment could mean higher tuition, fewer students, Regents learn. 2006. http://www.wisconsin.edu/news/2006/r060310.htm (accessed March 15, 2006).
Tilton v. Richardson, 403 U.S. 672 (1971).
Univ. of North Carolina refuses to recognize Christian fraternity for sticking to Christian membership. 2004. http://www.alliancedefensefund.org/story/?id=481 (accessed October 12, 2004).
Wallace v. Jaffree, 472 U.S. 38 (1985).
West Virginia Bd. of Ed. v. Barnette, 319 U.S. 624 (1943).

Widmar v. Vincent, 454 U.S. 263 (1981).
Wisconsin v. Yoder, 406 U.S. 205 (1972).
Yacovelli v. Moeser, 324 F. Supp. 2d 760 (M.D.N.C. 2004).

CHAPTER 4

Biological Basis of Spirituality

Dixie Dennis

> *Whether or not we find what we are seeking*
> *Is idle, biologically speaking*
> Edna St. Vincent Millay
> "I Shall Forget You Presently"
> 1920

Formed by combining the Greek *bios* (life) and *logos* (study of), biology is the study of life, including human life. Although biology is unlike physics in that biology can not always be described in terms of objects that obey immutable physical laws, it nevertheless encompasses genetics, which is based on DNA molecules that are responsible, for the most part, for a person's characteristics at birth (Wales 1999).

Before the late 1970s, health educators, practitioners who empower people to take control over and improve their lives by health promotion and health prevention activities (World Health Organization 1986), agreed that a person's biological characteristics at birth could be segmented into physical (e.g., fitness and working body parts and organs), mental (e.g., thinking), emotional (e.g., feelings), and social (e.g., temperament) dimensions. In 1979, Robert Russell, one of my teachers at Southern Illinois University, Carbondale, revolutionized the health education profession with his idea that spirituality belongs in the profession's Model of Health because it is a legitimate component of health. Furthermore, he believed spirituality is deeper than the other dimensions of health and is, therefore, the "directing" dimension. Currently, most health educators agree that spirituality is a viable, and directing component of health, and it is included in the agreed-upon Model of Health. Interestingly, though, the term *spirituality* still is not well understood by many health educators, including whether spirituality is biologically based.

Other health professionals, including physicians, who typically engage in disease and injury treatment, endorse the idea that spirituality affects health positively (Koenig 2002; Making a Place 1998; Rowe and Allen 2004). This thought is not new among physicians. Almost a half century ago when health was believed comprised only of physical and mental dimensions, Halbert Dunn (1959), a physician and Chief of the National Office of Vital Statistics at the Department of Health, Education, and Welfare, explained the importance of spirituality on those two dimensions of health by reporting that he did not believe he had ever seen a person who was sick in spirit who could maintain mental or physical health for long. Similar to many health educators, physicians, in general, though, do not understand *how* spirituality helps a person maintain his/her health or whether it is biologically based.

Understanding Spirituality

Many times, a concept is better understood by explaining what it is not. To explain, spirituality is not religion. A person's spirituality, though, may be enhanced by religion (Carr 2000). To further complicate any understanding of spirituality, a person may be spiritual and not religious or religious and not spiritual or neither or both. Yates (1997) differentiated religion from spirituality by explaining that spirituality is a journey of the heart, whereas religion is a journey of an established, institutionally patterned system of dogma and beliefs, including beliefs about God. Even though believing in God is not necessary to be spiritual (Spilka et al. 2003), because about 95 percent of Americans believe in God (Miller and Thoresen 2003) it seems reasonable to assume that what/who is spiritual for them may be God. For people (religious and/or spiritual) who believe in God, it makes more sense that God would be more interested in people living a positive, full, meaningful life (i.e., spirituality, which is later defined in this chapter) than about their obeying rules. Many religious people who attend church regularly and try diligently to live "the right way" (possibly God directed), nevertheless, live unfulfilled, negative lives (not possibly God directed). Only about 46 percent of Americans attend church (religion), but 58 percent of Americans say that they frequently think about what is meaningful (i.e., spirituality) in their lives (Inglehart 2004), which implies that many Americans may be more spiritual than religious.

Of interest regarding the degree of spirituality a person possesses is that, on tests designed to measure spirituality, females typically "out-score" men (Dennis et al. 2004). Hamer (2004) explained this by asserting women are more attuned to their emotional connections, which, he says, are the heart of spirituality. Some researchers and scientists may wonder, though, if females are more emotional and/or more spiritual from birth or if they are taught to be spiritual, which means, of course, men could be taught, too. Also worthy of note regarding spirituality among specific populations is that, on a recent survey, 68 percent of one segment of Americans, scientists, who in the past were frequently viewed as a-spiritual, classified themselves as "spiritual person[s]" (Harper 2005).

Definitions of spirituality include indices of values, principles, hopes, dreams, desires, goals, direction and eagerness for living (Reker 2003). Conversely, people with an unhealthy degree of spirituality, or spiritually ill people, are described as lazy, greedy, rude, sarcastic, prejudiced, and hostile (Seaward 2001). One health educator defined spirituality as the connection to oneself, others, nature, and to a larger meaning or purpose (Scandurra 1999). Likewise, most health educators currently agree that spirituality is the positive "feeling" (Abels, 2000), "experience" (Brussat and Brussat 2000), and/or "thing" (Dorsey 2000) that gives meaning to a person's everyday life. In other words, spirituality is merely living a fully alive, meaningful life. Ernest Becker (1975) concludes, "It [spirituality] is an expression of the will to live, the burning desire of the creature to count, to make a difference on the planet because he [sic] has lived, has emerged on it, and has worked, suffered, and died" (3). Hamer (2004) believes that humans are genetically predisposed to be spiritual.

Biologically Spiritual

The brain never stops working and fuels its work with glucose, a simple sugar. The brain takes up about 3 percent of the body's weight but consumes approximately 20 percent of the body's oxygen to help it burn glucose. To situate the mind-brain-consciousness discussion, which occurs through much of the remainder of this chapter, a basic understanding of the brain is needed. Although the brain has hundreds of structures and functions, only the most basic, relative to understanding the plausibility of the biological nature of spirituality, are presented.

The frontal cortex is the thinking part of the brain, called the "new" brain, wherein messages from other parts of the brain, including the limbic system (described in the following paragraph), are sent and received across the left and right hemispheres. Much of what can be seen on the surface of an exposed brain is the wrinkled "gray matter" of the new brain. The frontal cortex takes up approximately a third of the entire cortex. The frontal cortex depends on consciousness. The higher the percentage of the entire cortex that is frontal, the more complex cognitive tasks, like reasoning, can be performed. For example, unlike humans with about 30 percent frontal cortex, dogs only have about 7 percent, meaning, of course, that humans reason better than dogs! Could the frontal cortex be the biological basis for humans to understand that they are spiritual—because it just makes sense?

The limbic system, referred to as the "old" brain, makes up the inner section of the brain. All animals, including animals that predate humans, have limbic systems. This system is the place where drives (hunger, thirst, and sex), emotions and passions (love, sadness), and arousal are housed and where the brain's messages are biochemically placed into memory. The limbic system does not depend on reasoning/thinking/consciousness.

The mesolimbic dopamine pathway also is important for understanding later discussions about the possibility of biological spirituality. This pathway is the reward circuit in the brain, "hooking up" dopamine in the limbic system to create memories powerful enough to be remembered. Dopamine is a neurotransmitter (messages that signal nerve cells) responsible for motivating humans to have basic urges to eat, drink, have sex, and be fearful when necessary. Obviously, the dopamine pathway is believed to be needed for survival of the species. Are humans motivated, genetically and unconsciously, to be spiritual—for survival?

In efforts to understand the spiritual nature of humankind, Assagioli (1965), founder of psychosynthesis, and Jung (1964), a pioneer in the field of psychology who was fascinated with the unconscious mind, wrote about a "higher unconsciousness" in all humans. Jung referred to this region as the collective unconsciousness wherein he believed the essence of God in all people resides. According to Jung, this divine essence is manifest in the conscious mind partly through intuition and creativity.

At its core, consciousness refers to being aware, especially of that which is within oneself (*Merriam-Webster*, Collegiate Dictionary, 10th ed.). Still, according to Steven Smith (2001), scientist and engineer, scientists debate the nature of consciousness. Some claim consciousness arises from "unknown" interactions of Quantum Mechanics, while others believe consciousness is the operation of a complex machine—the brain. Others, Smith proclaims, claim the human mind (and consciousness) is distinct from the physical body. For example, Smith avers some scientists believe people are basically conscious beings who feel, contemplate the meaning of life, and freely decide how to think and act. These people appear to be fundamentally different from machine-like brain-operated people. In their book, *A Universe of Consciousness: How Matter Becomes Imagination*, Gerald Edelman (a Nobel-winning scientist) and Giulio Tononi (2001) describe consciousness as being purely neuron-based, with a particular kind of brain process. These authors never explain how consciousness arises but merely describe it as a machine-like brain operation. For example, these authors contend that "value messages" originate in the brain stem (the most primitive part of the brain) and that the higher brain matches them to perceptual categories, which creates a loop of correlations between events and those categories. Smith also offers a consciousness theory. Smith contends in his Inner Light Theory that, like Jung (1964) believed, inner reality (unconsciousness) is created by the sub-reality machine in the brain (consciousness). Said another way, spirituality (collective unconsciousness) is biologically made in and by the conscious part of the brain.

Whether humans can ever become "fully" conscious (and likewise fully spiritual), though, has not been resolved. Russell (1998) attributed Albert Einstein with proclaiming no problem can be solved from the same consciousness that created it. This view also can be said to reveal that people did not arrive in this world "spiritually naked...the operating instructions were clearly written in a language that the heart understands" (Seaward 2001, 100).

Clearly, if spiritual awareness is natural and part of consciousness, it likely also seems commonplace, meaning, of course, that it must be present in persons of all ages and cultures as well as different levels of education. Because of this universality, according to Hay and Socha (2005), a scientist can make only one type of substantiation for spirituality, which is to determine if it works for him/her. Others believe that spirituality can and should be measured and that it can be done so scientifically (Miller and Thoresen 2003).

Measuring Spirituality

Some people have opposed the scientific study and measure of spirituality. One philosophical basis for this opposition, according to Miller and Thoresen (2003), is some researchers' belief that there is nothing to be studied, implying spirituality is immaterial and, therefore, beyond the senses. Another possible reason for not studying spirituality is that science, by definition, is incapable of studying spirituality, meaning spiritual tenets are subjective and cannot be directly observed and replicated. Actually, though, throughout history, phenomena that were not directly observable have been scientifically studied and readily believed. Einstein's Theory of Relativity is an example. Possibly, some features of spiritual experiences, per se, may not be possible to study; nevertheless, it seems logical that spirituality can be both studied and measured similar to other biologically based health dimensions, such as physical, mental, emotional, and social. Many medical tests (blood pressure, blood work, and weight, for example) and many psychological tests to measure mental and emotional capacity, as well as social tests or personality tests, exist, providing a measure of the degree a person possesses these health dimensions.

Miller and Thoresen (2003) explain that much scientific research on spirituality already exists. Furthermore, many instruments are available for studying spirituality, such as one from Hill and Pargament (2003) and another from Reker (1999). In efforts to obtain spirituality "scores" of different populations (e.g., college students, African American college students, prisoners, exercisers), I have used Reker's valid and reliable survey, the Life Attitude Profile-Revised (LAP-R). The LAP-R contains 48 questions and was designed to measure meaning in life (i.e., spirituality) among individuals of all ages from adolescence to later adulthood. Because the word *spirituality* is not used in the survey and no religious practices such as praying or reading the Bible are mentioned, the survey appears not to bias people regarding any previous beliefs or practices regarding spirituality or its related concept—religion. In addition to ascertaining the degree of spirituality a person has, questions on this survey can be used to measure the innate yearning a person has to increase his/her spirituality (Hamer 2004).

Each of the 48 LAP-R questions (Reker 1999) is profiled in terms of six subscales (Purpose, Coherence, Choice/Responsibleness, Death Acceptance, Existential Vacuum and Goal Seeking) and two composite scales (Personal Meaning Index and Existential Transcendence).

1. Purpose: Having life goals, having a mission in life, having a sense of direction from the past, in the present, and toward the future. Implicit in Purpose is the notion of what is centrally important in a person's life.
2. Coherence: Possessing an intuitive understanding of self, others, and life in general. A score on this subscale provides an indication of a person's belief in his/her reason for existence.

3. Choice/Responsibleness: Demonstrating a perception of freedom to make all of life's choices. Choice/Responsibleness provides an index of the degree to which a person perceives that s/he is directing his/her life.
4. Death Acceptance: Having an absence of for regarding death as well as accepting death as a natural aspect of life.
5. Existential Vacuum: Having a lack of meaning and direction in life.
6. Goal Seeking: Having an eagerness to get more out of life.
7. Personal Meaning Index: Combining Purpose and Coherence, resulting in a more focused measure of personal meaning.
8. Existential Transcendence: Developing a global measure of attitudes toward life that takes into account both the degree to which meaning and purpose have been discovered and the motivation to find meaning and purpose. Existential Transcendence = Purpose + Coherence + Choice/ Responsibleness + Death Acceptance − the combination of Existential Vacuum and Goal Seeking.

One reason people may have different scores on spiritual assessments is that spirituality can be enhanced or lessened through life experiences. Cermak (1986), for example, believes parental alcoholism can diminish a child's spiritual nature. A child's spiritual growth is further dwarfed if s/he is not encouraged to develop a sense of spiritual identity, which is typically later revealed by an inner emptiness, i.e., less spirituality (Mull 1990). Another reason people may score differently on spiritual surveys is that some people "practice" their spiritual path and others do not. Just as a person would practice running, stretching, and weight-training before running a marathon (physical dimension), a person could practice his/her spiritual health dimension by taking deliberate steps to be more loving, kind, humble, and forgiving. Finally, people may have different spiritual scores in their spiritual dimension because they are inherently or genetically spiritually different—just as they are born with different physical, mental, social, and emotional dimensions.

Genetic Science

In his book, *The God Gene: How Faith Is Hardwired into Our Genes*, Dean Hamer (2004), a behavior geneticist, argues that spirituality is *in part* genetically based. As an impetus for this claim, Hamer defined spirituality as the capacity for self-transcendence, which includes self-forgetfulness, reverence, connectedness to other things/people, and intuitions. Next, in a survey Hamer assessed various populations regarding their temperament and character, paying particular attention to both identical and fraternal twins for their relative spirituality. Finally, he searched for genes that control serotonin and dopamine (both monoamine neurotransmitters) that play a role in mood, arousal, thinking, consciousness, and, by extension, spirituality, or the sense of self. The key to Hamer's argument is that the sense of self is derived from serotonin, dopamine, and other monoamines.

After collaborating with other scientists, and searching from over 35,000 genes and 3.2 billion chemical bases in the human genome, Hamer (2004) identified a "spiritual" gene, VMAT2, one of nine genes known to produce monoamines. Hamer showed that variances in the VMAT2 gene were associated with capacities for self-transcendence. He found that more often than not people with nucleic acid cytosine in one spot on this gene ranked high in spirituality, and those with nucleic acid adenine in the same spot ranked lower. Many people argue that Hamer possibly found one gene to indicate humans may be biologically spiritual, but many other "spiritual" genes likely exist. Hamer believes, however, that a person's genetic makeup determines, or at least helps to determine, how spiritual s/he is.

In reviewing Hamer's (2004) book, Keener (2005) proclaims that whether a person agrees or disagrees with Hamer is contingent on the degree s/he believes human personality is rooted in DNA (Deoxyribonucleic Acid), the nucleic acid that contains an organism's genetic instructions—the heredity molecule, or whether they believe it is shaped by environment. Many times, though, the old nature-versus-nurture choice (i.e., biology versus environment) is really nature *and* nurture, with percentages of each unknown. The same nature-and-nurture precursor seems plausible for spirituality.

Amy Nutt (2002) wrote about neuroscientist Rhawn Joseph, who spent many years studying history, myth, and biology to understand the universality of spirituality. According to Nutt, Joseph believes the connection between the brain and spirituality suggests humans are hardwired not just for spirituality but for God. Some people might argue that spirituality *is* God. Nevertheless, as an example to show that people are hardwired for God, Joseph said that the capacity to experience God is in the limbic system—the first-formed and most primitive part of the brain wherein urges originate. As explained previously, people naturally yearn to sleep, eat, and have sex, for example, and Joseph is saying that they, too, yearn to search for God. Joseph also offered an alternative explanation—evolution—for spirituality, meaning the limbic system neurons evolved over time to better cope with the unknown and to increase the likelihood of survival. Said another way, Joseph purported humans are genetically predisposed to be spiritual because belief in the divine makes them stronger and, therefore, able to survive longer than they would without it.

Clearly, D'Aquili and Newberg (1999), authors of *The Mystic Mind: Probing the Biology of Religious Experience,* argue that a person's sense of spirituality is a biological trait hardwired into genes by evolutionary design. Hamer (2004) and Joseph (Nutt, 2002) make similar arguments, and Jeffrey Kluger (2004) agrees, writing in *Time* magazine, "Even among people who regard spiritual life as wishful hocus-pocus, there is a growing sense that humans may not be able to survive without it" (64).

In addition to the belief that spirituality is a biological trait, so too is the extent of interest in pursuing spirituality. To explain, Borg, Andree, Soderstrom, and Farde (2003) believe variability in the serotonin 5-HT1A receptor may explain why people vary in spiritual zeal. Using the term *neurotheology*, Heffern (2001), like Joseph, reports that the brain's structure compels the spiritual urge. Neither concept, spirituality and the spiritual urge, contradicts the structure of the brain nor do they contradict the studies by Reker (1999), who measured both.

Through neurobiological research using image-scanning technologies, D'Aquili and Newberg (1999) reported that spirituality and spiritual experiences are too complex, evolving over millions of years, to be derived solely from one part of the brain. Interestingly, these authors use the terms "mind" and "brain" to be the same as did scientists who referred to light as both wave and particle. Just as a wave and particle are different but the same, at least, regarding light, so too are the mind and brain. To explain, the mind typically refers to thinking while the brain involves both thinking and feeling as appropriate functions. So thinking alone, as well as the combination of thinking and feeling, may be the impetus for and synonymous with spirituality and spiritual experiences.

In an analysis of Andrew Newberg's book, *Why God Won't Go Away,* Louise Palmer (2004) explained that Newberg believes there is a place in the brain, the Absolute Unitary Being (AUB), that mystics have claimed is far more real than daily "reality." Furthermore, Newberg claims that whether AUB is real or not, it provides a common source of all spiritual urges, which is not unlike Jung's (1964) theory of the collective unconscious. Palmer writes that many of the best scientific minds of the twentieth century (Albert Einstein, Robert Oppenheimer [theoretical physicist who helped create the atom bomb], and Edwin Schroedinger [physicist who helped create quantum theory]) believed the universe had a purpose that went beyond the material world. Newberg is quoted as saying a spiritual state is merely a neurological event, meaning that spirituality is real and biological.

Biological "Evidence"

Studies of twins are important tools for substantiating evidence about whether human traits are biological. Identical twins, or monozygotic twins, have identical DNA. These siblings' genotypes (specific genetic makeup) are duplicates of each other. For example, if one twin has an olive skin tone and blonde hair, so will the other. Fraternal twins, or dizygotic twins, share only half of their genes with each other. Their skin tone or hair color may be very different from each other. While twin studies using fraternal twins obviously do not serve as well for establishing biological evidence, they, nevertheless, serve ideally for a comparison to identical twins. If biology is more influential than environment, identical twins will be more similar than fraternal twins (Plomin et al. 1997).

Twins' studies have been used extensively to show biological basis for four of the dimensions of health—physical, mental, emotional, and social dimensions. As long as an environment exists, though, to show is not to prove, but it is as close as scientific studies can come. Among hundreds of examples of "proof" that the aforementioned dimensions of health are biological, the following are part: Liang and Eley (2005), who used twins to study depressive symptoms (emotional dimension of health); Jonsson et al. (2003) to study obesity (physical dimension of health); Hughes et al. (2005) to study theory of mind (mental dimension of health); and Daniels & Plomin (1985) to study infant shyness (social dimension of health). While fewer in number, there have also been twin studies conducted to provide evidence, sometimes biological evidence, of the spiritual dimension of health. Recently, Dr. Harold G. Koenig, professor of psychiatry at Duke University; director and founder of Duke's Center for Spirituality, Theology, and Health; editor-in-chief of *Science and Theology* News; and editor of the *International Journal of Psychiatry in Medicine,* used twin studies to show a genetic root for spirituality. Onion (2005) wrote that Koenig examined surveys completed by 169 identical and 104 fraternal twins. The findings revealed a genetic basis for spirituality, but his study was not the first to do so.

Among the first twin-spirituality studies was one led by one of Koenig's advisors, Thomas Bouchard, in 1979. Bouchard has been the Director of the Twin and Adoption Research since 1983, and he was awarded the Kistler Prize for his scientific research with monozygotic and dizygotic twins. In that now-famous study, Bouchard and fellow researchers tracked down 53 pairs of identical twins and 31 pairs of fraternal twins wherein spirituality was showed to be twice as strong among fraternal twins as the other twins. Over the years, Bouchard consistently found that spirituality is likely genetic ("Why do we believe" 2005).

Other compelling evidence regarding the likelihood of spirituality being biological is the pilot study by Tsuang et al. (2002). Tsuang and his fellow researchers conducted a study of spirituality and mental health using 100 pairs of twins and showed that a spiritual genetic linkage was strongly indicated. Nevertheless, it seems that just because a person is predisposed to be spiritual does not mean the trait does not need to be cultivated similarly to the other health dimensions.

Cultivating Spirituality

Alcoholics Anonymous (AA) is likely the oldest and best known program whereby people attempt to become more spiritual. In AA, a strong conviction to become more spiritual is not needed—only the willingness to become more spiritual. AA members tout that their newfound spirituality makes it possible to unlock the shackle of alcoholism and help them live spiritual lives, implying, of course, that spirituality can be learned—or possibly re-learned.

Many studies have been conducted by physicians, who also are researchers, trying to measure the effect they *see* that spirituality has on patients' health. Moreover, today more than 70 of the 125 United States medical schools offer specific courses in spirituality or incorporate it into the existing curriculum. Consequently, many physicians are taught to take patients' spiritual histories. When physician Walter Larimore (2003) asked a patient why he didn't mind being asked "spiritual questions," such as "Does praying give meaning to your life?", the patient replied, "…the fact that you ask, it tells most patients that it's important" (31). In a *Newsweek* article (Kalb 2003)

Harold Koenig said, "'keeping spirituality out of the clinic is irresponsible'" (47).

Over a half century ago, it was suggested that the continuing purpose of education was the development of moral and spiritual values (National Education Association 1951). Rachel Kessler (2000), author of *The Soul of Education*, contends "We decided to exclude the spiritual dimension from education because we adults couldn't agree on what 'it' was or how to teach 'it'" (xii). Furthermore, Kessler says many classrooms are spiritually empty, not by accident, but by design.

An impetus for spiritually empty classrooms—in schools and universities—likely hovers around the issue of constitutionality. Many Americans, including school teachers and college professors, mistakenly believe the Constitution forbids the study of religion in public houses of learning. While it is true the courts have removed the "practice" of religion from public education, the Supreme Court many times has upheld the "study" of religion (Nord 1995). Moreover, as previously stated, religion and spirituality are different concepts; and, in theory, even if practicing religion was forbidden by courts, the practice of and the study of spirituality is not (Dennis and Dennis 2002).

Others in the health field may believe they do not know how to help someone increase his or her spiritual dimension of health. To learn to do so is important, though. In a 2005 *Chronicle of Higher Education* article, Thomas Bartlett reported the results of a national study conducted in 2004 in which 112,232 college freshmen were surveyed. Approximately 80 percent reported they have an interest in spirituality and that they search for meaning and purpose in their lives. In contrast to this finding, Bartlett quoted Claire Gaudiani, former president of Connecticut College, who believes students are not educated in the spirit. She said, "'Right now students get the sense that we don't do spirituality'" (A40). According to another person quoted in Bartlett's article, Alexander Astin, director of the research center at UCLA (where the study was conducted), colleges should be searching for ways to incorporate spirituality into the curriculum even if it makes some professors uncomfortable. Dennis and Dennis (2002) believe spirituality can be taught by having professors, even those who are not comfortable teaching spirituality, offer activities and opportunities that allow each person to choose and apply processes that can result in increased spirituality—just like teaching students that eating a well-balanced diet and exercising can result in better physical health if they choose to comply.

An example of spiritual education is described by Kessler (2000). She offers a situation in which a teacher incorporated spirituality into her English class by organizing her entire curriculum around relationships and love, selecting literature related to those themes. In addition to readings, students kept journals to express their feelings about what they read. Once a week, students sat in council to share stories and feelings stirred from the required readings. Another avenue for spiritual education is Atkinson's (2001) "Student's Workbook for Exploring the Spiritual Journey." Students first look at different ways in which they can "be" spiritual through various workbook activities, such as readings, sayings, art, music, nature scenes, videos, and so on. The student is then called upon to reflect his/her personal thoughts by writing in the workbook. Students are offered the opportunity to discuss their thoughts/feelings with their classmates. Afterward, students are encouraged to explore and practice those spiritual activities that they discovered bring meaning to their lives.

In conclusion, I have explained what spirituality is, that it can be measured and increased, and that it can be done so in public school and university settings. In tandem with those explanations, though, is a compelling case that humans are more likely than not to be biologically spiritual with genetic spiritual yearnings. Therefore, educators would be remiss in trying to enhance other biological health dimensions but not the directing spiritual dimension. It makes sense that humans are spiritual—just like it makes sense that gravity exists, can be measured and taught, but cannot be seen or isolated except through manifestations of it. Whether or not researchers biologically isolate one spiritual gene or several spiritual genes, spirituality appears biological, probably consciously and unconsciously. As Edna St. Vincent Millay said about love, a related concept to spirituality, *whether or not we find what we are seeking is idle, biologically speaking.*

References

Abels, L., ed. 2000. *Spirituality in social work practice.* Denver, CO: Love Publishing Co.

Assagioli, R. 1965. *Psychosynthesis: A manual of principles and techniques.* New York: Viking.

Atkinson, D. L. 2001. The student's workbook for exploring the spiritual journey. *American Journal of Health Education* 32(1):96–99.

Bartlett, T. 2005. Most freshmen say religion guides them. *Chronicle of Higher Education* 22 April, A40.

Becker, E. 1975. *Escape from evil.* New York: The Free Press.

Borg, J., B. Andree, H. Soderstrom, and L. Farde. 2003. The serotonin system and spiritual experiences. *American Journal of Psychiatry* 160(11):1965–1969.

Brussat, F., and M. A. Brussat. 2000. *Spiritual R*. New York: Hyperion.

Carr, W. 2000. Some reflections on spirituality, religion, and mental health. *Journal of Psychology and Theology* 3(1):1–12.

Cermak, T. L. 1986. Diagnostic criteria for codependency. *Journal of Psychoactive Drugs* 18:15–20.

Daniels, D., and R. Plomin. 1985. Origins of individual differences in infant shyness. *Developmental Psychology* 21:118–121.

D'Aquili, G., and A. B. Newberg. 1999. *The mystical mind: Probing the biology of religious experience (theology and the sciences)*. Minneapolis, MN: Augsburg Fortress Publishers.

Dennis, D. L., and B. G. Dennis. 2002. Mental health: A case for spiritual education in public schools. *The Health Educator* 34(1):17–22.

Dennis, D. L., S. M. Muller, K. Miller, and P. Banerjee. 2004. Spirituality among a college student cohort: A quantitative assessment. *American Journal of Health Education* 35(4):220–227.

Dorsey, K. 2000. Spirituality added to curriculum. In C. Humphries, *The Southern Illinoisan*, 26 March, 5A–6A.

Dunn, H. L. 1959. What high-level wellness means. *Canadian Journal of Public Health* 50:447–457.

Edelman, G. M., and G. Tononi. 2001. *A universe of consciousness: How matter becomes imagination*. New York: Basic Books.

Hamer, D. H. 2004. *The God gene: How our faith is hardwired into our genes*. New York: Doubleday.

Harper, J. 2005. Scientists' spirituality surprises. *The Washington Times*, 15 August. http://washtimes.com/functions/print.php?StoryID=20050814-115521-9143r (accessed August 3, 2006).

Hay, D. H., and P. M. Socha. 2005. Spirituality as a natural phenomenon: Bringing biological and psychological perspectives together. *Zygon* 40(3):589–612.

Heffern, R. 2001. Exploring the biology of religious experience. *National Catholic Reporter Online*. http://www.natcath.com/NCR_Online/archives/042001/042001a.htm (accessed August 3, 2006).

Hill, P. C., and K. I. Pargament. 2003. Advances in the conceptualization and measurement of religion and spirituality: Implications for physical and mental health research. *American Psychologist* 58:64–74.

Hughes, C., S. Jaffee, F. Happé, A. Taylor, A. Caspi, and T. Moffitt. 2005. Origins of individual differences in theory of mind: From nature to nurture? *Child Development* 76:356–370.

Inglehart, R. F. 2004. *World values surveys*. Ann Arbor, MI: Author.

Jonsson, F., A. Wolk, N. L. Pederson, P. Lichtenstein, P. Terry, A. Ahlborn, and M. Feychting. 2003. Obesity and hormone-dependent tumors: Cohort and twin control studies based on the Swedish twin registry. *International Journal of Cancer* 106(4):594–602.

Jung, C. G. 1964. *Memories, dreams, reflections*. New York: Vantage.

Kalb, C. 2003. Faith and healing. *Newsweek*, 10 November, 43–56.

Keener, C. 2005. Review of *The God gene: How faith is hardwired into our genes,* by D. H. Hamer. *The Christian Century.* http://www.christiancentury.org/article.lasso?id=300 (accessed January 23, 2006).

Kessler, R. 2000. *The soul of education.* Alexandria, VA: Association for Supervision and Curriculum Development.

Kluger, J. 2004. Is God in our genes? *Time,* October, 64–68.

Koenig, H. G. 2002. An 83-year-old woman with chronic illness and strong religious beliefs. *Journal of the American Medical Association* 288:487–493.

Larimore, W. 2003. Cruising the highway of health. *Science & Theology* 3(9): 3, 31.

Liang, H., and T. C. Eley. 2005. Amonozygotic twin differences study of nonshared environmental influence on adolescent depressive symptoms. *Child Development* 76(6):1247–1260.

Making a place for spirituality. 1998. *Harvard Health Letter* 23(4):1–3.

Miller, W. R., and C. E. Thoresen. 2003. Spirituality, religion, and health. *American Psychologist* 58(1):24–35.

Mull, S. S. 1990. Help for the children of alcoholics. *Health Education* 21(5):42–45.

National Education Association. 1951. *Moral and spiritual values in public schools.* Washington, DC: Author.

Nord, W. A. 1995. *Religion and American education: Rethinking a national dilemma.* Chapel Hill: The University of North Carolina Press.

Nutt, A. E. 2002. *Researchers seek answers to faith's place in psyche.* Newhouse News Service. http://www.newhousenews.com/archive/story1a122302.html (accessed January 13, 2006).

Onion, A. 2005. Twin research links genetics and adult spirituality: As people enter adulthood, religious "genes" kick in. *ABC News.* http://abcnews.go.com/Technology/print?id=589469 (accessed January 5, 2006).

Palmer, L. P. 2004. What does he believe in? *Spirituality & Health* 10:28–39, 76

Plomin, R., J. C. DeFries, G. E. McClearn, and M. Rutter. 1997. *Behavioral genetics.* 3rd ed. New York: Freeman.

Reker, G. T. 2003. *Provisional manual of the spiritual transcendence scale (STS).* Peterborough, Canada: Student Psychologists Press.

———. 1999. *Life attitude profile-Revised manual.* Peterborough, Canada: Student Psychologists Press.

Rowe, M. M., and R. G. Allen. 2004. Spirituality as a means of coping with chronic illness. *American Journal of Health Studies* 19(1):62–67.

Russell, P. 1998. *Waking up in time.* Navoto, CA: Origin Press.

Russell, R. 1979. Some futures for health education in the 1980s. *The Eta Sigma Gamman* 12 (Suppl. 2):3–7.

Scandurra, A. J. 1999. Everyday spirituality. *Journal of Health Education* 30(2):104–109.

Seaward, B. L. 2001. *Health of the human spirit.* Boston: Allyn and Bacon.

Smith, S. W. 2001. *The inner light theory of consciousness.* San Diego, CA: California Technical Publishing.

Spilka, B., R. W. Hood, Jr., B. Hunsberger, and R. Gorsuch. 2003. *The psychology of religion: An empirical approach.* 3rd ed. New York: The Guilford Press.

Tsuang, M. T., W. M. Williams, and J. C. Simpson. 2002. Pilot study of spirituality and mental health in twins. *The American Journal of Psychiatry* 159(3):486–493.
Wales, J. 1999. Biology. *Wikipedia.* http://en.wikipedia.org/wiki/biology (accessed January 28, 2006).
Why do we believe in God? 2005. *Metareligion,* http://www.meta-religion.com/Psychiatry/psychology of religion/why_do_we_believe.htm (accessed January 28, 2006).
World Health Organization. 1986. *Guidelines for training community health workers in nutrition.* Geneva: Author.
Yates, W. 1997. Today's spirituality: An exploration. *Religious Humanism* 31(1, 2):11–24.

CHAPTER 5

Spirituality, the Professorate, and the Curriculum

Al DeCiccio

In Search of the Spiritual Professorate and Curriculum

I was able to hear Stanley Fish speak at the Annual Meeting of the Association of American Colleges and Universities in January 2004. Fish, a literary critic famous for his ideas about understanding and how reader-response theory can help us to *understand* understanding, became Dean of Arts and Sciences at the University of Illinois (Chicago). In traveling to UIC, Fish brought with him many notables, including his wife—also a literary critic—Jane Tompkins, whose spirituality has led her to be a compassionate, transformative professor.[1] Fish was well-published in many venues during this time, extolling the ideals of the academy. He authored a column for *The Chronicle of Higher Education*, in which some of what he said in January 2004 was originally published. Repeated in *The New York Times* in May 2004, Fish's bottom line was that professors should do their job (and only their job) well; that professors should not attempt to do the jobs of others for which they are not qualified; and that professors should not let others do their jobs. Here's a provocative citation from Fish:

> You can reasonably set out to put your students in possession of a set of materials and equip them with a set of skills (interpretive, computational, laboratory, archival), and even perhaps (although this one is really iffy) install in them the same love of the subject that inspires your pedagogical efforts. You won't always succeed in accomplishing these things—even with the best of intentions and lesson plans there will always be inattentive or distracted students, frequently absent students, unprepared students, and on-another-planet students—but at least you will have a fighting chance given the fact that you've got them locked in a room with you for a few hours every week for four months.
>
> You have little chance, however (and that's entirely a matter of serendipity), of determining what they will make of what you have offered them once the room is unlocked for the last time and they escape first into the space of someone else's obsession and then into the space of the wide world.

And you have no chance at all (short of discipleship that is itself suspect and dangerous) of determining what their behavior and values will be in those aspects of their lives that are not, in the strict sense of the word, academic. You might just make them into good researchers. *You can't make them into good people, and you shouldn't try.* (emphasis added)

Starting with Fish may seem odd, given that I will be writing about spirituality, the professorate, and the curriculum. In so doing, I will emphasize the transformative mission of the professorate and the curriculum, that is, how professors can nurture "good people" through their teaching and the courses they develop. I will point out that such change can occur only if professors are "rooted," to call Simone Weil to mind,[2] and I will argue that being rooted is being spiritual. Finally, I will maintain that it is in the community of the academy where we should be encouraged to be spiritual and, it is in the community of the classroom where we should hold mature conversations[3] that will lead to the kind of abundance Parker Palmer (1990) says is possible for the academy. "Community and its abundance are always there," Palmer writes, "free gifts of grace that sustain us. The question is whether we will be able to perceive those gifts and receive them. That is likely to happen only when someone performs a vulnerable public act, assuming abundance but aware that others may cling to the illusion of scarcity" (138).

For the professorate, Palmer's "vulnerable public act" might well be the conversation(s) professors engender by making their classrooms Burkean parlors.[4] In this way, students should be prepared to engage in the ongoing public debates about the important questions of the day, fortified with the knowledge, wisdom, and charism of a rooted education. Such a student will journey through a Newman-like, inquiry-based curriculum in which she or he contemplates, studies, and sees revealed what the poet Hopkins (1965) called "God's Grandeur."

Such a student will learn that meaning is charged with the supernatural. Such a student will understand the difference between the way of life and the way of death, truth and falsehood, heaven and hell, darkness and light. Such a student, in the end, will be armed against reductionism. As Mark Schwehn (1993) writes, "Spiritually grounded education in and for thoughtfulness seeks the cultivation of those virtues that make the communal quest for the truth of matters possible, an undertaking that is in every sense prior to…the explication of various systems of meaning…this conception of higher education insists both that religion needs Enlightenment and that Enlightenment needs religion" (135–136). Schwehn has certainly provided an answer to Stanley Fish. What, then, should the professorate undertake in the twenty-first century and beyond? In the words of Augustine, they "who [seek] to teach in speech what is good, spurning none of these three things, that is to teach, to delight, and to persuade, should pray and strive that [they] be heard intelligently, willingly, and obediently" (142).

Engaging Faculty and Students for a "Rooted" Academic Community

Fish may have a point in asking faculty to do best what they have been prepared to do: teach research, create, produce, and disseminate. When faculty allow their political ideologies and social programs to take precedence in their classrooms, they risk losing their hold on teaching the content for which they are compensated and risk dismissing the educational needs of their students. Fish may also be following a tradition in offering his own perspective to the so-called culture of suspicion to which nineteenth- century thinkers such as Marx, Freud, and Nietzsche contributed. In such a culture, the idea of character formation cannot thrive and will not be accepted. Moreover, if we affirm Ronald Mahurin's (2006) recent historical analysis about the academy, we may view Fish's assertions as his attempt to delineate the roles higher education itself has ascribed to members of the academy. "Any knowledgeable student of the history of higher education in America understands," Mahurin writes, "that most colleges and universities were formed around an explicit and purposeful set of educational objectives (today, we would use the phrase 'desired outcomes'), which included the intellectual, aesthetic, moral and spiritual development of students. Read any history of the great Ivy League universities, and one finds that these objectives permeated the curriculum and the life of the institution at virtually all levels. And as we know, these institutions and many others no longer embrace a mission that would include in any specific sense a moral and spiritual formation of students, beyond a general assumption that it is a student's responsibility to figure these things out for themselves." While Mahurin goes on to write, "Many would applaud these developments in higher education," he also points out, "for some, this 'great divorce' between the spiritual and the intellectual has produced a cultural, moral and intellectual vacuum in the leadership in our businesses, nonprofit organizations and even in our [academic] institutions."

Fish's caveats notwithstanding, I would argue that we should all take very seriously Mahurin's point about the cultural, moral, and intellectual vacuum caused by the divorce between the spiritual and intellectual in higher education. In so doing, we might call to mind Augustine, who argued that the ultimate revealer of all things hidden is love, not suspicion. I submit, therefore, that the academy has to have a common object, and that we may find it in the love of learning fostered by a liberal education. Moreover, to avoid what may be the most significant problem on campuses today—reductionism and a resulting corporate myopia—colleges and universities should seek to provide students a core curriculum that is, if not a classical, certainly a postmodern trivium. As a result, reasoning, rhetoric, and the poetic or spiritual may be taught in a collaborative, Freirean setting to help ensure mature conversation will ensue, bringing hope to the suspicious.

To be sure, Fish's critique of character-building efforts by professors becomes less biting when one recognizes that his reader-response theories are predicated upon a notion—social constructionism—which has as its ideological locus the transformation of society and extols collaborative learning (i.e., dialogue among peers leading to critical consciousness) as its pedagogical practice. In some ways, Fish wants it both ways. Fish calls to mind Schwehn, an advocate of Clifford Geertz and the scholar who coined the phrase "exile from Eden," himself an exile from the University of Chicago.[5] Fish asks faculty to nurture the intellectual life, in a community of knowledgeable peers, ultimately, teasing tender minds into thought—what he attempted to do at UIC after his tenure on the Faculty at Duke. As Schwehn (1993) elegantly writes in *Exiles from Eden*, rooted, spiritual colleges and universities strive "to keep certain questions alive, such as questions about the relationship between religious faith and the pursuit of truth..." (vii). Indeed, as Schwehn intimates, passionate engagement must be the hallmark of the college or university. It is this passionate engagement which leads thinkers (Fish's and Geertz's knowledgeable peers, as well as those who wish to become knowledgeable peers—their students) toward community and the quest for truth and, ultimately, against reductionism.

Roughly two thousand years ago, Quintilian recognized the importance of three disciplines—grammar, rhetoric, logic—as he tried to assemble good men to carry on the ideals of Roman culture in his *Institutes of Oratory*. Much more recently, John Henry Newman (1907), in *The Idea of a University*, writes an extension to Quintilian: "If then a practical end must be assigned to a university course, I say that it is that of training good members of society...It aims...at cultivating the public mind, at supplying true principles to popular enthusiasms and fixed aims to popular aspirations,...at facilitating the exercise of political power, and refining the intercourse of private life." Today, in colleges and universities, we may return to these ideas and Quintilian's trivium (adding the poetic or the spiritual to grammar), even as we acknowledge new literacies brought about by technological advances, new genre studies that prepare young men and women for the public discourses that await them, debates about the environment, stem cell research, human reproductive health, and so forth. General education, core curriculums, at colleges and universities attempt these "greater expectations"[6] by preparing students for living in and contributing to a world in which individuality—human dignity, individual rights, personal choice—is more and more interconnected with global systems of commerce and telecommunications. At colleges and universities, curriculums can initiate this process by using reading, oral and written communication, critical reasoning, and spiritual reflection to explore the interaction among individuals and the various communities within which personal identity is cultivated. And they might advance these skills in multicontextual teaching and learning communities, both inside and outside the classroom.[7]

Let me spend a few minutes sketching out a curriculum in which this return to the trivium may help academic workers meet the goals Quintilian established. Contrary to Fish, I believe we must surely meet these goals in the dangerous world we currently inhabit. Since faculty live in a broken world, they also accept a responsibility to teach in and for this broken world, rooted in and oriented by faith, hope, and love. The brokenness of the world is nearly ubiquitous. Consider, for example, the so-called "war on terror." Whether it is a "clash of civilizations" or a struggle between competing powers, this war marks in violent ways the ruptures in our world. At a more domestic level, the seemingly intractable problems arising from what W.E.B. DuBois called the "color line"[8] is an example of the world's brokenness. Despite advances made since the civil rights movement broke down legal barriers and established legal guidelines (see the *Brown* decision), people of color, on the whole, continue to lag behind their White counterparts in many indices of social success, among them access to higher education. To be sure, professors are neither preachers nor priests; colleges and universities are not churches. However, professors have a responsibility to manifest faith, hope, and love in their teaching. These virtues, embodied by the professor and passed on to be embraced by the student, will help to heal our broken world.[9]

In an April 2005 study conducted by Alexander and Helen Astin, "Researchers released data…that offers the most complete portrait to date of new college students' attitudes about spirituality and religion, and the study suggests that freshmen care far more about spiritual matters than is widely believed. More than three-quarters of freshmen say they are looking for meaning in life, for example, and more than two-thirds engage in prayer" (Jaschick 2005). As the Astins noted in the study, "'the relative amount of attention that colleges and universities devote to the 'exterior' and 'interior' aspects of students lives has gotten out of balance…we have increasingly come to neglect the student's inner development—the spheres of values and beliefs, emotional maturity, spirituality and self—understanding'" (quoted in Mahurin 2006). Can a curriculum create from the outset conditions for students and faculty to engage in mature conversations about values and beliefs, maturity, spirituality, and self understanding? Can it lend itself to being collaborative, multicontextual, and transformative? I think the answer to these questions is yes.

The Engaged Classroom within the "Rooted" Campus

The First Year Seminar movement in higher education is one reason why I think we may answer the above questions affirmatively. As evidenced by their success nationwide, First Year Seminars should be the centerpiece of the student's first year. While I understand their purpose, I am not writing about first year experience seminars that indoctrinate students to college or university life. I am writing about first year seminars that are based on dialogues involving the arts of rhetoric, reasoning, and the spiritual or poetic. They can be designed to do the following:

1. To introduce the student to the ways in which liberal arts disciplines contribute to the study of the nature of the human individual, the relation between the individual and community, how that relationship could help to heal a broken world, and to do so in ways that overlap, support, and challenge each other;
2. To deepen and broaden the student's ability to read, write, speak, contemplate, and reason;
3. To create a community of learners who apply these skills to engage subject matters and each other actively.

The First Year Seminar rhetoric course should teach the student to read and write about ways in which texts contribute to the study of the nature of the human individual, the relation between the individual and community, and how that relationship could help to heal a broken world. The First Year Seminar logic course should teach students to identify, analyze, and evaluate instances of reasoning and to practice applying these critical reasoning skills to support their own beliefs, with special emphasis on the centrality of good reasoning to the nature of the human person, to individuality, and to human communities. The First Year Seminar religion or theology or literature course should examine the theme of individual and community from the perspective of the spirit or poetic, teaching the student how to reflect on meaning, beauty, the transcendent value of faith, contemplation, and the kinds of bold actions that will lead, ultimately, to global healing.

In the context of a community of knowledgeable peers to which everyone contributes and in which everyone participates, the student will take these initial competencies through her or his undergraduate career, learning how to make the connections between and among the other courses of study in the liberal arts and sciences and even the professions. Then, I would argue that a Junior Year Seminar should serve as a culmination of the student's education in the liberal arts and sciences. If we regard the First Year Seminar as a first "bookend," the Junior Year Seminar can be considered the other bookend. The Junior Year Seminar will require higher-level exercise of the foundational competencies begun in the First Year Seminars: reading, writing, speaking, contemplating, reasoning, and taking action. The Junior Year Seminar will expand the thematic focus of the First Year Seminars (individual and community) out to the globe; it will integrate the outcomes of a liberal education with those of career and vocational training; and, ultimately, it will enhance the student's connection with the vision of the college or university through the focus on ethics in the workplace, social justice, service to the larger community, and global responsibility. Ideally, to engage the entire faculty, each individual Junior Year Seminar will reflect the discipline of the instructor in both content and perspective but will be "clustered" thematically with other Junior Year Seminars, allowing students to engage in cross-disciplinary conversation.

Surely, it will take transformative leadership to show us all how to bring together spirituality, the professorate, and the curriculum. About such leadership, Palmer (1990) is sage, warning us against an "effortful and self-defeating" leadership, which makes community-building and abundance "a goal to be achieved" (136). "Why?" you may ask. "Because as long as we are the makers," Palmer answers, "we remain in control; and as long as we are in control, we will not be vulnerable to the risks of true community" (136). This is why Palmer cautions us, saying "as we act to evoke community, we must remember that community itself is a gift to be received..." (136). For Palmer, true leadership is risky business: "When we cut through the scarcity illusion and trigger a communal act of abundance, we take the considerable risk of angering the powers-that-be. Political power often depends on perpetuating the illusion of scarcity, and anyone who reveals the communal potential for abundance may feel the wrath of those in high places" (137). Moreover, when we practice a pedagogy of hope, love, or faith, we have no reassurances that we will be well received. However, as Palmer's story tells us, we just might evoke "a similar vulnerability" in those with whom we work, "giving them a chance to acknowledge and act upon the abundance each of them possesses" (137).

It seems apparent that the rooted, spiritual college or university is a community in which those who work there want to assume abundance, "a mixing of our ideas and energies" (Palmer 1990, 129). In such an environment, professors will neither be sullen nor downtrodden, seeking sustenance elsewhere—at professional meetings, away from their campuses, away from the persons they should be bringing inside their disciplinary circles and teaching their particular habits of mind. The current practice for enticing faculty to revitalize themselves is to send them away to professional meetings or to provide them sabbatical leaves of absence. These are fine benefits to provide the faculty. But a complementary course of action might be to provide faculty strategies to fashion, in a sustaining community, transdisciplinary programming. Such programming that aims at extending to all the academy's constituencies an opportunity to be contemplative and then to take action will certainly effect positive societal change. I have related Palmer's thoughtful discussion about *scarcity* and *abundance* to this discussion, particularly to *isolation* (which results from *scarcity*) and to *hope* (which results from *abundance*). I also think that what Palmer has to say in his eloquent voice about contemplation and action is what all of us want to believe about the academy in which we work: It is *that* place where people may actively share what gifts they have and are willing to receive and to reflect upon these gifts, adding to what they and their students already possess cognitively, socially, and materially.

Kafka's "Metamorphosis" and Spirituality in Colleges and Universities

As I bring this chapter to a close, I would like to do so by writing a little about Franz Kafka's (2001) short story, "The Metamorphosis." If nothing else, the story's title fits the topic of this chapter because I have been writing about a stance that affects change. I have written about changing the way people in the academy relate to one another, about changing the way they then are able to think about the communities they join and depart, and, ultimately, about the way in which they bring about positive change for those communities as well as for themselves. In "The Metamorphosis," we find out that the protagonist, Gregor Samsa, "awoke one morning from uneasy dreams [to find] himself transformed in his bed into a gigantic insect" (280). Gregor has certainly undergone an enormous change, but what if we were to examine that change as Palmer might? What if we were to consider Gregor's metamorphosis as his taking a vulnerable risk to bring about change to his family's situation, coaxing them into becoming a community able to withstand the modernist forces that are driving them apart and, as in his own case, mad?

In the story, Gregor takes three additional risks before his ultimate demise. While this story has been critiqued from every possible perspective, suffice it to say that, as Gregor changes from brow beaten human being to caterpillar-like insect to death, Gregor's family, in a cocoon for a long time, changes from isolated individuals (the asthmatic mother, the overweight and aging father, the frail and frivolous seventeen-year-old girl with few prospects) to a community that is able to stand up to the society of bloodsuckers, represented by the three boarders, thereby getting their sustenance from one another, not from someone else.

Kafka's story ends in the following manner:

> Then they all three [Gregor's father, mother, and sister] left the apartment, which was more than they had done for months, and went by tram into the open country outside the town. The tram, in which they were the only passengers, was filled with warm sunshine. Leaning comfortably back in their seats they canvassed their prospects for the future, and it appeared on closer inspection that these were not bad at all, for the jobs they had got, which so far they had never really discussed with each other, were all three admirable and likely to lead to better things later on...it struck both Mr. and Mrs. Samsa, almost at the same moment, as they became aware of their daughter's increasing vivacity, that in spite of all the sorrow of recent times, which had made her cheeks pale, she had bloomed into a pretty girl with a good figure...And it was like a confirmation of their new dreams and excellent intentions

that at the end of their journey their daughter sprang to her feet and stretched her young body. (313)

The change here is unmistakable. We have witnessed the metamorphosis: from caterpillar-like Gregor—suffocating, alone, unloved in the city—to butterfly-like Grete—breathing in the air and the sunshine, adored, and loved in the country. Gregor's family has become a community, now with opportunities for sharing in the corporate abundance of their environs. Of course, Gregor's old ways of doing things are replaced with his death. Yet, all the change may be viewed, if we import Palmer here, as a result of Gregor's risky actions. (In fact, how reminiscent of Plato's *Phaedrus* is this story![10]) The bottom line is that we want to bring our students inside our circles, our sacred spaces for teaching and learning, nudging them to complete projects we have started and may not be around to see through to fruition. To drive home this final point, I will cite Thomas M. Landy, founder and director of Collegium at Fairfield University and a member of the faculty at the College of the Holy Cross. Landy (2001) himself borrowed from Walter Ong's exegesis of Matthew 13:33—the parable about kneading dough into bread—when he talked about the value of a spiritual education. Landy (2001) writes, "the function of [rooted][11] intellectual life [is] to be leaven in the world, both to help transform creation and to be transformed by it" (xv). A rooted, spiritual academy can certainly instigate such change—one that will bring together our professors and their students to heal our broken world.

Notes

1. In her book *A Life in School: What the Teacher Learned,* Jane Tompkins argues that academics ought to nurture the individual, not just the intellect. During the early nineties, Tompkins was a member of a team of teachers and scholars who helped Departments of English revise their curriculums in just this rooted way. Her spirituality came under severe attack by academics who found her new work too warm and fuzzy for their rigorous regimens. Nevertheless, Tompkins was unwavering in her efforts to help students to learn what they needed to find personal fulfillment, believing that, in so doing, they would effect positive change.
2. When Simone Weil could not join the French resistance movement against the Nazis, she published *The Need for Roots: Prelude to a Declaration* of *Duties towards Mankind* in which she illustrated the problems of the modern world. Surprisingly contemporary for the purposes of this chapter (and book), Weil calls for a rooted and passionate search for truth, which will bring about a long-lasting, positive change.

Spirituality, the Professorate, and the Curriculum 95

3. Tracy Schier, co-editor with Cynthia Russett of *Catholic Women's Colleges in America* and co-director of Boston College's Institute for Administrators in Catholic Higher Education (IACHE), offered the idea that rooted colleges and universities must act by developing courses and programs in which these mature conversations can take place as a way to ensure positive change in the future.
4. Based upon the ideas of Kenneth Burke, arguably America's most spectacular theorist of rhetoric, the Burkean parlor is that place where people enter and exit an ongoing, rooted conversation about all that confronts humankind.
5. Mark Schwehn has been the Director and remains heavily involved in the Lilly Fellows Program in Humanities and the Arts at Valparaiso University. Schwehn and his fellows have long endorsed the idea of rooted, spiritual education being located in the liberal arts of the academy's colleges and universities.
6. Released in September 2002, the AAC&U's report, entitled *Greater Expectations: A New Vision for Learning as a Nation Goes to College*, "calls for a dramatic reorganization of undergraduate education to ensure that all college aspirants receive not just access to college, but an education of lasting value. The panel offers a new vision that will promote the kind of learning students need to meet emerging challenges in the workplace, in a diverse democracy, and in an interconnected world."
7. Roberto A. Ibarra, Senior Consultant at the Southwest Wing of Ibis Consulting Group, Special Assistant to the Provost, and Associate Professor of Sociology at the University of New Mexico, is writing about how to reframe the context of higher education. Ibarra's current research focuses on developing models for changing academic and corporate cultures. His *Beyond Affirmative Action* is based on an ethnographic research project funded by the Ford Foundation to study Latino graduate students, faculty, administrators and non-academics across the country. That study uncovered a new approach to diversity (an active, collaborative-learning, multi-contextual model) that is becoming recognized as a new paradigm for educational change.
8. See *The Souls of Black Folks* where DuBois makes this argument elegantly, eloquently, and passionately. See also Cornel West's *Race Matters* where DuBois' point is validated even nearly ninety years after first establishing it.
9. My Rivier colleague, Dr. Bradford Stull, has argued this perspective in a recent mission-related proposal for the VPAA and President, entitled "Engaging the Times." To view this proposal, contact Dr. Stull via email at bstull@rivier.edu.
10. In *Phaedrus*, Plato has Socrates lead Phaedrus away from the city to the country, not so much to enhance a seduction, but to change the location of the mature conversation in which they will engage. They need to learn how to love one another so as to effect a dialogic interaction.
11. In this instance, Landy is writing about the Catholic college and university.

References

Augustine. 1958. *On Christian doctrine*. Translated by D. W. Robertson, Jr. Indianapolis, IN: Bobbs-Merrill.

DuBois, W. E. B. 2003. *The souls of black folks*, centennial ed. New York: Modern Library.

Fish, S. 2004. Why we built the ivory tower. *The New York Times*, 21 May, Op-ed.
Freire, P. 1972. *Pedagogy of the oppressed*. Translated by M. B. Ramos. New York: Herder and Herder.
Hopkins, G. M. 1965. *God's grandeur*. In *Poetry of the Victorian period*. 3rd ed. Eds. J. H. Buckley, and G. B. Woods. Glenview, IL: Scott Foresman.
Ibarra, R. A. 2000. *Beyond affirmative action: Reframing the context of higher education*. Madison: University of Wisconsin Press.
Jaschick, S. 2005. God and freshmen. *Inside Higher Ed*. http://insidehighered.com/news/2005/04/14/spirit (accessed August 3, 2006).
Kafka, F. 2001 The metamorphosis. In *Literature and its writers: An introduction to fiction, poetry, and drama*, ed. A. Charters and S. Charters, compact 2nd ed. Boston: Bedford/St. Martin's.
Landy, T. M., ed. 2001. *As leaven in the world*. Franklin, WI: Sheed and Ward.
Mahurin, R. P. 2006. Faith, scholarship and the college classroom. *Inside Higher Ed*. http://insidehighered.com/workplace/2006/02/01/mahurin (accessed August 4, 2006).
Newman, J. H. 1907. *The idea of a university*. New York: Longman's.
Ong, W. J. 1990. Yeast, a parable for Catholic higher education. *America* 162:347–363.
Palmer, P. 1990. Loaves and fishes: Acts of scarcity or abundance. In *The active life: A spirituality of work, creativity, and caring*. Ed. P. Palmer, 121–138. Boston: HarperCollins.
Plato. 1981. *Phaedrus*, trans. W. C. Helmbold and W. G. Rabinowitz. Indianapolis, IN: Bobbs-Merrill.
Quintilian. 1987. *Quintilian on the teaching of speaking and writing*. Ed. J. J. Murphy. Carbondale and Edwardville: Southern Illinois University Press.
Schier, T. and C. Russett. 2002. *Catholic women's colleges in America*. Baltimore: Johns Hopkins University Press.
Schwehn, M. R. 1993. *Exiles from Eden*. New York: Oxford University Press.
Tompkins, J. 1996. *A life in school: What the teacher learned*. Reading, MA: Addison Wesley.
Weil, S. 2002. *The need for roots: Prelude to a declaration of duties towards mankind*. Classics ed. London: Routledge.
West, C. 2001. *Race matters*. New York: Vintage.

CHAPTER 6

Spirituality and Student Development

Deborah M. Cady

Introduction

In recent years, college student spirituality has been the focus of student development research, with many researchers suggesting a rise in student interest in spirituality (Astin and Astin 2004; Chickering 2003; Hindman 2002; Love 2001; Mahoney, Schmalzbauer, and Youniss 2001; Parks 2000; Schwartz 2001; Stamm 2003). In particular, the spiritual development theories of Fowler (1976) and Parks (2000) are of crucial importance to the literature on student spiritual development. This chapter draws upon the work of Fowler and Parks to provide a theoretical framework for students' spiritual development and discusses ways in which spirituality acts as a tool for students to engage in religious difference so that they develop a sense of wholeness and learn to practice discovery dialogue.

Theoretical Framework

Early documents defining the student affairs profession announced the goal of developing the "whole person," including the intellectual, emotional, recreational, cultural, vocational, and *spiritual* lives of students (American Council on Education 1986). As the profession matured, spiritual development theories were grounded in two theoretical perspectives. First, the theories borrowed from the cognitive development theorist family, including the theories of Perry (1981), Kegan (1994), and Gilligan (1982). Spiritual development as a cognitive development theory requires increased cognitive complexity in the ways in which one makes meaning in the world (Love 2002). To move through each cognitive stage, students encounter challenges, dilemmas, and diverse viewpoints that provide the occasion for developing higher-level thinking skills. The cognitive stages begin with a reliance on an authority for meaning, and, as this authority is questioned, students make cognitive progress by seeing multiple perspectives that do not promote any one true answer. Fowler (1976) and Parks (2000) have both constructed a theoretical model for student spiritual development through the lens of these student development theorists.

Second, spiritual development theories also drew from the person-environment theorists, such as Bronfenbrenner (1993), Tisdell (2003), Cross and Helms (as cited in Evans, Forney, and Guido-DiBrito 1998), because such theorists focus on a relational context necessary for meaning making. For example, Astin (1993) shows that students make meaning of their lives through their peer relationships. Thus, through peer relationships, students are engaged in meaning-of-life conversations that empower their spiritual development process. Parks (2000), in addition to using cognitive developmental theories, sees the concept of spiritual development through the person-environment lens by examining community relationships. In her study of young adults, Parks (2000) examines forms of community that influence the spiritual development of college students. Understanding that life in community enhances student faith development (Hindman 2002), Parks explores how community can best challenge and support students (Sanford as cited in Evans, Forney, and Guido-DiBrito 1998) in their spiritual development. Parks (2000) describes five forms of community, including conventional community, diffuse community, mentoring community, self-selected group, and a community open to others. The mutual shaping relationship between one's identity and his or her community results in a developmental progression not unlike the cognitive theories where students progress from a closed, like-minded community to a more open, inclusive, and diverse community.

Particularly salient to the traditional college student, Parks's (2000) mentoring community involves a peer group in which members challenge and support each other in the process of making meaning. Parks (2000) suggests the mentoring community as the primary avenue for spiritual development of traditional-aged college students. However, the peer group and campus culture must strike a delicate balance between challenge and support (Sanford as cited in Evans, Forney, and Guido-DiBrito 1998) to deal with life's complex questions (Parks 2000). When life's questions become so complex, without the necessary supports to confront the challenge of trying to understand complexity, students face the danger of feeling foreclosed to further exploration or meaning-making processes. Parks (2000) discusses this foreclosure as "shipwreck." Students feel stranded when challenges that overwhelm them require support for students to progress in their development, but that support is not available. Shipwreck is inevitable if adequate support is not available because college students ask "big questions" in search of their life vocations, dreams, and truths (Parks 2000). However, when these big questions are asked in the mentoring community, students have the support necessary to promote spiritual development because the mutual shaping between environment and identity plays a significant role in students' spiritual development.

As with cultural identity theories described by Cross, Helms and others (Evans, Forney, and Guido-DiBrito 1998), Tisdell (2003) and Parks (2000) suggest that activities of immersion and emersion challenge and support this spiritual spiraling process. Tisdell (2003) also makes a distinct connection between spiritual development and racial identity development, and racial identity development theories have been associated with the person-environment interaction family of theories. To progress toward committed, internalized, and autonomous racial identity, students need to cross racial borders for learning and growth (Evans, Forney, and Guido-DiBrito 1998). This process is similar to the spiritual development experiences of college students. The connection between the "immersion/emersion stage" of racial identity development outlined by Cross and Helms (as cited in Evans, Forney and Guido-DiBrito 1998) and Tisdell's (2003) and Parks's (2000) notion of "encountering otherness" identify implications for spiritual development practice.

The theoretical foundations of student development theory inform the directions of student spiritual development. Spirituality acts as a tool for college students as they understand religious diversity, develop a sense of wholeness, and ultimately grow into their understanding of self, the other, the world and faith.

Spirituality as a Tool for Religious Understanding

Students are increasingly reporting multiple religious and cultural identities as they arrive on campus, and the growth of a racially diverse campus provides for a multi-faith student body, early evidence of a return to spiritual life (Cherry, DeBerg, and Porterfield 2001; Eck 2001). Parks (2000) and Tisdell (2003) suggest that student encounters with "otherness" provides a vehicle for an awareness and appreciation of identity differences, particularly around spiritual development. In her study on diversity and inter-group relations, Hurtado (2005) states, "students appear to be engaging in difficult discussions and realizing they have much to learn from their differences—and perhaps are even more confident about dealing with conflict" (605). These friendships of "otherness" act as the primary catalyst for student spiritual development (Parks 2000; Pettigrew 1998) and ultimately as a tool for student understanding regarding religious diversity.

This friendship connection through the encounter of "otherness" enables students to be aware of differences and to understand the experiences of another. As students encounter another, they reach new levels of engagement either by challenging their development process and forming new values or confirming their values. For the impact of the "encountering other" experience to be effective, the conditions of the interaction require contact with people of different races, religions, cultures, sexual orientations, and physical abilities, to name a few. The impact of these interactions is further enhanced when supported by significant mentors who have regular contact with students in their daily lives. Student growth and development around issues of difference require encouragement of inclusive, working communities that involve meaningful friendships among their members (Allport as cited in Ben-Ari 2004). In other words, students learn from those perceived as the "other" or as "different" when in relationships with each other. This encounter of "otherness" within one's immediate peer group provides lessons of multi-culturalism in this relational context. Students engaging in conversations of difference can learn conflict engagement and gain confidence in engaging in such conflicts (Hurtado 2005).

The peer group, to be effective, needs to expand beyond a supportive community to include discussions that question assumptions, attitudes, and beliefs, so the peer group should expand to include new members with viewpoints that challenge the group. For example, students are more likely to gain competence on religious understanding when in a friendship with members from diverse religious perspectives. Not only do students' perceived assumptions regarding their friends' religious traditions change, their preconceived notions of other religious traditions are expanded or changed. Friendship groups of otherness act as the primary conduit of the conversation where new insights transcend the immediate intergroup friendship to include other identity differences.

The college environment, including course material, campus events and faculty lectures, offers a wide circle of relationships that often stimulate peer conversations around meaning-of-life questions. In fact, when discussing such questions, students can refer to spirituality as the common neutral language to understand religious differences (Cady 2006). Students use spiritual language rather than religious terms to express their questions because spiritual language provides a neutrality that allows students to safely engage in discussing potentially contentious issues. Religious language, on the other hand, might be judged as being harsh, disallowing dialogue. In addition, everyone has questions about the meaning-of-life, the values of love and hope, the future and our place within the world, and those common spiritual questions allow students to engage in deeper religious questions using neutral spiritual language without fear of diverse answers that could divide.

In addition to neutral language, students learn a systematic conversation strategy often resembling the following: An event such as the war in Iraq, a campus event, or engaging classroom discussion provokes a meaning-of-life question. The event encourages students to ask several valid questions and often inspires self-reflective thought about the potential consequences of their own values, beliefs, and attitudes concerning a particular issue. Students then "test out" their ideas, beliefs, and questions with a group of trusted, which often means "like-minded," peers. As students feel more confident over their four years of college, they might further "test out" their "truth" by debating their ideas in conversation with peers of "otherness." Conversations of religious difference particularly require the final step of engagement for students to encounter others as a way of learning and growing.

In light of the spiritual development literature (Fowler 1976; Love 2002; Parks 2000), it makes sense that students question religious authority and consider more relative ways of seeing their spiritual lives through meaning-making processes. Students then use the "divine neutral" language of spirituality as a strategy to enter cautious conversation regarding meaning-of-life questions in a multi-faith setting. The language of spirituality allows students to defer the hard questions that religious difference raises. This use of caution is reminiscent of other conversations on our campuses, particularly around issues of race and gender (Alemán 1997; 2000). As a result of this cautious conversation in the context of religion and spirituality, students see the peer group as a resource to engage in faith-based discussions that ultimately inform their values, beliefs and attitudes.

A new religious pluralism has reached the college campus, and educators would be well served to examine the role of religion in the spiritual lives of college students. Eck (2001) shares the following definition of pluralism: "the language of pluralism is the language not just of difference but of engagement, involvement, and participation. It is the language of traffic, exchange, dialogue and debate….Pluralism is the dynamic process through which we engage with one another in and through our very deepest differences" (69–70). Pluralism, in this view, is an evolving process that engages students in conversations about religious diversity that provide the conduit for student spiritual growth.

Spirituality as a Tool for Developing a Sense of "Wholeness"

Not only should students engage in conversations about religious diversity to inform their own views about religion but also the inclusion of spirituality in the consideration of a whole person identity indicates the important role of spirituality in one's overall wellness. Developing the sense of "wholeness" that is identified with wellness is critical to students during "shipwreck" moments, and spirituality can facilitate students' attempts to reconnect their lives after the shipwreck. As students struggle with suffering, for example, they turn to their spiritual identity for comfort, support, and answers. Students can also turn to spiritual mentors on campus through the chaplain's office or student services for guidance in navigating the process of achieving "wholeness" again in their lives (Cady 2006).

Often, the college experience provides shipwreck moments when a campus event or encounter is challenging enough to lead students to ask meaning-of-life questions (Parks 2000). Sometimes the shipwreck moments have nothing to do with college, but rather life circumstances that humans must deal with, such as death, loss, illness, relationship break ups, poverty, etc. The peer group plays an important role during these shipwreck moments (Astin and Astin 2004; Parks 2000) by providing the most supportive environment for students to seek answers in light of their despair. Students, however, tend to avoid the peer group conversation in facing life shipwrecks for fear of appearing vulnerable (Cady 2006). Instead, students seek out "wise mentors" to explore these tough life questions.

As a result of an oncoming crisis in college or with their family, students engage in a process for understanding their spiritual journeys and development (Cady 2006). The pattern for spiritual growth often resembles the following. The shipwreck provokes a spiritual "crisis." Much like the spiritual conversation process, the shipwreck event prompts students to internalize the potential consequences and reflect individually on the questions the event provoked. Students then realize that they can not "sit" alone with their suffering and often reach out to wise mentors—faculty, staff or upper-class students—for support. In addition to seeking wise mentors for support, students turn to religious practices, places of worship, meditation, or the contemplation of nature during times of crisis. When confronting grief, students turn to scripture reading, prayer, meditation, religious services, bodies of water, or religious teachers for support (Cady 2006). Although students struggle with the utility of such religious and spiritual practices in every day life, they also realize the importance of such practices in achieving "wholeness" once again. Students often re-engage in the peer conversation as they begin to achieve spiritual "wholeness." In this renewed conversation, students share their lessons from adversity with other peers now experiencing personal shipwrecks. Students desire to support other students through life curveballs by sharing their own personal stories of despair as an upper-class student might have done for them. Despite the limited role of the peer group in life's shipwreck moments, students return to the peer group to find ways to support peers through other college curveballs as a method of achieving personal wholeness.

Spirituality as a Tool for Student Cognitive Development

In addition to achieving wholeness, spirituality empowers students to make meaning of life's complexity (Parks 2000). Students, engaged in the spiritual conversation, encounter questions that enable them to understand four areas of their lives. In understanding the self, others, the world, and faith, students discover their own skills and abilities to engage in the peer conversation. Parks (2000) described these conversations of meaning as an exploration of "big questions." It is through this process of exploring big questions that students describe a process of growth and discovery (Cady 2006). Baxter (1992), Chickering and Reisser (1993), Gilligan (1982), and Perry (1981) describe the identity and cognitive development process of college students as a progression toward autonomy and inter-dependence with less reliance on authority as sources of validation, information, and "truth." Students utilized spiritual conversations as one tool to understand their identity. These spiritual conversations often present paradoxes in their lives and ultimately lead toward a comfort with the unknown—a stage described in cognitive development theories. Student engagement in spiritual conversations acts as the discovery tool in understanding the self, other, world, and faith during the cognitive development process.

Spiritual conversations allow students to engage in the process of self-discovery. In developing their own identity, students ask themselves questions about their identity, values, skills and vocation. While engaging in self-exploration, students ask: Who am I? What do I believe? How do I accept the things I can not control? What has shaped me to be who I am today? And, where am I going? These questions encourage self-reflection, value clarification, and discernment. The peer conversation, centered on these questions, not only leads to the self-discovery process but also prompts further engagement to understand one another in community.

In exploring the self, students are more curious and open to hearing the stories of others and exploring the questions that cross identity boundaries. Students ask questions of their peers as a method to enhance their own self-discovery and deepen their understanding of the other. Students ask questions such as, "How do I connect my own experiences with the journeys of others?" "How do I fit in when I'm unsure about who I am and who you are?" "Will my friendships last when my world changes?" "How do the opinions of others fit into my views, beliefs and values?" The process of understanding others requires students to engage in the conversation itself in addition to the questions asked during the conversation. As students learn how to engage in conversations that seek to understand others, they develop the skills to engage in dialogue that attempts to understand the world.

Global events, particularly in a post-September 11 world, provoke students to ask a variety of meaning-of-life questions. The questions reveal the urgency in which students feel compelled to understand the world. Students explore the inevitable "why" questions. "Why do bad things happen in the world?" "Why is there inequality and suffering?" "Why are we at war?" "Why am I privileged, and what should I do with such privilege?" Students realize the complexity of these questions and feel challenged to find their role in addressing world concerns. Exploring world questions teaches students lessons of privilege that can lead to their commitment to social change and justice. Many students turn toward questions of faith to understand the world and their role in changing it.

In students' quest to understand themselves, each other, and the world, they ask questions of their faith. At the core of this conversation, students question the role faith has in understanding "truth." Students ask questions such as, "Do I believe in the divine?" "Does it matter if there is a transcendent realm?" "How does my spirituality shape my view of the world?" "Should faith and society interact?" "Why would a divine power allow all this suffering in the world?" Many of the questions students ask regarding faith center on making sense out of that which could not be reasonably explained and making the connection between faith and life.

Students, through these discovery conversations, come to terms with the "tension of opposites" (Fowler 1976). Students describe a series of conflicting feelings and struggle to balance these often opposing feelings in the conversation. In this conversation process, students are often presented with two opposing yet "true" values, feelings, or opinions. A series of reactionary opposites, in response to the meaning-of-life dialogue, include comfort/challenge, peace/despair, responsibility/powerlessness, gratitude/resistance, individual/community, and action/reflection. In exploring these opposites, students attempt to reconcile the many different aspects of their identity, each other, the world, and faith. Students feel conflicted, confused, and challenged to understand how two opposing parts of their lives can, in fact, co-exist. "Chaos" and "confusion" within students' exploration for understanding create that opportunity for growth.

Students' spiritual conversations provide a forum for change and development as students explore the variety of roles they assume on campus and in their lives. Through the discovery process facilitated by spiritual conversations, students develop conversational skills, self-confidence, openness to others, an understanding of privilege and their role as leaders in a complicated world. Exploring meaning-of-life questions enables students to make the developmental leap as they come to terms with the tension of opposing "truths." Spirituality, as a tool for students to engage in religious difference, to develop a sense of wholeness and to develop cognitively in ways that encourage discovery dialogue, provides educators with an opportunity to engage students in new practices that promote student development and growth.

Recommendations for Practice

Higher education and particularly student affairs plays an important role in supporting students' spiritual development and engaging students in conversation regarding religious diversity. The conversation on religious diversity is particularly salient in today's complicated world struggling with accepting religious differences. As Hurtado (2005) asserts, "we can no longer leave intergroup relations to chance, because they play a central role in ensuring that students can function in a diverse work force and pluralistic democracy" (607). The following are five sets of recommendations for higher education in addressing the spiritual and religious developmental needs of college students to provide forums for greater cognitive growth.

First, student life staff can play a critical role in teaching spiritual practices on campus and can promote spirituality as a method of coping during difficult times. Students often rely on their religious traditions and spiritual practices most often during college "curveballs." Often the peer conversation is not sufficient to help students cope with a curveball situation, so students turn to "wise mentors" to seek support. Student life needs to find ways to reach students who experience "shipwrecks" that do not rise to our immediate attention, particularly those students who experience challenging moments associated with some of the more everyday disappointments. However, student affairs can also provide students with coping strategies prior to the actual shipwreck event. For example, orientation programs should address spiritual wellness. Students should be made aware of various resources, including the religious and spiritual life staff. In addition, collaborative meetings between several areas of student life, including first year programs, counseling center, residential life, health center, and religious and spiritual life, should address the spiritual needs of students in addition to other aspects of wellness within crisis management.

Second, student affairs staff could develop faculty partnerships that connect the cognitive and spiritual development of students. The classroom is a central element for students in engaging in meaning-of-life questions. Faculty and student life staff could engage in discussions regarding the ways in which courses inspire meaning-making processes with students. This conversation could also uncover ways in which to engage students around issues of difference. In partnership, faculty and student life staff can approach the developmental moment of holding the tension of opposites through a language of understanding, an encouragement of questioning, and an engagement of curiosity rather than cautious conversation.

Third, student affairs staff could develop connections between multicultural and multi-faith education to engage students in conversations of difference. The literature suggests a deep connection between religious and cultural identity development, so developing competencies and learning outcomes for multi-faith and multi-cultural dialogues could enhance student engagement in difficult conversations. Such skills include asking clarifying questions, engaging in self-reflection, developing critical-thinking skills, and engaging in conversation that encourages curiosity rather than caution. In addition, as professionals continue to learn student conversation strategies, programs can be developed that use these strategies for discussions of difference.

Fourth, student life staff should partner with religious and spiritual life staff in the student spiritual development process. To have connected partnerships between these departments, chaplains would benefit in learning the language of student development theory to connect with student life staff. This language is often most helpful to students when they are engaged in the student development and growth process. The theological model could often inhibit student growth, particularly around religious diversity. In addition, student life staff could enhance their work with students when comfortable with spiritual development theory. Using the spiritual development lenses could aid student life professionals in engaging with the spiritual life conversation. Student life staff could be most helpful in the spiritual development process when ready to engage students in the big meaning-of-life questions. Students are asking themselves and each other these questions and could benefit from student life professionals ready and willing to act as "wise mentors" to them in their growth process.

Fifth, student life programs could develop intentional communities on campus that enhance the "encountering other" experience. Creating a multi-faith living and learning community within the residence halls is a great opportunity for collaboration between residential life and religious and spiritual life. Through this community, students would be encouraged to develop relationships across religious traditions, to explore spiritual questions with their neighbors, and to discover new learning through multi-faith dialogue. Student activities also could partner with religious and spiritual life staff as student religious organizations continue to form on college campuses. In addition to specific religious organizations on campus, an umbrella multi-faith organization could provide opportunities for students to discuss collaborative opportunities in spiritual life and religious diversity programming on campus.

Providing spiritual programming or services for those not involved in a particular religious tradition is also important. To reach these students, student affairs should use language that reaches those wanting to engage in meaning-of-life conversations without depending upon a religious organization to act as the catalyst of the conversation. In engaging students unconnected with a religious organization with those students connected to a religious organization, student affairs can help students truly become understanding and tolerant of the beliefs and values of others. Ultimately, student affairs staff need to develop programs, partnerships, and services that engage students in conversations of difference that enhance cognitive development.

Conclusion

Clear student interest in spiritual life and the changing religious diversity on campus urges higher education to take seriously the role of spiritual development in the life of college students. The combination of spirituality and religious diversity is today's "causal movement" of students' identity exploration on the college campus. As today's institutions of higher education search for the language to engage in spirituality and religious diversity, students are having the conversation. Students crave opportunities to share their college spiritual journey. Their journeys are often filled with hope, despair, dreams, anxiety, truth, and uncertainty during a time in our history plagued by war, terrorism, and economic insecurity. Although student stories are diverse, student experiences are grounded in a shared curiosity for life meaning, shared desire for self-understanding, and a shared hope for a better future. Spirituality acts as a catalyst for student development by providing students with a way to ask meaning-of-life questions often explored in the peer conversation. Higher education serves students well when attending to their spiritual needs by providing resources and services that enhance the learning outcomes of peer conversations.

References

Alemán, A. M. 1997. Understanding and investigating female friendship's educative value. *Journal of Higher Education* 68(2):119–159.

———. 2000. Race talks: Undergraduate women of color and female friendships. *The Review of Higher Education* 23(2):133–152.

American Council on Education. 1986. The student personnel point of view. In *Student affairs: A profession's heritage,* eds. G. L. Suddlemire and A. L. Rentz, 74–87, 122–140. Washington, DC: ACPA.

Astin, A. W. 1993. *What matters in college? Four critical years revisited.* San Francisco: Jossey-Bass.

Astin, A. W., and H. Astin. 2004. *Spirituality development and the college experience* (Research Report). Los Angeles: University of California, Higher Education Research Institute.

Baxter, Magolda M. 1992. *Knowing and reasoning in college: Gender-related patterns in students' intellectual development.* San Francisco: Jossey-Bass.

Ben-Ari, R. 2004. Coping with the Jewish-Arab conflict: A comparison among three models. *Journal of Social Issues* 40(2):307–322.

Bronfenbrenner, U. 1993. The ecology of cognitive development: Research models and fugitive findings. In *Development in context: Acting and thinking in specific environments,* eds. R. H. Wozniak and K. W. Fisher, 3–44. Hillsdale, NJ: Erlbaum.

Cady, D. 2006. *College student spiritual development: A narrative of peer conversation.* Ph.D. diss., Boston College.

Cherry, C., B. De Berg, and A. Porterfield. 2001. Religion on campus. *Liberal Education* 87(4): 6–14.

Chickering, A. W. 2003. Reclaiming our soul: Democracy and higher education. *Change* 35(1): 38–45.

Chickering, A. W., and L. Reisser. 1993. *Education and identity.* San Francisco: Jossey-Bass.

Eck, D. 2001. *A new religious America: How a Christian country has become the world's most religiously diverse nation.* San Francisco: Harper.

Evans, N. J., D. S. Forney, and F. Guido-DiBrito. 1998. *Student development in college: Theory, research, and practice.* San Francisco: Jossey-Bass.

Fowler, J. W. 1976. Stages of faith: The structured developmental approach. In *Values and moral development,* ed. T. C. Hennessey, 176–234. New York: Paulist Press.

Gilligan, C. 1982. *In a different voice.* Cambridge, MA: Harvard University Press.

Hindman, D. M. 2002. From splintered lives to whole persons: Facilitating spiritual development in college students. *Religious Education* 97(2):165–182.

Hurtado, S. 2005. The next generation of diversity and intergroup relations research. *Journal of Social Issues* 61(3):595–610.

Kegan, R. 1994. *In over our heads: The mental demands of modern life.* Cambridge, MA: Harvard University Press.

Love, P. 2001. Spirituality and student development: Theoretical connections. In *The implications of student spirituality for student affairs practice,* ed. M. A. Jablonski, 7–16. San Francisco: Jossey-Bass.

———. 2002. Comparing spiritual development and cognitive development. *Journal of College Student Development* 43(3):357–373.

Mahoney, K. A., J. Schmalzbauer, and J. Youniss. 2001. Religion a comeback on campus. *Liberal Education* 87(4):36–42.

Parks, S. D. 2000. *Big questions, worthy dreams: Mentoring young adults in their search for meaning, purpose and faith.* San Francisco: Jossey-Bass.

Perry, W. G. 1981. Cognitive and ethical growth: The making of meaning. In *The modern American college,* ed. A. W. Chickering, 76–115. San Francisco: Jossey-Bass.

Pettigrew, T. F. 1998. Intergroup contact theory. *Annual Review of Psychology* 49:65–85.

Schwartz, A. 2001. Growing spirituality during the college years. *Liberal Education,* 87(4):30–36.

Stamm, L. 2003. Can we bring spirituality back to campus? Higher education's re-engagement with values and spirituality. *Journal of College and Character.* http://www.collegevalues.org/articles.cfm (accessed July 25, 2003).

Tisdell, E. 2003. *Exploring spirituality and culture in adult and higher education.* San Francisco: Jossey-Bass.

CHAPTER 7

Spirituality and Higher Education Leadership

Sherry L. Hoppe

> *All work is spiritual.*
> —Richards 1995, 57

Introduction

Spirituality is as mysterious and as elusive as the wind. Unlike the wind, though, it cannot be measured or felt on your skin. Its evidence cannot be heard in the rustling of leaves or be seen in the swaying of trees. You know it is there, but you cannot see it or hold it against your bosom. To believe in spirituality is thus to suspend disbelief. Spirituality can only be described with indefinable words like "meaning." Chavez (2001) found meaning and thus guidance for his entire life in the advice his mother gave him when he was growing up: "Go out and walk by the river and think about life. Consider your place in the world" (69). Throughout the ages, many have followed this wisdom, even though they may never have heard the words of Chavez' mother. We are drawn to mountaintops and valleys, sunrises and sunsets, oceans and deserts, and nature's birth and rebirth because these scenes touch our souls—they feed our spiritual beings. Dicarlo (1999) reminds us Abraham Maslow called these "'peak experiences,' since they represent the high moments of life where we joyfully find ourselves catapulted beyond the confines of the mundane and ordinary" (xvii). Dicarlo notes Maslow might have called them *peek* experiences, in that "during these expansive occasions, we sneak a glimpse of the eternal realm of Being itself" (xvii). That glimpse, though, is often elusive in the workplace. Nature may be a reservoir for spirituality, but finding spirituality in the workplace is like chasing an angel—it is ethereal and alluring, but the search is perplexing. Pierce (2001) describes work spirituality as an oxymoron: "two ideas that at first do not seem to go together, like 'jumbo shrimp' or 'tough love'" (2).

Leadership itself is difficult to define; adding the dimension of spirituality further complicates describing how to lead with spirit. Despite this challenge, the changing context and demands of leadership in the twenty-first century have opened the door to a paradigm shift that dictates a dimension beyond what is found in traditional approaches to leadership. Spirituality in leadership amplifies and complements the concepts in leadership theories, encompassing and indeed embracing wholeness, meaning, authenticity, and conceptual understanding. The interlocking of these concepts and related ones provides the basis for this chapter's integration of leadership theory and spirituality.

Leadership Theories

Leadership theories abound, but space does not allow a thorough review of all of them. However, to provide a frame of reference for the discussion of spirituality in the context of leadership theory, four major classifications will be summarized, primarily as described by Lussier and Achua (2003).

- *Leadership trait (or attitude) theories* base leadership effectiveness on distinctive patterns of characteristics that most leaders possess. Some of the identified traits include high energy level, attitude, appearance, self-reliance, persuasiveness, stability and integrity. Within this category, perhaps the most commonly known theories are Theory X and Theory Y, developed by McGregor in the 1960s. These theories are based on the leader's positive or negative feelings about people, motivation, and issues. Simplistically described, Theory X holds that workers respond mainly to the "rewarding carrot" and the "disciplinary stick." (The best description of Theory X may have occurred long before it was conceived by McGregor. Niccolo Machiavelli [1908] noted in the sixteenth century that people could be motivated through two ways: love or fear. Avowing that love is too fickle, he believed we should motivate through fear.) In contrast to Machiavelli's premise and Theory X, Theory Y is based on the belief that people work hard because of personal drive and the resulting satisfaction from striving to do their best at all times. Leaders who subscribe to Theory Y believe employees are self-motivated and seek input from them because they believe all workers are capable of being creative and innovative if they are encouraged.
- Behavioral leadership theories describe the way effective leaders act and are influenced by trait *leadership* theories because relationships are often based on the good or bad traits of the leader. In addition, behaviorists believe actions and patterns of actions can be predicted

based on people's needs, Abraham Maslow's well-known hierarchy of needs (physiological, safety, belongingness, esteem, and self-actualization) under girds this approach to leadership theory. A leader who recognizes this hierarchy will behave in ways that support basic as well as higher order needs of followers so that in turn their behaviors will meet the needs of the organization.
- Contingency leadership theories explain leadership in the context of situations and individuals. First *introduced* by Fred E. Fiedler in 1951, this approach describes how situational variables interact with personalities and behavior of leaders. It includes an examination not only of situations but also of the level of a leader's power, the nature of the tasks (e.g., repetitive or nonrepetitive), and leader/follower relationships. It thus not only focuses on the style of the leader but also on the nature of the work to be performed, the external environment, and the characteristics of the followers.
- Integrative leadership theories combine trait, behavioral, and contingency theories to explain successful leader-follower relationships. These are obviously the most comprehensive of the theories since they draw from and integrate the three others in explaining how the traits of leaders, *combined* with situations and how leaders interact with followers, result in their ability to influence followers to work hard and make personal sacrifices for the good of the organization. One example of an integrative theory is Theory Z, developed by William Ouchi after studying the success of Japanese companies, which involves collective decision making and shared leadership responsibilities (Lussier and Achua 2003). Another, submitted by Komives, Owen, and McMahon (1998), concentrates on relationship-building as requisite to leaders and followers working together to accomplish change or make a difference to benefit commonly held goals. Similarly, a very popular leadership theory originated by Robert Greenleaf (1977) evokes images of the leader as a servant and the leader as a relationship builder. Greenleaf believed leadership should begin with a natural desire to serve—that a leader must first be a servant.

Even with the above referenced conceptual family approach, leadership theory remains diverse and fragmented. It is, I believe, the addition of the spiritual dimension that enables one to bring together a theory applicable to needs in today's workplace. The spiritual leadership theory presented in this chapter draws from all of the previously described leadership approaches. Although the remainder of this chapter will deal with the spiritual aspect of leadership, occasional references will illustrate how leading with spirit dovetails with traditional leadership theories.

What Is Spirituality?

...And the end of all our exploring
Will be to arrive where we started...
—T. S. Eliot in Palmer 2004, 48

Although spirituality is currently a hot topic in literature on the workplace, the myriad books on this topic rarely agree on a common definition. Attempts to quantify this ethereal concept range from something as simple as "team spirit," which may be no more than working together in harmony as a group, to a more traditional approach relating it to a higher power or the divine. Marcic (2000), after reviewing about 100 books and another 100 journal articles on spirituality published over the preceding 10 years, noted that less than 20 percent of the publications mention God or a higher power. Instead, the literature focuses on topics such as group spirit, team spirit, human spirit, centeredness, morality, meditation, or creativity. Writers who describe spirituality in such non-material terms generally avoid tying spirituality to religion. Greenstreet (1999) describes one author who takes a different approach: "Heriot (1992) differentiates between religion and spirituality and in doing so brings many of these dimensions of spirituality together. She sees spirituality as a broader notion, an umbrella under which religion and the needs of human spirit are found. Spirituality is described as being concerned with the personal interpretation of life and the inner resources of people. Religion is seen as an external, formal system of beliefs" (650). Greenstreet (1999) explains that the needs of the human spirit referred to by Heriot (meaning and purpose in life, meaning in suffering, love and relatedness, forgiveness, sense of transcendence, and sense of awe and wonder about life) include some that might be filled by religion while others may be fulfilled without any notion of a deity or higher power. Clark (2001) sees some congruence between spirituality and religion but also notes distinctions in his definitions of the two: "Spirituality refers to that noncorporal aspect of each human being that is separate from the mind. Religion refers to an organized set of doctrines around faith beliefs within an organization" (38).

Daniels, Franz, and Wong (2000) approach spirituality from a worldview perspective. They believe our worldviews (generally defined as a set of presuppositions that affect the way we view our world) have enormous implications for how we view leadership. They draw on a Christian perspective on human nature that holds dichotomous views: "Humans are made in God's image and therefore have the potential for enormous good, yet as fallen beings they are also selfish and rebellious toward God" (553). Such a Christian worldview would not presume people are either purely good or purely evil. This Christian notion of human nature seems to contradict McGregor's Theory X/Theory Y approach since those theories are based on the presupposition that people/human nature are either inherently bad (X) or inherently good (Y). A Christian worldview allows for both human natures in every person. Manning (2000) seems to hold this position when he describes himself (and perhaps all mankind) this way: "When I get honest, I admit I am a bundle of paradoxes. I believe and I doubt. I hope and get discouraged. I love and I hate. I feel bad about feeling good. I feel guilty about not feeling guilty. I am trusting and suspicious. I am honest and I still play games" (26).

Even with our flawed humanity, I believe being a spirit-filled leader is possible. But, what *is* spirituality? I will not delve into the debate except by noting a dichotomy and by offering my own definition for the purposes of this chapter. Blanchard (1999) clearly realizes that trying to define spirituality raises more questions than answers when he says, "We are not human beings having a spiritual experience. We are spiritual beings having a human experience" (92). Not disagreeing with Blanchard, to undergird the theory I propose, for the purpose of this chapter I offer a broad-based definition of spirituality: "The search for depth and meaning in our entire being" (Hoppe 2005, 84).

Leading with Spirit

Building on the above definition of spirituality, I submit that leading with spirit requires:

- meaning that derives from connectedness and unity,
- wholeness that comes from an integrated and balanced life,

- authenticity that comes from congruence between beliefs, values, and behaviors; and finally,
- contextual understanding that begins with acceptance and tolerance and moves toward forgiveness.

The following diagram captures these components and illustrates their relationships to each other and to the center of being in our lives. As noted in the introduction to this chapter, these concepts are interlocking. They are not, however, sequential, since their relationships vary based on the dynamics of situations and individuals.

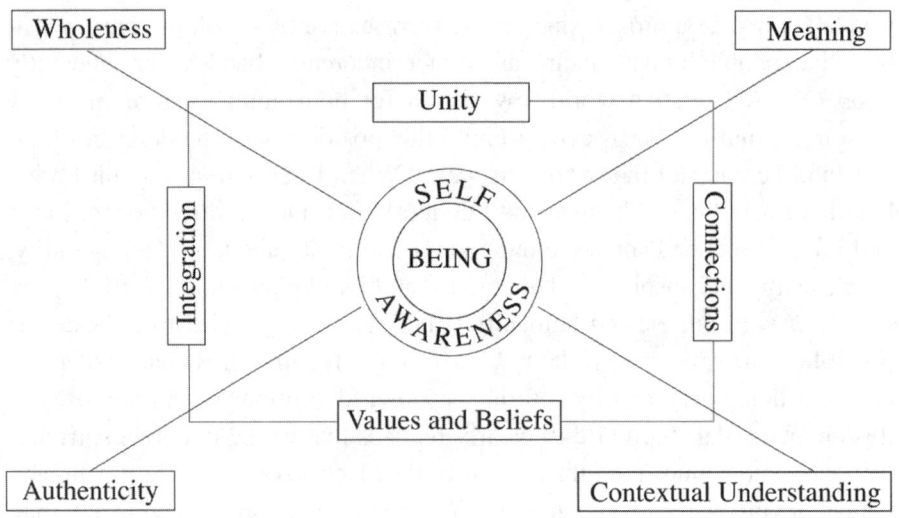

To apply the above model and achieve a practicing and consistent leadership spirit will undoubtedly necessitate a paradigm shift for many leaders. Riding the waters of change is never easy—the ripples throughout the organization often increase in intensity and threaten to envelope the desired peace and calm. Despite the potential tsunami, spirituality has swirled into corporate towers and even flooded manufacturing floors over the past few years, perhaps prompted by the changing nature of work. No longer can employees look forward to a lifetime with the same organization, to assurances of retirement benefits or even generous health benefits. In the absence of a patriarchal employer, stress and uncertainty increase as mutual loyalty diminishes. The search for meaning in work, where most people spend the majority of their waking hours, has become increasingly important in an environment where bottom line profits have often reduced the role of employers to human "resources," providing little room for appreciation of their contributions as human "beings."

Higher education is not immune from such environments, but it may also be less likely to wholeheartedly embrace spirituality in the workplace. Despite the honoring of both intellect and spirit in the earliest colleges of Colonial America, most of the twentieth century saw a chasm erupt between liberal education and anything spiritual, especially if it smacked of religiosity. Today, though, the beginning of a distant tidal wave of spirituality is seeping into higher education in much the same way it has in corporate America, and higher education leaders must find ways to respond despite the reticence inside some ivy-covered walls.

While the infusion of work teams into all types of organizations has attempted to address the "meaning" need (primarily through integrative leaders), it is not enough. A true paradigm shift requires that meaning extend beyond such work groups into the broader context of the organization as well as life outside the workplace. Biberman and Whitty (1997) contend that even Deming's total quality management theories (which fit the integration model) lack the essence needed for a postmodern management paradigm that emphasizes spiritual principles and practices. Citing Rose (1990), they paint a picture of a paradigm that contains two main components: interconnectedness and empowerment. Asserting this paradigm is continuing to emerge, Biberman, Whitty, and Robbins (1999) believe "persons operating from a spiritual paradigm perspective would be open to change, have a sense of purpose and meaning in their lives, appreciate how they are connected with a greater whole, and have individual understanding and expression of their own spirituality" (133).

In contrast to organizations operating from a modern paradigm that includes "rigid bureaucratic structures and hierarchal chains of command," the postmodern or spiritual paradigm opens the dam for sharing information, trusting others, accomplishing mutual objectives and empowering others (Biberman and Whitty 1997, 133). This opening of previously held sacred power and information has the potential to help all employees seek meaning and find purpose through a sense of contribution to work life (Biberman and Whitty 1997). Such a connection is critical as leaders (especially those subscribing to contingency theories) and thus followers attempt to live and work in what Vaill (1989) describes as a *permanent white water*. We seek permanency in spirit as the one part of our lives that remains constant, connects our inner and outer beings, and gives us inner peace despite the chaos and change in our physical world. Russell and Evans (1992) aver individuals must possess both a sound rudder and strong anchor to navigate uncertain seas. Remaining not only afloat but also spiritually stable requires pointing the internal compass toward our "being," the core or essence of what and who we are.

Know Thyself

In Act I, scene iii of *Hamlet*, Polonius prepares his son Laertes for travel abroad with a speech in which he directs the youth to commit a "few precepts to memory." Among these percepts is this dictum: "This above all: to thine own self be true,/And it must follow, as the night the day,/Thou cans't not be false to any man" (ll.78–80).

Polonius' advice was sound, but he falls short of telling us how to *know* "thine own self." And yet, an inner journey is required if we are to find our "being." Higher education administrators, like our counterparts in business and industry, must discover who we are by looking deep inside ourselves if we are to set our compass for the search for meaning as individuals and as leaders (Hoppe 2005). In the absence of internal clarity about what we want for our lives, our leadership will lack clear purpose, leaving us open to leading others to places we do not necessarily want them to go. Without an internal map, we will have no foundational sense on which to build our leadership potential (Lee and King 2001). I believe the foundation we need comes from answering questions such as these:

- Who am I?
- What do I value?
- What do I believe?
- What do I want to become?
- Who inspires me?
- What gives me energy?
- What makes me feel creative and intuitive?

(Lee and King 2001)

While answering these questions is more difficult than asking them, the exercise is necessary in our search for self-awareness. Bolman and Deal (2001) point in the direction of the classics in advising us to lead an examined life and to have a spirit of inquiry and experimentation, noting that the "contemporary search is grounded in the age-old journey of the soul that has been a core preoccupation of every human culture since the beginning of time" (4). We are driven to search by our spiritual hunger and restlessness, and Bolman and Deal (2001) are convinced that "what's really missing is soul and spirit" (5). If we dedicate time for reflection and self-examination, if we plunge into the depths at the core of our being, our inner journey will lead us to our desired destination: we will find our soul. Spirituality, defined for the purpose of this chapter as "the search for depth and meaning in our entire being" (Hoppe 2005, 84), begins with such an inner examination and moves toward questions about the meaning of life itself and the meaning of our individual lives. Meaning ultimately requires connections to one another and to the world beyond ourselves (Conger 1994).

Meaning

The purpose of life is a life of purpose.
—Robert Byrne

At the heart of the search for meaning is a desire for peace. Rolheiser (1999) says this desire "lies at the center of our lives, in the marrow of our bones, and in the deep recesses of the soul" (3). He describes us as "driven persons, forever obsessed, congenitally dis-eased, living lives, as Thoreau once suggested, of quiet desperation, only occasionally experiencing peace" (3). Reminding us that this desire lies at the heart of all great literature, poetry, art, philosophy, psychology and religion, he offers Anne Frank's story as one haunting example. He also mentions several others: the journals of Thérèse of Lisieux and Etty Hillesum; the work of Sigmund Freud and Karl Jung; and the writings of James Hillman and Doris Lessing. I would add Victor Frankl to his list. Frankl, seemingly hopeless in a Nazi concentration camp, found his thirst for life renewed in what he called "will to meaning." Frankl believed that, regardless of conditions, "it becomes clear that the sort of person the prisoner became was the result of an inner decision, and not the result of camp influences alone. Fundamentally, therefore, any man can, even under such circumstances, decide what shall become of him—mentally and spiritually. He may retain his human dignity even in a concentration camp" (Frankl 1992, 75). Frankl (1992) told his fellow prisoners "that human life, under any circumstances, never ceases to have a meaning, and that this infinite meaning of life includes suffering and dying, privation and death...that the hopelessness of our struggle did not detract from its dignity and meaning...and finally I spoke of our sacrifice, which had meaning in every case" (90–91).

In more recent times, *The Moviegoer* illustrates that the search for meaning continues. Raper (2001) tells us that in this book Percy Walker avows all people would undertake the search for meaning if we were not sunk in the "everydayness" of life. Those who become aware of the possibility of the search see hope; it is those who are not even aware that they can try to make sense of the world who despair. Walker, according to Raper, illustrated the reason for the quest using Nietzche's famous lines: "he who has a *why* to live for, can bear almost any *how*" (Raper 2001, 24). Frankl poignantly used Nietzche's quote on more than one occasion. Jung (1933) expresses a similar premise, telling us everything depends on how we look at things: "The least of things with a meaning is worth more than the greatest of things without it" (66).

Despite the overwhelming human need for meaning and its constancy over the centuries, the search is not often discussed outside the confines of the classroom. Indeed, in leaders' circles, we rarely have time to pause and consider the "bigger picture" of life and how what we do relates (or should relate) to our inner being. We are all about data, productivity and accountability. We may subscribe to integrative leadership theories, but we do it at the highest levels—not with the lower ranks of the organization. We often do not take the time to share enough information for followers to see how their role contributes to the corporate good.

Beyond the basic striving for meaning about life itself is an attendant striving for meaning in our daily work. Bennett (2003) notes, "At the institutional level organizational divisions too often isolate us from each other and separate our inquiries about things that in nature are continuous" (3). He uses the perennial separation of academics from student affairs as an example of our failure to "seize the advantages that closer cooperation would generate" (3). To address such deficiencies, Allen and Kellom (2001) suggest that we "amplify meaning making" (168). They, like Bennett, realize that when we are very busy, we often fail to link the tasks to something larger than ourselves, thus missing an opportunity to create meaning. Concomitantly, we miss an opportunity to practice spirituality in the workplace. Allen and Kellom note, "Using meaning as a form of cohesion in an organization builds on the spiritual need in all of us to work toward a higher purpose" (168). (This statement pushes us toward behavioral leadership, recognizing the highest order of needs.)

Connections

> *We cannot live only for ourselves.*
> *A thousand fibers connect us with our fellow men.*
> —Herman Melville

Cohesion begins with connections, and the first connection we must make is with our being. Tolle (1999) tells the story of a beggar who sat by the side of the road for more than 30 years. One day, after mumbling his usual, "Spare some change," he was told that the stranger had nothing to give him but that he should look inside the box on which he was sitting. The beggar thought that was crazy, but at the insistence of the stranger he got up and pried off the top of the box. To his utter amazement, the box was filled with gold. Tolle uses this story to illustrate that what we are searching for so relentlessly can be found deep inside ourselves. "Those who have not found their true wealth, which is the radiant joy of Being and the deep, unshakable peace that comes with it, are beggars, even if they have great material wealth" (9). Tolle goes on to describe a "natural state of *felt* oneness with being" as a "state of connectedness with something immeasurable and indestructible, something that, almost paradoxically, is essentially you and yet is much greater than you" (10).

Connectedness with being is the supreme goal—an outcome that brings one in touch with his or her essence. As noted in the introduction to this chapter, being at one with Nature often brings a sense of serenity and peace. Indeed, one must live in a world of humanness; and while connectedness with Being is a desirable state, connections to other people are a necessity for a steady and stable life. Neck and Milliman (1994) state, "core spiritual beliefs often involve a strong sense of community and need to contribute to the betterment of others and society" (7). The goal of spirituality, they assert, is often to achieve a high state of attainment of the potential in one's own life, which in turn leads to organizational commitment. This occurs through a sense of community and connections within that community (reminiscent of servant leadership theory). Allen and Kellom (2001) advise us to "Treat others as sacred" (167). They ask "What would happen if we treated each other as if we were worthy of reverence and respect? How would this change what we talk about, how we interact, and what would we believe about each other?" (168). "The Rabbi's Gift" illustrates the answer: Trying to save a monastery that had fallen on hard times, the Abbott visited a Rabbi to ask for help. The old man offered no solution to the monastery's problems but did whisper to him that "The Messiah is among you." After the Abbott shared this message with his fellow monks, they begin to wonder which one of them was the Messiah—cantankerous Brother William? mean and spiteful Brother Stephen? dirty and sloppy Brother John? moody Father Matthew? or crotchety Brother Thomas? Unable to decide, the monks began to treat one another with extraordinary respect, on the off-chance that one of them might be the Messiah. Visitors sensed the human, yet divine, quality about the monks and were moved to help the monastery. Within a few years, the monastery became once again a thriving order, and—thanks to the Rabbi's gift—a vibrant community of light and love for the whole realm (Zander and Zander 2000).

If we as leaders could see our colleagues as the monks saw each other, we would be on the path not only to connections but also to unity. Unfortunately, in the jet age unity is hampered by the splintering of the extended family. Conger (1994) asserts that although churches and temples historically served as important places for unity and connections, their impact has been seriously diminished as engagement with rituals has been pushed out of our daily lives. In an era where the workplace is our primary source of community, it is there where we form many of our friendships and relationships, where we discover many of the challenges of our lives, and where we contribute to society (Conger 1994). We must thus acknowledge that the search for spirit and unity will also be a part of the connections we make in our work lives. Connections thus form the basis for our search for unity in spirit.

Unity

"No man is an island, entire of itself; every man is a piece of the continent."
—John Donne

Morris (1997) asserts that numbers alone bring a certain strength. He illustrates his point with old Ethiopian folk wisdom: "'When spider webs unite, they can tie up a lion'" (194). He adds a statement by Homer from *The*

Iliad, "'Not vain the weakest, if their forces unite'" (194) to remind us that union with others is requisite in both life and work. As higher education leaders, we must acknowledge the need among our employees for networks that support and nourish them when they face uncertain or traumatic times (a lower level need for safety, calling for behavioral leadership). Barrentine (1993) reminds us that in times of transition, networks tend to expand and deepen because during these times people experience a strong need to build unity with each other and find truth together. Unfortunately, as Mitroff and Denton (1999) assert, too many organizations continue to separate spiritual concerns from the workplace and thus force employees to compartmentalize their lives. This results from a failure to recognize the workplace as one of the most important settings where people join together to achieve what they cannot do alone—that is, to realize their full potential as human beings (a higher order need for self-actualization). Unless organizations support the unity necessary for individuals to meet not only their individual but corporate needs, they will fail to benefit from full engagement of their employees. Strangely, the organizations that have the greatest potential for infusing spirituality and unity into the workplace are the ones creating the major impediment to progress. According to Mitroff and Denton (1999), business schools and academe in general typically omit any acknowledgment of the soul in their lessons or discussions. Consequently, leaders go into the workplace ill-prepared to deal with employees who are seeking connections and unity as part of their search for meaning in their lives.

Unity (oneness within and oneness in our community or workplace) is imperative if academic leaders are to avoid what Bennett (2003) describes as "insistent individualism." "Insistent individualism promotes the isolated self—it advances disconnection among faculty and staff as well as between faculty, staff, students, and institutions. It works against internal integration and separates personal from professional lives. It encourages exclusiveness rather than relationality, self-protection rather than openness to the other. It celebrates instrumental rather than relational knowledge. Insistent individualism encourages disciplinary and specialty boundaries, isolated departments, and fragmented institutions…" (23). Fragmentation works against wholeness and integration, and leaders must thus find ways to support unity.

Wholeness

"there is in all things...a hidden wholeness"
—Merton in Palmer 2004, 4

With connections and unity in place, we are well on the way to wholeness in our lives and in the workplace. We must recognize, though, that the struggle is constant and never-ending. While people do not *want* to compartmentalize their lives, many leaders either expect their followers to leave their "souls" at home or just fail to acknowledge this aspect of a person's life as a necessary ingredient of wholeness (Mitroff and Denton 1999). As leaders, we often fail to accept Thomas Carlyle's words (as quoted by Morris 1997): "It is the spiritual that determines the material." Expanding this premise, Mitroff and Denton (1999) also cite, from the seventeenth century, the great mathematician and scientist Blaise Pascal's identification of three orders of reality: "the physical realm, or the order of the body; the intellectual realm, or the order of the mind; and the spiritual realm, or the order of the heart" (178). They assert that most people often live in just one or two of these realms, crowding out spirit and thus robbing themselves of a deep need that is ultimately the source of wholeness as it brings integration to all parts of our lives. McMillen (1993) believes that without this wholeness, "we will be forever distracted...We will fail to acquire that larger, mystical awareness of the interconnectedness of life" (107).

How do academic leaders bring wholeness not only to themselves, but also to their followers? Bolman and Deal (2001) believe we derive this capacity from an ethic in which one sees leadership as a "higher calling" (106). We must see our roles as occurring in more than just a business or rational enterprise; and we must avoid seeing our institutions as "atomistic and unconnected curricula, isolated disciplines, and fragmented departments" (Bennett 2003, 25). Instead, we must see the wholeness not only of the enterprise but also of individuals. That requires us to acknowledge the notion that "spirituality, more powerfully than most other human forces, lifts us beyond ourselves and our narrow self-interests....It helps us to see our deeper connections to one another and to the world beyond ourselves" (Conger 1994, 17). Palmer (1987) calls to our attention that such connections extend beyond people to historical events, to nature, to vision and to things of the spirit. This larger reality also encompasses our understanding of the world and beyond (Hoppe 2005). Wholeness thus brings together the fragmented parts of our lives and weaves them into a tapestry that makes sense.

Integration and Balance

> *The best and safest thing is to keep a balance in your life,*
> *acknowledge the great powers around us and in us.*
> *If you can do that, and live that way, you are really a wise man.*
> —Euripides

As noted previously, integrative theories of leadership explain how the traits of leaders, combined with situations and interactions between leaders and followers, contribute to their ability to influence followers to work hard and make personal sacrifices for the good of the organization. Leading with spirit adds another dimension to that combination, enabling a leader to help followers achieve greater integration and balance.

Richards (1995) identifies four energies within all people: physical, mental, emotional and spiritual. (While some might say they do not have spiritual energy, I would assert that this energy is there in all human beings—it is just buried more deeply in some than in others.) Richards describes physical energy as tangible and solid, residing in tissue, muscle, organs, and cells. Physical energy enables us to move our bodies, to work, and to play. Mental energy resides in our brains and consists of our thoughts, ideas, and memories. The third energy, emotional, is less definable but brings us feelings of joy or sorrow, pride or shame, wonder or dismay. Richards says, "it flows like a broad river, at one moment turbulent and muddy, at the next serene and clear" (14), and he notes that it is not often welcome in the workplace. The same is true for spiritual energy, which arises from our search for being and concerns beliefs about "unseen forces that shape our reality and…relationships to those forces" (14).

Richards (1989) sees the four energies as entwined in ways that form a complex web of interdependence and connectedness, resulting in wholeness. He describes this as "centering" (15). We are brought full circle back to "being," which must be the basis for that centering. Whether centering a lump of clay in the process of forming a vase or bowl or centering a life, spinning is requisite to the final form of wholeness. Without centering, we will have no balance in our lives—and especially not in our leadership.

Balance is likely a recurring theme in most people's lives as we juggle work, community, and personal responsibilities. For many, finding time for spiritual development is even more difficult than just finding time for oneself. In the race for success and the desire for peace, we find conflicting demands within and without.

Biberman, Whitty, and Robbins (1999) use *The Wizard of Oz* to explain one way an individual or an organization can achieve balance in the multiple facets of life or energy. In the story, Dorothy's reclaiming of her balance results in her spiritual transformation. While changes from within allow Dorothy and other characters to achieve inner victory over their darker sides, Biberman, Whitty, and Robbins (1999) assert that it is the integration of the experiences along the path that allows the changes to occur. Likewise, organizations need to support integration of individuals and their workplace in ways that allow for the four energies (physical, mental, emotional, and spiritual) to be present and accepted. Biberman, Whitty, and Robbins (1999) believe organizations need to balance recognition of employees' inner strengths "with responsiveness both to ideas and to shifts in their environments" (250), echoing contingency leadership theories. Only then can an organization be open to spiritual transformation.

Such a transformation faces many difficulties in higher education. Balancing the need to secure needed resources with the need to preserve institutional autonomy and academic freedom often leaves little room for spiritual exploration or even leading with spirit (Astin and Astin 1999). This conflict is exasperated by a litany of other struggles: "the commitment to advance the frontiers of knowledge versus the commitment to educate students well and to serve the community; the commitment to academic excellence versus the commitment to educational opportunity and equity; the quest for individual professional achievement and recognition versus the desire to nurture and sustain an intellectual community" (2). And that's not all. Today higher education leaders are faced with scrutiny over every decision in an ever-increasing environment of accountability to multiple constituents. How does one combat the competing demands and expectations yet simultaneously achieve a balance in organizational life that includes tenets of spirituality? The answer is found, I think, in our beliefs and values. We must not let the pressures of daily leadership move us away from our authentic selves—what we believe and what we stand for. Too many times in recent history, leaders in all types of organizations have lost that authenticity through the lack of congruence between their espoused values and beliefs and their actions.

Authenticity

The first key to greatness is to be in reality what we appear to be.
—Socrates

Barrentine (1993) describes authenticity as being "*all* of yourself" (11). She believes we should resist society's expectation that we leave "ourselves" at the door when we enter our workplace. Splintering our inner being from our work life will, as noted previously, lead to fragmentation. If authenticity means that what I believe, what I say, and what I do are consistent, then my beliefs cannot be left at the door. Throughout the earliest history of American higher education, the president was clearly an institution's moral leader (Chickering and Mentkowski 2006). With religion as part of the founding mission of most colonial institutions, this was not only expected but required. Today, with religious doctrine virtually absent in the leadership of most institutions (including many sectarian ones), being authentic is sometimes difficult if one presumes that includes sharing one's beliefs. I purport that leading with spirit can exist without such overt expressions. Authenticity does not require I tell my followers that I am a Christian or a Jew or a Moslem or whatever. What it does demand is that my actions consistently reflect my beliefs and values, whatever they may be. We cannot be chameleons. Wood (2001) graphically supports this assertion:

Jack pines...are not lumber trees [and they] won't win many beauty contests either. But to me this valiant old tree, solitary on its own rocky point, is as beautiful as a living thing can be...In the calligraphy of its shape against the sky is written strength of character and perseverance, survival of wind, drought, cold, heat, disease....In its silence it speaks of...wholeness...an integrity that comes from being what you are. (3–4)

Palmer (2004) notes that we humans are often less revealing of ourselves than are jack pines. "Afraid that our inner light will be extinguished or our inner darkness exposed, we hide our true identities from each other. In the process, we become separated from our own souls. We end up living divided lives, so far removed from the truth we hold within that we cannot know the 'integrity that comes from being what you are'" (4).

Beliefs and Values

Leadership ultimately becomes moral in that it raises the level of human conduct...of both leader and led, and thus transforms both.
—Burns 1978

Barrett (1998) notes that while all organizations are value-driven, the real issue is whether the values are "conscious, shared and lived" or remain behind the scenes in the unconscious or just not discussed. He notes that shared values build trust and create community, as well as cohesion and unity. Fortunately, many of today's approaches to leadership—teams, partnerships, alliances—work toward relationships that allow for sharing of spirituality, sometimes explicitly but more often implicitly, through our actions (à la relational leadership theory). One courageous example of an initiation entailing a discussion of spiritual growth as a core value can be found at Bowling Green State University (OH) under the leadership of President Sidney Ribeau. Strange (2000) reported that a task force on building community at Bowling Green eventually resulted in a campus study group on spiritual growth, beginning a process of musings about spirituality, with reflections on meanings of spirituality and their connections to the learning, growth, and development of students at a public institution. Although Strange does not describe the motivation for Ribeau's foray into uncharted waters, I suspect his journey began within himself. Allen and Kellom (2001) believe the "starting point for enhancing the spiritual development of ourselves, our staff, and our organizations is our own deep soul work, reflection on our own lives and what gives them meaning. What is it that matters? What are the values that guide our lives?" (161).

Kanungo and Mendonca (1994) state, "To develop spiritually, we need both intellect and will" (166). Intellect "enables us to ascend from the domain of the senses to the domain of ideals. It is here in the domain of ideals that spirituality resides" (166). From ideals come our values. Kanungo believes, at a cognitive level, "cardinal values and capital vices" (167) are at the core of human existence. Lussier and Achua (2003) note that the basis for meaning comes from values. They define values as "stable and enduring beliefs about what an individual considers to be important" (361). What then, are those values or ideals that represent what is good and right and how do we as leaders not only advocate them but also live them?

Bennis (1989) espoused the following values for leaders:

1. Communication that is full and free, without respect to rank and power
2. Consensus that comes without conflict or coercion
3. Influence based on competence and knowledge rather than personal whims or privileges of power
4. An environment that encourages spirit along with tasks
5. An acceptance of conflict and a rational approach for dealing with it

Bennis's list is a good beginning, but it fails to address what Mitroff and Denton (1999) believe is the cornerstone of value-based organizations: trust. They believe a socially responsible organization is run with good family values, and trust is essential not only in our natural families but also in our extended work families if relationships are to flourish (pointing us again toward a relational leadership theory). Quoting from Marcic's *Managing with the Wisdom of Love: Uncovering Virtue in People and Organizations* (2000), they use the Golden Rule as the basis for protecting these relationships. A universal law underlying all of the world's great religions and philosophies, the Golden Rule derives from love, which in turn is the most basic underlying value or virtue (Marcic as cited by Mitroff and Denton 1999). Although the words may sometimes vary, the message remains essentially constant: "Love your neighbor, be honest, live in justice, control your impulses, avoid corruption, let your intentions be pure, and serve your fellow humans" (Marcic as cited by Mitroff and Denton 1999, 149). Following the spiritual law to love our neighbor and treat our neighbor as we would want to be treated is central to developing our spiritual natures and acquiring virtues, such as trustworthiness, respect, patience, and so on (as cited by Mitroff and Denton 1999).

As higher education leaders, we must ensure that our followers understand our values. Jack Welch, CEO of General Electric, boiled it down to one requirement: ethical behavior (Mitroff and Denton 1999). Employees must understand that certain behaviors, such as cheating or covering up bad quality, are never acceptable. That begins with congruence between our values and our actions as leaders.

Congruence

> *It is no use walking anywhere to preach*
> *Unless our walking is our preaching.*
> —Francis of Assisi

Barrett (1998) tells us, "values talk (109)." If our behaviors visibly demonstrate our values, then we have congruence. A popular phrase, "walk the talk," illustrates the principle that discrepancies should not exist between our values and our behaviors. If we as academic leaders make open declarations about our values and how we expect our followers to behave, we must not make exceptions ourselves. Many organizations print their values and post them in conspicuous places, but talking and writing about our values is not enough. Values become tangible only when they are seen in behaviors. As Bennett reminds us, "It is not what I say but what I do that informs you of my values" (187). Alignment between stated values and behaviors results in integrity and trust only if the congruence is always visible, regardless of circumstances: under stress or at leisure, in good financial times or financial uncertainty, in conflict or in peace, in competition or in cooperation. The situation or context matters not; values and actions must be congruent. Context can be important, though, in other ways.

Contextual Understanding

> *The blizzard of the world*
> *... has overturned*
> *The order of the soul.*
> —Leonard Cohen from Palmer 2004, 1

I have never been in a blizzard, but I have seen movies where people run a rope from the back door of their house out to the barn to avoid wandering off and being frozen to death while in a whiteout that keeps them from seeing the house just a few feet away. Palmer (2004) tells us, "Today we live in a blizzard of another sort. It swirls around as economic injustice, ecological ruin, physical and spiritual violence, and their inevitable outcome, war. It swirls within us as fear and frenzy, greed and deceit, and indifference to the suffering of others" (1). Within this blizzard, people can wander off and become separated from their own souls, Palmer says. Competitiveness and generational changes (from baby boomers to generation x to millennials), combined with shifts of power from the top to employee rights and input, make leading an organization a difficult task. In a highly competitive environment, organizations of all kinds struggle with finding ways to help employees see the value of service, quality, and responsiveness. No easy solutions are available, but I believe the answer begins with understanding people where they are—accepting them in the context of their lives rather than just in the context of the workplace. The acceptance of employee needs begins with Maslow's hierarchy but goes far beyond. For both leaders and followers, understanding "is a fundamental condition for satisfaction and deep fulfillment in what we do as well as for who we are" (Morris 1997, 206). I should note that understanding must be three fold: (1) the more followers understand about the organization, the greater their contributions to the common goals; (2) the more leaders understand about their followers, the more they can do to support them in achieving both personal and corporate goals; (3) the more leaders understand about the vagaries of life, the more they can accept people who may be less than perfect, people who make mistakes, and people who hurt us in various ways (Morris 1997).

Tolerance, Forgiveness, and Acceptance

"Wholeness does not mean perfection:
it means embracing brokenness as an integral part of life"
—Palmer 2004, 5

We only have to recall the destructive eruption of the volcano at Mount St. Helens and the eventual (and quick) healing of nature's wounds through rebirth of vegetation in the midst of devastation to know that healing is not only possible but an act of our nature if we are in touch with our being on a daily basis.

If we are truly in touch with our being, we will acknowledge that both leaders and followers are flawed. As leaders, we must first be in touch with our own imperfections if we are to avoid disconnecting from our soul (Bolman and Deal 2001). Hoppe (2005) advises, "to avoid such a disconnection with its concomitant spiritual bankruptcy, leaders must recognize their own limitations and those of their followers: some based on personal experience with the history of the institution, some based on personal experience outside the organization, and some just based on inherent human fallacies" (88). As a university president, I am keenly aware of my own weaknesses when I deal with the flaws of others. A book that spoke to my heart about how to develop an attitude of acceptance rather than criticism is *The Ragamuffin Gospel* by Manning (2000). I once used this book as part of the basis for a convocation address in an attempt to "mend the fences that are inevitably and continuously in need of repair between administration and faculty on most campuses" (Hoppe 2005, 88).

Manning (2000) wrote his book not for the "super spiritual," but for the "bedraggled, beat-up, and burnt out" (15). While followers may think they have the edge on such feelings, leaders often experience such low ebbs themselves. At times, we can all be described as "inconsistent, unsteady humans whose cheese is falling off their cracker" (Manning 2000, 15). "Leaders, like followers, sometimes grow weary and discouraged along the way" (Hoppe, 2005, 88). Manning's goal is to help us understand that we are all ragamuffins—and thus we should accept others in their ragamuffin state. "Usually we see other people not as they are, but as we are....If we have made peace with our flawed humanity and embraced our ragamuffin identity, we are able to tolerate in others what was previously unacceptable in ourselves....Solidarity with ragamuffins frees the one who receives compassion and liberates the one who gives it in the conscious awareness, 'I am the other'" (Manning 2000, 151–153).

Mahatma Gandhi told us, "The weak can never forgive. Forgiveness is the attribute of the strong." Accepting that we are all imperfect human beings makes forgiveness of others' failures and hurts possible. So it was that Pope John Paul II walked into a prison and forgave the man who had tried to kill him. If we follow this pope's example, we will not allow ourselves to be broken and bent by what others do and say; otherwise, we will end up like the birches in one of Frost's poems: "You may see their trunks arching in the woods/ Years afterwards, trailing their leaves on the ground" ("Birches" Frost [1916] 1963). A better option is offered by Palmer (2004), who believes hope comes from embracing brokenness rather than being hurt by it; human wholeness (including our imperfections and flaws)—mine and yours—"need not be a utopian dream, if we can use devastation as a seedbed for new life" (5). That seedbed is at the core of our being, and it is always fertile. As leaders, we must care about people enough to look beyond their idiosyncrasies and see their virtues. We must be compassionate and forgiving. Bolman and Deal (2001) contend that "love is the true hallmark of great leaders—love for their work and love for those with whom they work" (108). In a later book (2003), Bolman and Deal point out that loving others makes one vulnerable but note that "confronting vulnerability allows us to drop our masks, meet heart to heart and be present for one another" (339). In doing so, "We experience a sense of unity and delight in those voluntary, human exchanges that mold 'the soul of the community'" (339). Bennis (1989) describes this focus on others as a true calling that is an inevitable outcome of leaders who have fully integrated lives.

Conclusion

Nobody knows what the soul is,
It comes and goes
Like the wind over the water.
—Mary Oliver quoted in Palmer 2004, 33

If Bennis (1989) is right, our calling as leaders may inevitably lead us to be servant leaders. However, servant leadership will not necessarily open the floodgate to spirituality for higher education leaders nor is it the only way to lead with spirit. Rather, we must draw from multiple leadership theories if we are to position ourselves as spiritual leaders. Regardless of the theory held, many leaders have experienced "a sea change in the way they must approach the problems of business and work" (Nash and McLennan 2001, 4). That "sea change," according to Nash and McLennan, is spirituality. Furthermore, even though we can not penetrate the mystery of the soul any more than we can the see the wind itself, we can feel its impact in our lives as individuals and as leaders. Richards (1989) advises us to "trust the invisible gauges we carry with us" (27), while Palmer (2004) notes that our soul strives to keep us "rooted in the ground of our own being" (33). From that being, we find meaning in connectedness and unity; for it is there we build our lives in relationships not only among humankind but also in nature. To be effective spiritual leaders, we must not have divided lives. Instead, we need a wholeness in our lives that comes from integration of the four energies while allowing for a balanced life. We must also achieve authenticity through congruence between our beliefs/values and behaviors. Most importantly, we must understand and accept the contexts in which we live and work so that we will not only tolerate but respect our fellow workers. If we can do all this, we may not *know* what the soul is, but we will recognize it when it comes and goes like the wind over the waves. We will then be prepared to lead with spirit.

References

Allen, K. E., and G. Kellom. 2001. Learning to connect: Spirituality and leadership. In *Transforming campus life: Reflections on spirituality and religious pluralism*, eds. V. M. Miller and M. M. Ryan, 161–168. Studies in Education and Spirituality, vol. 1. New York: Peter Lang.

Astin, A., and H. S. Astin. 1999. *Meaning and spirituality in the lives of college faculty*. Los Angeles: Higher Education Research Institute, University of California.

Barrentine, P. 1993. Introduction to women as harbingers of business transformation. In *When the canary stops singing*, ed. P. Barrentine, 105–116. San Francisco: Berrett-Koehler Publishers.

Barrett, R. 1998. *Liberating the corporate soul*. Boston: Butterworth-Heinemann.

Bennett, J. B. 2003. *Academic life: Hospitality, ethics, and spirituality*. Bolton, MA: Anker Publishing Company, Inc.

Bennis, W. 1989. *Why leaders can't lead: The unconscious conspiracy continues*. San Francisco: Jossey-Bass.

Biberman, J., and M. Whitty. 1997. A postmodern spiritual future for work. *Journal of Organizational Change Management* 10(2):130–138.

Biberman, J., M. Whitty, and L. Robbins. 1999. Lessons learned from Oz: balance and wholeness in organizations. *Journal of Organizational Change* 12(3):243–254.

Blanchard, K. 1999. *The heart of a leader: Insights on the art of influence*. Escondito, CA: Honor Books.

Bolman, L. G., and T. E. Deal 2001. *Leading with soul*. San Francisco: Jossey-Bass.

———. 2003. Reframing ethics and spirit. In *Business Leadership*, ch. 20. San Francisco: Jossey-Bass.

Burns, J. M. 1978. *Leadership*. New York: Harper and Row.

Chavez, A. F. 2001. Spirit and nature in everyday life: Reflections of a Mestiza in higher education. In *The implications of student spirituality for student affairs practice*, ed. M. A. Jablonski, 69. New Directions for Student Services. San Francisco: Jossey-Bass.

Chickering, A. W., and M. Mentkowski. 2006. Assessing ineffable outcomes. In *Encouraging authenticity and spirituality in higher education*, eds. A. W. Chickering, J. C. Dalton, and L. Stamm, 220–242. San Francisco: Jossey-Bass.

Clark, R. T. 2001. The law and spirituality: How the law supports and limits expression of spirituality on the college campus. In *The implications of student spirituality for student affairs practice*, ed. M. A. Jablonski, 37–46. New Directions for Student Services, no. 95. San Francisco: Jossey-Bass.

Conger, J. A. 1994. *Spirit at work: Discovering the spirituality in leadership*. San Francisco: Jossey-Bass.

Daniels, D., R. Franz, and K. Wong. 2000. A classroom with a worldview: Making spiritual assumptions explicit in management education. *Journal of Management Education* 24(5):540–561.

Dicarlo, R. E. 1999. Preface to *The power of now*, by E. Tolle. Novato, CA: New World Library.

Frankl, V. E. 1992. *Man's search for meaning*. Boston: Beacon Press.

Frost, R. Birches. In *Selected poems of Robert Frost. Introduction by Robert Graves*. New York: Holt, Rinehart and Winston, 1963. (Originally published 1916).

Greenleaf, R. 1977. Servant leadership—A journey into the nature of legitimate power and greatness. Mahwah, NJ: Paulist Press.

Greenstreet, W. M. 1999. Teaching spirituality in nursing: A literature review. *Nurse Education Today* 19:649–658.

Hoppe, S. L. 2005. Spirituality and leadership. In *Spirituality in higher education*, eds. S. L. Hoppe and B. W. Speck, 83–92. New Directions for Teaching and Learning, no. 104. San Francisco: Jossey-Bass.

Jung, C. G. 1933. *Modern man in search of a soul.* Translated by W. S. Dell and C. F. Baynes. New York: Harcourt, Brace & World.

Kanungo, R. N., and M. Mendonca. 1994. What leaders cannot do without. In *Spirit at work: Discovering the spirituality in leadership*, eds. J. Conger and Associates, 166–178. San Francisco: Jossey-Bass.

Komives, S., J. E. Owen, and T. R. McMahon. 1998. *Exploring leadership: For college students who want to make a difference.* San Francisco: Jossey-Bass.

Lee, R. J., and S. N. King. 2001. *Discovering the leader in you.* San Francisco: Jossey-Bass.

Lussier, R. N., and C. F. Achua. 2003. *Leadership: Theory, application, and skill development.* Mason, OH: Thomson South-Western.

Machiavelli, N. 1908. First included in Everyman's Library in 1515. New York: Alfred A. Knopf.

Manning, B. 2000. *The ragamuffin gospel.* Sisters, OR: Multnomah.

Marcic, D. 2000. God, faith, and management education. *Journal of Management Education* 24(5):628–649.

McMillen, K. 1993. The workplace as a spiritual haven. In *When the canary stops singing*, ed. P. Barrentine, 105–116. San Francisco: Berrett-Koehler Publishers.

Mitroff, I. I., and E. A. Denton. 1999. *A spiritual audit of corporate America*. San Francisco: Jossey-Bass.

Morris, T. 1997. *If Aristotle ran General Motors.* New York: Henry Holt and Company.

Nash, L., and S. McLennan. 2001. *Church on Sunday, work on Monday.* San Francisco: Jossey-Bass.

Neck, C. P., and J. F. Milliman. 1994. Thought self-leadership: Finding spiritual fulfillment in organizational life. *Journal of Managerial Psychology* 9(6):9–16.

Palmer, P. J. 1987. Community, conflict and ways of knowing: Ways to deepen our educational agenda. *Change Magazine*. http://www.couragerenewal.org/?q=resources/writings/community (accessed August 8, 2006).

———. 2004. *A hidden wholeness: The journey toward an undivided life.* San Francisco: Jossey-Bass.

Pierce, G. FA. 2001. *Spirituality at work: 10 ways to balance your life on-the-job.* Chicago: Loyola Press.

Raper, J. 2001. Losing our religion: Are students struggling in silence? In *Transforming campus life: Reflections on spirituality and religious pluralism*, eds. V. M. Miller and M. M. Ryan, 13–32. Studies in Education and Spirituality, vol. 1. New York: Peter Lang.

Richards, D. 1995. *Artful work: Awakening joy, meaning, and commitment in the workplace.* San Francisco: Berrett-Koehler Publishers.

Richards, M. C. 1989. *Centering in pottery, poetry, and the person.* Middletown, CT: Wesleyan University Press.

Rolheiser, R. 1999. *The holy longing.* New York: Doubleday.

Rose, F. 1990. A new age for business? *Fortune*, December 2, 156–164

Russell, P., and R. Evans. 1992. *The creative manager: Finding inner vision and wisdom in uncertain times.* Jossey-Bass Business and Management Series. San Francisco: Jossey-Bass.

Strange, C. 2000. Spirituality at state: Private journeys and public visions. *College Values.* http://www.collegevalues.org/articles.cfm?a=1&rid=134 (accessed September 20, 2004).

Tolle, E. 1999. *The power of now.* Novato, CA: New World Library.

Vaill, P. B. 1989. *Managing as a performing art.* San Francisco: Jossey-Bass.

Wood, D. 2001. *Fawn Island.* Minneapolis: University of Minnesota Press.

Zander, B., and R. Zander. 2000. *The art of possibility.* Boston: Harvard Business School Press.

CHAPTER 8

Moral Conversation: A Theoretical Framework for Talking about Spirituality on College Campuses

Robert J. Nash
DeMethra LaSha Bradley

Introduction

We are two teachers, one a young administrator and one a veteran professor, in a Carnegie I, "Public Ivy" university, who have co-taught undergraduate and graduate college students how to talk with one another about spirituality and religion in a secular setting. We teach two courses that feature this subject matter: "Higher Education in the United States," and "Religion, Spirituality, and Education." Our main challenge is always the same: how to establish a safe, yet invigorating, space for discussing and writing about very sensitive topics such as spirituality and religion. We strive to create this safe space not only in our seminar room, but also in conference halls, campus offices, and any other sites where teachers, administrators, and students might come together to be fully present to one another. We find that the best way to provide a safe, evocative atmosphere for conversing about spirituality and religion is to be mindful always of the wonderful, Zen-like words of the poet, May Sarton. The one reality that we know for sure in our teaching this controversial, yet important, subject matter is that both teachers and students "face one another in this place…Right now, right away, right here" (Sarton 1993, 155).

We are convinced that spirituality comes in all shapes and sizes. It can be personal, or it can be institutional. It can be driven by the head or by the heart. It can be communitarian or individualistic. It can be mystical or doctrinal. It can be political or apolitical. It can be inspired by a sacred text or by a sunset. It can spring from doubt or from certainty. It can be metaphysical or naturalistic, or it can be a complex combination of all of these, some of these, or, even, none of what we have identified here but something else entirely.

Several religious studies scholars tend to use the word "spiritual" to differentiate an institutionally based belief system from a personally based one, as do so many young and older people today. This distinction is crucial to most of our students, and we try always to be respectful of the strong sentiments behind it. However, we are also careful to recognize the fact that conventional religious believers can be spiritual, and vice versa. So we recognize the importance of both terms in our teaching, and we use them frequently. Notwithstanding the differences, however, what both terms have in common for us is that they represent the universal search of all individuals to discover and create worldviews/narratives that give meaning to their lives in particular places and particular times. In Neil Postman's words, the major purpose of religion and spirituality is to help all of us create "a sense of personal identity, a sense of community life, a basis for moral conduct, and explanations of that which cannot be known" (Postman 1996, 7). How our students do this, of course, is played out in multiple belief and action systems.

At this point, we will make a few comments about our use of the language of *narrative*. We believe that spiritual and religious stories are indispensable in communicating meaning, inspiring praiseworthy behavior, and in bringing people together in a spirit of compassion and social justice. All the great religious traditions teach best by telling stories. Neil Postman (1996) goes so far as to assert that "...the word 'narrative' is actually a synonym for god—with a small 'g'. God is the name of a great narrative, one that has sufficient credibility, complexity, and symbolic power to enable one to organize our lives around it" (6).

We hold that the brilliance of all the religions and spiritualities the world has ever known lies in their peculiar narrative power. Religion is basically a story lived out by people to give meaning to their lives at various times throughout human history. If this is true, then we must continually ask how a particular narrative created at a particular point in history still speaks to our needs today. How does it help us to understand who we are, whom we belong to, how we should behave, and how we might come to grips with the mystery of our existence?

Thus, with students, we advocate using the word "narrative" to describe each of the various religious and spiritual traditions. We mean no disrespect by the term. We do not mean to imply at all that religions and spiritualities are mere fictions or myths manufactured mainly to comfort and placate people. Rather, we use the word "narrative" in its original Greek, Latin, and Sanskrit senses: a way of knowing and telling that confers important survival benefits on both the tellers and hearers. For example, we agree with sociobiologists and evolutionary psychologists that narrativizing could very well be a deep-structure behavior hard-wired into the human brain. Thus, the ability to construct religious and spiritual narratives in our lives allows us to create order and meaning out of apparent chaos. It also enables us to reach out to others across our differences and to unite with them. This skill is as fundamental to human survival as our ability to satisfy our needs for love, food, sex, and shelter. All of these needs define, and complete, our basic humanity.

Eight Spiritual Narratives

At this point, we want briefly to sketch eight miniature portraits of the types of students representing several narratives who show up in our classes, as well as in a number of other campus venues, seeking spiritual knowledge, understanding, inspiration, and engaging conversation (Nash 2001a; 2001b). We find these religious and spiritual types to be represented among every age, gender, racial, ethnic, and socio-economic group in our work with students. No single type of student, or narrative, exists as a pure stereotype, of course, and, at least in theory, none of them need be monistic in their beliefs. In fact, some are pluralistic, some are syncretistic, most are inclusivists, and only a minority of students in our experience are spiritual or religious exclusivists. Most importantly, however, we find that most students only need a little encouragement, the right questions, and a supportive dialogue space to tell their stories of meaning to each other and to us.

- The *Orthodox Believers* come in all religious and philosophical stripes. With only a few disturbing exceptions, they usually remain humble but unyielding in their claims to be in possession of an absolute, revealed truth that most of their classmates obviously lack. Their confident, sometimes gentle, sense of certainty attracts, more than repels, many of us throughout the semester. In class, a small coterie of anti-orthodox skeptics, however, always manages to remain unconvinced, and they often have great difficulty concealing their disdain for any expression of uncompromising, orthodox belief. The core leitmotif for the Orthodoxy story is this: *There is a Truth that is unimpeachable, immutable, and final; and it can only be found in a particular book, institution, prophet, or movement. The mission of the Orthodox Believer is to deliver this Truth to others as an act of love and generosity.*

Spirituality for Orthodox Believers exists only as a minor piece of their religious narratives. They may speak about spirituality in terms of a gift given to a "prophet" who then went on to establish a religious movement.

They may adopt religious lifestyles completely in line with specific dogmas, doctrines, and inerrant passages found in sacred books. Thus, their spirituality is rooted in a very fixed, and tightly defined, religious narrative. We frequently hear orthodox believers talk about their religion without speaking of spirituality, but we rarely, if ever, hear them talk about spirituality without talking about their religion.

- The *Mainline Believers* constitute a very large group of college students. These students are neither excessively conservative nor avant-garde. They dislike authoritarianism in religion as much as they dislike faddism. They prefer a life of traditional worship that balances traditions, standards, self-discipline, and moral conscience with a degree of personal freedom, biblical latitude, and the *joie de vivre* of close community life. Often, they remain in the Catholic and Protestant churches (and Jewish temples) of their parents and grandparents. They are the proud holdouts against postmodernity and the religious experimentation and deconstruction that so often accompany it. The controlling theme in the Mainline narrative is this: *People need an organized, sacred space, one that provides clear boundaries between the sacred and the profane, a stable support community, a sense of order, and a moral bulwark against the excesses of secularism.* Although Mainline religion appears to be alive and well in America, some of us, nevertheless, ask Mainliners two complementary questions. When does the need for religious stability and rootedness turn into a denial of those changes that any denomination needs to remain vital, responsive, and pastoral? Moreover, is it possible for the mainline denominations to make reasoned compromises with the world without the cooptations and dilutions that too often accompany those compromises?

For Mainline Believers, an emphasis on spirituality may lean too much toward a postmodern view of religion. It is true that, for Mainliners, a sense of spirituality may be present in their conventional devotions, because many do practice their religions with at least a modicum of personal freedom and biblical latitude. But, on the whole, spirituality is not the most vital component of their religious being. Spirituality is sometimes seen by Mainline Believers as a secular New Age compromise with the world that causes a dilution of more traditional forms of religion.

- The *Wounded Believers* include those students who define their religious experience mainly as a reaction to the physical and mental abuse (often perpetuated in the name of religion) that they have suffered at the hands of hypocritical, over-zealous clergy, lovers, parents, relatives, and friends. Their self-disclosing narratives of suffering, denial, reconciliation in some cases, and eventual healing always win our attention, believer and non-believer alike. Sometimes Wounded Believers embarrass us, sometimes they inspire us, but they never fail to captivate us. The thematic thread that winds throughout all Wounded Belief narratives is this question: *If there is a good, all-loving God, why has there been so much unbearable pain in my life?*

For Wounded Believers, spirituality is often experienced as the safe space of connection. They will clearly assert that religion has wounded them and has turned them away from the doctrines or rules of their specific religions. Nevertheless, the spiritual remnants of their formal religious upbringings give them the opportunity to remain close to their religions without having to participate in the institutionalized structures of those religions. Wounded Believers may not believe in, or have faith in a "God" (conceptualized as a major prophet or as a supernatural ruler of the universe), yet they still seem drawn to a spiritual way of being in the world. They often acknowledge that they are present in the world in a spiritual way, and they move in the world because of some kind of supernatural "force." They may refer to this force as "The Universe," a "Higher Power," or even, in Tillich's (1968) phrase, the "Ground of Being." But few Wounded Believers will give a definitively dogmatic name, or even offer an acknowledgment, to a particular religious prophet or deity. The "Universe," or some such abstract term, is about as close as they will come to naming an outside power that guides their lives.

- The *Mystics* remind us continually that more often than not a genuine faith requires a discerning silence on the part of the believer, instead of a learned, theological disquisition. Some turn to the East; some to alternative American religions; some to folk religions; and some to private forms of spirituality. Most express a love for mystery, stillness, and attunement that eludes those of us who too easily fit the stereotype of the fitful, ambitious, hard-driving Westerner. At the heart of the Mysticism narrative is this motif: *The transcendent is best experienced, not through idle chatter or abstract concepts, but by way of meditation, mindfulness, and, above all, a pervasive calmness.* The rest of us listen, learn, and wonder how on earth we can ever find the mystical "stillness" that is said to inhabit the center of all our frenetic activity. Some students, however, reject the Mysticism narrative outright as too quiescent and self-absorbed.

The notion of a non-dogmatic spirituality fits quite well with the Mystics' way of faith. When we look at spirituality as a personally based belief system, and we look at the Mystics' way of being in the world, the fit is highly compatible. Mystical students often declare their own unique spiritualities with as much conviction as Orthodox Believers do their religions. But, unlike Orthodox Believers, the Mystics are more likely to offer their testimonies from a strictly personal perspective, based on their own private faith understandings and practices. Their avenues for private spiritual connection with the world are far less doctrinally or institutionally driven. Mystics prefer to speak the language of practice and connection, the language of personal meditation, oneness, and mindfulness. For Mystics, this holistic experiential language is the best way to achieve their own spiritual connection with the world.

- The *Social Justice Activists* urge us throughout the semester to consider the possibility that believers must be responsible for building the Kingdom of God in the here-and-now, rather than waiting for some distant paradise to come. They advocate an activist faith dedicated to the liberation of oppressed peoples, equal rights and social justice for all, and radical social transformation marked by full democratic participation in decision-making. For them, religious leaders are judged to be effective only according to their commitment to bring about massive social reform on behalf of the least among us. The common theme in the Activism narrative is this: *Religion makes the most sense whenever it tells a story of human rights and social transformation; whenever it invites believers to criticize existing structures of power and privilege such as the wealthy, white, male hierarchies in the churches, universities, businesses, media, and government.* While many students are drawn to the transformative elements of the Activism narrative, others dismiss it as merely partisan liberal politics with a religious gloss.

For Social Justice Activists, spirituality is the essence of human rights and social transformation. The language of spirituality is salient in Activists' recollections of great historical social movements such as the Civil Rights revolution in the United States. They appreciate the social movements in which being "people of faith" was the only way, for example, that oppressed people of color, among others, endured regimes of tyranny and persecution. Social Justice Activists, for example, who are knowledgeable about an Afro-

Caribbean religion such as Rastafarianism (which has a profoundly spiritual grounding), may commend a particular religion because its inherent spirituality of grievance and liberation has resulted in significant social justice and change. Some Social Justice Activists, like the Latin American liberation theologians, believe that spirituality can actually be a tool for small- and large-scale social change, because it reinforces the human need for freedom and for social justice.

- The *Existential Humanists* help us to understand that all too often believers turn to the supernatural to escape from the difficult responsibilities of individual freedom. For them, a humanistic, "self-centered" ethic can stand on its own as a defensible way of a person's being in the world and living an authentic human life. What is necessary is that all of us confront the inescapable fact of our human finitude and make a conscious choice to create ourselves through our daily projects, through our courageous strivings to make meaning in an absurd universe. The recurring idea in the Existential Humanism story is this: *The stark truth is that God has forever disappeared —if He ever existed in the first place—and now it is up to us to get on with our lives.* After listening to the Existential Humanists, some of us begin to understand, for the first time, the significance of Jean Paul Sartre's (1946) assertion that we are all unique selves "condemned to freedom," and Paul Tillich's postulation of a "Ground of Being" as a viable substitute for a personal God, the traditional God of theism. We proceed to look for constructive, alternative ways to cope with the loss of absolutes. Others find the story too bleak and individualistic.

Some Existential Humanists view spirituality as the "last stop" for those who might be seeking answers to the riddles of human existence from a source (not necessarily metaphysical) outside themselves. Existential Humanists, in the tradition of Christian thinkers like Kierkegaard, Marcel, and Tillich, are quietly comfortable with expressing the belief that spirituality might actually be an expression of a larger will to exist in the world with authenticity and meaning. Religious notions of spirituality, say some Existential Humanists, are really "cover-ups" for the secular realization that individuals alone must be accountable and responsible for their own choices. This may or may not be a "spirituality" that is religious or spiritual in the traditional sense. However, it is a spirituality that connects us to the larger human quest for making meaning and purpose—a universal amidst particulars.

• The *Postmodern Skeptics* are also deeply suspicious of any and all religious claims to absolute truth. In contrast to the Existential Humanists, though, they reject the existence of an unsituated, context-free self or soul. As committed moral relativists, they openly challenge our religious and moral certitudes, our ethical universals, and our grand spiritual narratives. They frequently encourage the rest of us to accentuate rather than integrate our many differences, to recognize our cultural situatedness as a critical fact of life, and to put our faith, not in metaphysical doctrines or dogmas, but in the awareness that we are all social constructors of our own religio-spiritual realities. The leading theme in the Postmodern Skepticism narrative is this: *An informed sense of contingency, irony, and doubt, and a willingness to repudiate religiously grounded, patriarchal systems of social domination, are what make us truly human and our lives truly worth living.* In reaction to the Skeptics, some of us confess a gnawing pessimism over life's ultimate prospects. A few, fearing the onset of a corrosive cynicism and nihilism, refuse to take these people seriously.

According to some Postmodern Skeptics, a spirituality of doubt and questioning keeps religion "honest." In this respect, spirituality plays the "devil's advocate" to religion. Postmodern Skeptics ask the question, "Why are the beliefs we take for granted in religion this way or that way?" This is a question that few Orthodox or Mainline religious worshipers are willing, or able, to ask. A spirituality of doubt, in the eyes of Postmodern Skeptics, is like the "heckler" in the back of the religious room. Even so, most of these hecklers are not out to embarrass or denigrate religion. Their mission is mainly to remind those listening exclusively to the official strictures of religious teachers that, at best, religion is an imperfect human creation, and, as such, it does not have all the answers.

• The *Scientific Empiricists,* while genuinely open to the possible existence of a cosmological God who created the universe, nevertheless argue that the evidence of astrophysics, organic evolution, biology, and the brain sciences effectively contravenes this hypothesis. No empirical evidence is able to establish incontrovertible proof of a supernatural power greater than nature or ourselves but the alleged existence of a transcendental power cannot be controverted scientifically, either. The core of the Scientific Empiricism story is this: *We are utterly alone in the universe, beyond final Divine revelations and interventions, and left to our own human devices, accompanied by the findings of science, to create a better world for everyone.* In response, some of us express the hope that religion and science can indeed be compatible. Others, however, can never get beyond what they think is the fundamental irreconcilability of faith and reason.

For Scientific Empiricists, spirituality is even more unquantifiable than religion. For example, many scientists believe that for something to be said to be "real," it must, at least, be measurable, verifiable, and replicable, and its variables must be controllable. Unpredictability, or untestability, is unacceptable to most Scientific Empiricists. Ironically, in this empirical assumption lurks a type of "spirituality" that, at the edges, is congenial with the quest for certainty found in so many religions.

For example, some Empiricists might ask, how can one measure, let alone understand and predict, a conception of spirituality, with its potentially endless array of variables (shapes and forms)? At least, several of the world's so-called "wisdom" religions have a set of permanent doctrines that do not change. But a belief system based on the ephemera of spirituality, and separated from the moorings of the historical Wisdom traditions, is simply too diverse, slippery, and individualistic to predict and control. How then, some Scientific Empiricists will ask, is it possible to find measurable truth in something that is always changing and never stable? Thus, ironically, the scientist and the religious believer find common ground in their suspicions regarding the validity of a privatized spirituality. Each, in their own way, subscribe to a spirituality of certainty—one empirical, the other supernatural.

Having Difficult Conversations with One Another

Given the diversity of spiritual and religious meaning makers like all of the above who make their way to our classroom, the major question for us as educators is how to get proponents of each of these narratives to talk with one another about what they believe, and practice, without going to war with one another. Thus, we start with the assumption that there is nothing inherently erroneous or immoral about any initial presumption of religious or spiritual truth. What is destructive, however, is any attitude that one individual (or group) possesses all the truth, and those who disagree do so because they are in error or there is something wrong with them. Barbara Herrnstein Smith puts it this way: "If a particular claim to an absolute truth is that which is manifestly obvious, self-evidently right, and intuitively and universally preunderstood, then how is it that its absolute truth and rightness elude the skeptic? The absolutist answer to this question is familiar: profound defects and deficiencies of intellect and character..." (Smith 1997, 123).

We have learned in our work with proponents of each of these types of spiritual and religious narratives that conversation begins with an awareness of the wisdom in Michael Oakeshott's words: "Taste the mystery without the necessity of at once seeking a solution" (Oakeshott 1950, 424). Another bit of insight, in David Bromwich's paradoxical words, is this: "The good of conversation is not truth, or right, or anything else that may come out at the end of it, but the activity itself in its constant relation to life" (Bromwich 1992, 131–132). We believe that Oakeshott and Bromwich are on to something. Their observations lead precisely to where open and safe conversation about religion and spirituality should begin, and, ideally, where it ought to end: in a fondness for mystery; in a commitment to cooperative story-construction; in the tireless support of the other person's flourishing; in an ethic of do no harm and do much good; in an awareness that virtue and vice are constructs that people must decide, and act upon, collectively, but always starting from a base of compassion; and in a love of spiritual and religious conversation for its own sake, absent all the usual off-putting, dialogue-stopping, ideological prerequisites.

Moral Conversation

To achieve our purposes, one of the authors has created a dialogue-framework that he calls moral conversation (Nash 1996). The Latin root of the word conversation, *conversari*, is to live with, to keep company with, to turn around, to oppose. Thus, a conversation is literally a manner of living whereby people keep company with each other, and talk together, in good faith, to exchange sometimes agreeable, sometimes opposing, ideas. A conversation is not an argument, although it can get heated. A conversation is at its best when the participants are not impatient to conclude their business, but wish instead to spend their time together to deepen and enrich their understanding of an idea, or, in our case, the ideas in a text.

A conversation that is moral, from the Latin root, *moralis*, is one whose customs emphasize the fundamental worth and dignity of each participant in the exchange, and this includes the authors of our texts as well. We believe that the best way to get a person to talk about a topic as controversial as spirituality is to treat that person with the utmost respect. As moral conversationalists, we always try to treat students with the highest regard in the sense that we believe all of them have at least a partial share of truth. No single one of them, or us, inhabits the spiritual high ground *a priori*. No single one of us has the final word on an issue like spirituality. We operate from the basic assumption that we are all *viators* (travelers with a purpose) on a journey to find meaning in the life we live, and because our journey is our own, it possesses intrinsic worth, and is to be respected.

The ground rules for moral conversation in our classes, as well as in our consultancies in a variety of campus settings, are as follows, and we make them very clear at the outset:

- We must recognize that every single person deserves a presumptive respect for any views expressed. The core responsibility of all participants in moral conversation is to find the truth in what they oppose and the error in what they espouse—before they go on the critical offensive.
- We need to display empathy and understanding for others at all times. Moral conversation begins with the resolution to see others as possible allies instead of enemies. It attempts to find common ground and overlapping middles in discussions rather than establishing irreconcilable dichotomies. It progresses from there to mutually constructive encounters. Unfortunately, the traditional model of discourse in the academy, particularly in its scholarly publications, has been more adversarial and polemical than reconciling.
- We need to listen to, and to read, one another with generosity, trying always to attribute the best, not the worst, motives. This works best when people speak, not simply in the voice of an omniscient third person, but from the heart of what they personally believe—from their subjective "I."
- In the interest of intellectual integrity, we also need to listen to one another critically and, whenever appropriate, be willing to change or to modify our own, previous positions on spiritual and religious topics, given the persuasive force of what we hear.
- Ethically, we need to commit ourselves to the principle of nonmaleficence: at all times, we must refrain from going on the attack only for attack's sake. We must engage in spoken and written dis-

course always on the supposition that a genuine attempt to understand another's spiritual and religious views is the prerequisite for active engagement with those views.
- We should acknowledge that the ideal end of moral conversation is to reach a point where there are only conversation starters rather than conversation stoppers. At the very least, moral conversationalists must be able to have their say and leave the conversation with their dignity and integrity fully intact.
- We must understand that moral conversation is not without its internal contradictions and epistemological biases. Its basic philosophical premises tend to tilt toward a liberal-postmodern view of the world. Its highest value is civil dialogue. Its ultimate objective is to find common ground and overlapping middles. It sees all truth claims in spirituality and religion as being up for grabs, as being infinitely interpretable and contestable. This approach is bound to be offensive to those who believe that they possess the Whole Truth, or even that there is Truth.

All views in moral conversation, including the eight narratives we described earlier, deserve at least an initial respect. We assume *a priori* that our students are each unique makers of meanings, looking frequently to express them, hoping to find others to confirm them, and wanting to live their lives in a manner that is consistent with them. It is rare, however, that many of them, ourselves included, will actively seek out others to change them. Schwehn (1993) proposes that four virtues in particular—humility, faith, self-denial, and charity—are necessary for respecting, rather than changing, the spiritual and religious views of others.

Four Virtues in Moral Conversation

Humility presumes that we attribute at least a modicum of wisdom and insight to others. We should avoid too quickly dismissing the truth in another person's view until we have heard it and understood it from that person's perspective, as well as from our own. We should try to comprehend (from the Latin, *comprehendere,* to grab hold of, to seize) the other's truth from the inside-out as well as from the outside-in.

Faith means trusting that what we hear from others is worthwhile in some way. We need to have some confidence that what others have to offer us might indeed be able to enhance our own understandings. In the matter of religion, for example, this does not mean accepting religious truths uncritically, but rather with an open mind, trusting in the fundamentally good intentions of the other. Schwehn (1993) puts it this way: "Believe what we are questioning and at the same time question what we are believing" (49).

Self-denial suggests that at some point, we need to consider the possibility of abandoning at least a few of the beliefs we cherish. Self-denial is the core of intellectual integrity and honesty; without it, minds would never change, and mere opinions would ossify into sacred certainties. Schwehn (1993) says that we need to cultivate a "disposition to surrender ourselves for the sake of the better opinion" (49). Self-denial is the inclination to give up the delusion that we are omniscient gods. Intellectual arrogance and selfishness are the vices that exist in opposition to the virtue of self-denial.

Finally, *charity* is all about attributing the best motive to those who are willing to express their most cherished political, philosophical, or religious truths to us. This does not mean ignoring or excusing errors in judgment, faulty reasoning, or one-sided zealotry. Rather, in Schwehn's (1993) terms, it means trying to be "more cautious in appraisal, more sympathetic with human failings, less prone to stereotype and caricature" (51). Charity is all about generosity and graciousness, and it is a virtue tragically missing in higher education today.

The golden rule of moral conversation is a willingness to find the truth in what we oppose and the error in what we espouse, before we presume to acknowledge the truth in what we espouse and the error in what we oppose. This concept is not to suggest that truth is always an illusion or that every view of truth is equally true or equally false. Truth-denial and truth-equivalence—what some call nihilism and relativism—have nothing to do with authentic moral conversation. Further, this principle is not meant to relieve truth-proclaimers (or truth-repudiators) of the responsibility to explain and defend their truths (or lack of them) or, even when necessary—under the weight of compelling, countervailing evidence—to modify them.

Moral conversation is our way of teaching students how to deal with the ubiquity of pluralism in all aspects of their lives, but particularly in the spiritual and religious domains. Furthermore, in our classes, the reality of spiritual and religious diversity becomes more and more obvious to us each and every semester, as it is in the world at large. This is a truth that all of us in the twenty-first century have begun to accept as a global reality, as the risks

"Truth" in Moral Conversation

During moral conversation, students need to recognize that what might represent "definitive" or "inerrant" truth for some, may represent just the opposite for others. Moreover, this does not mean that others are necessarily defective in intellect, religious and spiritual conviction, or moral character. In matters of spirituality and religion, a conflict of beliefs may be based less on a stubborn, ignorant, or "sinful" refusal to embrace revealed absolutes than on a sincere difference of opinion rooted in personal interpretation or perspective. It is necessary, therefore, for all of us to try to understand the special appeal of an opposing view to the actual truth-holder or truth-proclaimer.

We have found that asking ourselves the following types of questions whenever representatives of our eight spiritual and religious types of students on college campuses get together might help: What is there in the other's perspective that makes the truth-claim ring truer than it does for me? Is there any validity to the other's truth-claim, no matter how slight it might seem to me, given the total narrative-context out of which the other is operating?

We encourage these types of questions because we believe that a person's perception of spiritual and religious truth is inevitably shaped by taste, temperament, perspective, and background. As Felipe Fernandez-Armesto (2001) says: "To see things from no point of view is not even theoretically possible" (97). We would add: To see things outside of our socialization is an impossibility. Even when we might be in agreement that truth claims in spirituality and religion need to meet one or another of the tests of objective revelation, coherence, logical consistency, tradition, self-interest, or practical utility, a person's perceptions of these criteria will always be mediated through particular sociocultural and psychological perspectives.

The conclusion is inescapable for us: To engage in empathic moral conversation about spirituality and religion, the reality of multiple perceptions of "invariant" or "objective" truths will require us to listen carefully for the impact of the socialization process on the other's proclamations of truth. Stated more simply, we must always work hard to detect even a little bit of truth in what each of us feels is the biggest bunch of nonsense. What constitutes "truth" and "nonsense" in spiritual and religious matters depends, of course, on *our* perspective, just as it does on *theirs*.

Joseph Natoli (1997) recommends several additional moral conversation questions that we ask ourselves to genuinely hear the voices of "others" in our classroom. Here are some of them, expressed in our own words: Which personal world, or story of the spiritual and religious world, is this student presenting to us? How do things come to meaning within this narrative frame? What exactly do the student's words signify within this narrative frame? How are we to place ourselves within this narrative world to communicate effectively? What is it about this particular time and place that shapes our seeing and understanding of the student's story? What shared cultural stories might forge a connection among all of us here? Why is what we are hearing from this student unsettling and offensive to us, or to others? What story of ourselves is here being challenged and questioned?

Finally, in a nutshell, moral conversation that is genuinely pluralistic, according to the comparative religions scholar, Diana Eck (1993), aims to "build bridges of exchange and dialogue...and this must include constant communication—meeting, exchange, traffic, criticism, reflection, reparation, and renewal" (197–198). In our opinion, pluralistic moral conversation about religions and spiritualities in the classroom, as in the campus at large, requires direct, give-and-take participation with all types of religious and spiritual otherness. It insists that we allow the "other" to get under our skins, to engage with us, to disturb us, and even, if the circumstances warrant, to *change* us. Simple tolerance, respect, and celebration of difference must always give way to the active seeking of understanding, and a willingness to consider transforming or modifying our previous religious and spiritual views. We believe that an appreciation of religious and spiritual diversity begins with an understanding that the world of spirituality is radically diverse and constantly changing, and nobody has a corner on the whole truth (Eck 1993).

The Test of Good Moral Conversation

We both know that we are engaging in good moral conversation with our students when the following is happening more and more frequently in our class discussions:

- Students make an honest effort to read texts, and to understand others, *on others' terms* as well as on their own terms.

- Students acknowledge that while they do indeed "construct" their own types of spiritual and religious meanings when reading a text and listening to others, they also have biases and blind spots that can be exposed, and reconstructed, by others who might be wiser than they are.
- They maintain an open-mindedness about the possibility of learning something from both the author *and* their peers in the conversation.
- They show a willingness to enrich and deepen their current spiritual and religious narratives, because they just might be incomplete.
- They make a conscious effort to refrain from advancing their own current spiritual and religious narratives as the best ones.
- They work hard to listen intently to grasp the meaning of other people's worldviews for expressing their own particular spiritual and religious truths.
- They publicly agree with, and put into practice, the principle that clarifying, questioning, challenging, exemplifying, and applying spiritual and religious ideas are activities always to be done in a self- and other-respecting way.
- They realize that classes will frequently get off course in conversations about spirituality and religion because a spirit of charity, intellectual curiosity, and even playfulness will characterize many of their discussions.
- They appreciate the fact that it will take time to get to know one another, and they understand that eventually they will be able to find ways to engage in robust, candid, and challenging conversation about controversial spiritual and religious topics without being so "nice" they bore one another to death, or without being so hostile that they cripple one another other emotionally and intellectually.

Moral Conversation Aphorisms

Finally, we have a few pithy aphorisms that we find useful in helping to foster moral conversations about spirituality and religion each semester. We often share these aphorisms with our students at the beginning of each term they spend with us in the classroom:

- *Do not force premature closure on the moral conversation.* Genuine discourse about spirituality and religion rarely speaks in clear and unambiguous messages. Rather it speaks in subtleties, sometimes in riddles, occasionally in circles and haltingly at that, and always in ambiguities, paradoxes, and unfinished business. Beware of the tyranny of quick-fix directives, and impatient "final" calls to action.

- *First, find the truth in what you oppose. Find the error in what you espouse.* Then and only then declare the truth in what you espouse, and the error in what you oppose.
- *Listen as you would be listened to.* Question as you would be questioned. Pontificate only if you would be pontificated to.
- *T. S. Eliot* once *said that Hell is where nothing connects. Thus, speak with, not at, or separate from, each other.* Conversational Heaven is where every comment is a link in an unbroken chain.
- *If you don't stand for something, you'll fall for anything.* But know how to stand up for what you believe without standing over, or on top of, others.
- *Accept no spiritual or religious narrative for yourself uncritically; it might be false. Reject no spiritual or religious narrative for yourself uncritically; it might be true.*
- *Find and express your own voice but also find the right time to lower your own voice so that others might find theirs.* The paradox is that we discover what we know as much by listening as by speaking. Is this why we have two ears and one mouth?
- *Once you acknowledge your right to speak up, even if your ideas are only half-formed or even half-baked, do not be afraid of appearing less than brilliant in your conversation about spirituality and religion.* It will be the joint responsibility of each and every one in the classroom to discover the "brilliance" in those observations you consider merely ordinary.
- *Know that, at times, the moral conversation will be heated, even emotionally upsetting.* We are bound to hurt each other's feelings at least a few times during the semester, because we will be discussing important spiritual and religious topics and personal beliefs—ideas each of us takes very seriously. Please do not take misguided attacks on your most precious convictions personally. If our past experience is any indication, nobody in this class (especially the instructors!) will be fully able to live up to the ideals of the moral conversation. In the words of a famous theologian, Joseph Pieper, our "fat, relentless

egos" will take care of that. Even though we will be awkward as we learn how to converse with each other in a morally considerate way, we promise that with your help we will improve each meeting.

References

Bromwich, D. 1992. *Politics by other means: Higher education and group thinking.* New Haven, CT: Yale University Press.

Eck, D. 1993. *Encountering God: A spiritual journey from Bozeman to Banaras.* Boston: Beacon.

Fernandez-Armesto, F. 2003. *Truth: A history and a guide for the perplexed.* New York: St. Martin's Press.

Nash, R. 1996. Fostering moral conversations in the college classroom. *Journal on Excellence in College Teaching* 7(1):83–106.

———. 2001a. *Religious pluralism in the academy: Opening the dialogue.* New York: Peter Lang.

———. 2001b. Constructing a spirituality of teaching: A personal perspective. *Journal of Religion and Education* 28(1):1–20.

Natoli, J. 1997. *A primer to postmodernity.* Malden, MA: Blackwell.

Oakeshott, M. 1950. The idea of a university. *The Listener* 43:424.

Postman, N. 1996. *The end of education: Redefining the value of school.* New York: Vintage.

Sarton, M. 1993. *May Sarton: Collected poems (1930-1993).* New York: W. W. Norton.

Sartre, J. P. *No exit and the flies.* Translated by S. Gilbert. 1946. New York: Alfred A. Knopf.

Schwehn, M. 1993. *Exiles from Eden: Religion and the academic vocation in America.* New York: Oxford University Press.

Smith, B. 1997. *Belief & resistance: Dynamics of contemporary intellectual controversy.* Cambridge, MA: Harvard University Press.

Tillich, P. 1968. *A history of Christian thought.* New York: Touchstone.

PART TWO

Practice in the Disciplines

CHAPTER 9

Art, Spirituality, and Teaching

Laurel Campbell

Scenario

"Critique day" is well known among art and design students. It is typically the day their projects are due as well as when they are asked to justify their work by answering questions and receiving feedback from their peers and professor. On one such day, looking weary and annoyed, Mindy walked slowly into the room and placed her work of art in front of her on the table. The other students were already positioning themselves in the same manner; the class began the critique at my prompting, focusing on one person and one work of art at a time.

The assignment to be viewed was the culmination of several weeks of reading about empathic understanding, spirituality as it relates to teaching, and teacher development. As a visible expression of their own personal development as teachers, I asked the students to create an altar or shrine that either literally or metaphorically represented their devotion or attachment to another person, pet, or a special event or place in their lives. One goal in the altar/shrine activity was to illustrate how uncovering and expressing layers of meaning in objects might also include representing the sacred in our everyday world. The requirements for the project were left very open-ended so that students could choose how to engage with the concept of an altar/shrine. They were also encouraged to reinterpret traditional religious views of this art form in a more contemporary manner that focused on the meaning of "place" and juxtaposition of objects. As an inspiration for the project, visual images were provided, ranging from Hispanic altars in "Day of the Dead" rituals to shrines made from objects with special meaning placed in a windowsill above the kitchen sink.

The students seemed anxious to explain the meaning of their work; many of the shared narratives were touching, revealing aspects of the students' lives that were previously unknown to the group. Empathy for others and personal growth were clearly being expressed both in the works of art and in the critique. All were willing participants except for Mindy, who had remained quiet until it was her turn to discuss her work. Her body language had already sent a clear message of uneasiness. She asked, "What do our personal beliefs have to do with the teacher we want to become? I don't think that our spirituality has any relevance in an art education methods course." I was surprised at first; we had discussed the conceptual objectives of the studio activity, as well as the need for personal reflection, at length. I paused a moment, and then replied, "How you see the world has everything to do with how you see your students and how you teach. When you create and teach visual art, you also project your own beliefs, sometimes unknowingly, onto others." As we talked more, Mindy indicated that her spiritual development was private and discussion of this topic should not be required in this course. She then seemed more relaxed but, because I knew her well by this point in the semester, I was sure she remained skeptical as we parted. My thoughts were confirmed two weeks later when she wrote an evaluation of the course in which she criticized the altar/shrine project as an unnecessary activity. A majority of the other 13 students commented that their favorite activity that semester was constructing the altar/shrine, which they felt had been enlightening and helpful in their quest for growth and development as a person, an artist, and a teacher. No one else expressed disdain for the art activity, although by nature some students do not complain. It is too unrealistic to hope for 100 percent approval for every lesson, but this particular event spoke volumes to me about how and if spirituality can be integrated into the art education curriculum.

Analysis of Scenario

The scenario represents a common dilemma: the discussion of spirituality in the context of secular education. This incident could have happened in almost any classroom, in any institution. In analyzing this particular scenario, it is first necessary to deconstruct how the prior readings and classroom discussions in the course were used to conceptually frame the art project described in the scenario; second, consideration must be given to how spirituality can be defined in secular settings; and third, appropriate activities that respect students' privacy and beliefs should be designed.

The general course objectives of the teacher education course in question focused on learning how to blend theory and practice, as well as on acquiring methods for instruction and curriculum development through reading, writing, studio production, and classroom discussion. Several of the course readings introduced the pre-service teachers to "spiritual reflective practice"

(Campbell 2005), which suggests that new teachers need to explore their personal beliefs about what they value, how they find purpose in their lives (which can become a spiritual endeavor), and the manner in which this relates to their own teaching philosophies. The project that culminated on critique day was designed to promote an investigation of personal meaning through the creation of shrines/altars, including the actual art making experience and the discussion of the concepts, meaning, craftsmanship, and expressive qualities of the art object.

Several questions had occurred to me as I designed the activity: How do I encourage university students to understand the importance of self-knowledge and the necessity of asking the *bigger* questions about life? How do these questions and their answers help formulate one's own teaching philosophy? Does it matter if this philosophy is rooted in spiritual concerns? How is spirituality manifested in art making and art teaching? The answers I found to help me with this project came from the research literature about spirituality and holistic education, from personal experience with research on spiritual teaching (Campbell 2003), and from teaching preservice teachers for several years.

The course readings chosen and the discussions held in the classroom focused on convincing examples of real teaching experiences, shared by the teachers themselves and the researchers who interviewed art teachers in various stages of their careers. In addition to anecdotal narratives that focused on teaching caring and empathy to art students and cooperation in the classroom, we also read about and discussed life stories by teachers of art. These artist/teachers found that their own art work, as well as their teaching, was greatly influenced by inward reflection about their purpose in life and their mission as teachers. Many of these testimonials revealed that by first searching inwardly and by articulating a teaching philosophy, which changed as their experiences widened, teachers found a spiritual connection between their inner motivations and sense of purpose and the manner in which they taught their students. This spiritual connection was frequently described as a sense of unity or complete integration after serious involvement in reflection. By basing my own practice on this understanding of teacher development, I assigned readings that focused on these issues. Classroom discussions were held that encouraged individual interpretations of these concepts.

After lengthy reflection about the scenario and my months of work with Mindy, I realized that she might have rejected the idea that spirituality could be distinctly different from religion. Her idea of an altar might not have expanded beyond religiosity as my own definition had. For example, during our discussion of altars/shrines, we talked about temporary altars made on the roadside where a loved one had perished, a non-religious activity, although perhaps Mindy and others could have seen that as a religious experience.

Such reflections made it apparent that when spirituality is mentioned in secular settings, a considerable amount of time must be spent defining the meaning of the words spirit and spirituality in a manner that allows for either secular or religious interpretations, depending on one's choice. Adhering to a distinct separation between religion and state in secular institutions at present and historically tends to dominate our philosophy and practice. In addition, to create an appropriate classroom environment that is respectful of multiple perspectives, we need to be mindful of how spirituality is interpreted by our students and colleagues.

Spirituality can be defined for this discussion by merging several viewpoints. Cousins (1996) states that the "spiritual core is the deepest center of the person" (xiii); Feldman (1992) considers spirituality to be manifested in questioning our own existence; and, Assagioli (1965) finds spirituality in those people who have "wider and deeper levels of realization" (193). Wright (2000), who defines spirituality as "our concern for the ultimate meaning and purpose in life" (7), seems to reflect what could be seen as a more secular definition, which has broad application in educational contexts. More importantly for this scenario, Abbs (2003) advocates for an open-ended, less restrictive definition of spirituality that may be useful in a variety of contexts. It has been my experience that a spiritual person is one who strives to nurture those aspects of the self that are reflective of higher values, as well as a consideration of the relationship between the self and others. This definition disavows a type of narcissistic view of the world; instead, the goal or mission of a spiritual person is often centered on peaceful negotiation, social justice, and care and empathy for others.

It is appropriate to attempt to resolve the issue of Mindy's objection to this assignment, although some of her thoughts and reasoning will never be known. It would have been ideal for her to raise her objections during the session in which the assignment was first explained; an excellent opportunity to dispute the definitions of spirituality offered in our classroom discussions was evidently overlooked. Unfortunately, until Mindy actually created her artwork, she was not vocal in her concerns and possibly not even conscious of the reasons for her reaction. Her annoyance might have stemmed from the feeling that she was still searching for some sense of purpose or that she could define this purpose intellectually but not spiritually with the language she possessed. The meaning in the shrines and altars could be withheld; no one was asked to reveal anything they wished to keep inside. What about her right to not disclose her personal beliefs? The parameters of the assignment allowed for an interpretation that focused solely on objects that had meaning for the artist creating the altar/shrine and seemed respectful of one's privacy.

Perhaps the words *altar* and *shrine* were too traditionally bound in religion to be viewed as secular, even though many examples were given where one's idea of sacred was idiosyncratically constructed. Many of the students in the class seemed to grasp the secular concept quite well. For example, one student converted a fishing tackle box into a tribute to her husband who had survived cancer and began to go fishing once again. Another student converted a breath mint metal tin, adding decorative painted motifs, to carry mementoes of her deceased husband who had died in a motorcycle accident. Copper tubes, which held special poems about life's pain and joy, were connected metaphorically by twisting and turning copper wire, creating a private haven for personal expression by another student. The process of creating this form of expression was the main focus, not the revelations or the finished product.

The resolution of this problem for Mindy is not in the way the assignment was presented, but more in the lack of attention to deconstructing the beliefs that we bring to the classroom. As teachers and students, we have to suspend prior conclusions and consider the possibility that traditions are changing in our contemporary world, that while for many religion may indeed hold the answers to the *big* questions we carry with us each day, religious answers do not work when working with a diverse group of people. There are, in fact, many ways to express our lived experiences, including visual arts, and becoming open to a variety of choices is the first step many fear to take. One answer to my dilemma about Mindy is that perhaps she rejects both spirituality and religion, no matter how well the concept of spirituality is presented as a secular concept. There is no proof of this position, but this possibility always exists among students and therein we see the issue teachers must face: to confront spirituality or leave it alone. I suggest that we forge ahead, aware of the pitfalls, conscious of how we define and discuss spirituality.

Perhaps this incident occurred precisely because art and spirituality are often conflated, because many believe, as do I, that art and spirituality share a common place in our lives and consciousness. Hall (2000) explains that art has been historically connected with religion and spirituality in many cultures throughout time. Humans in almost every culture on earth have expressed their social, religious, political, and cultural beliefs as well as their inner sense of purpose or their humanity through art, which has allowed diverse people to create common bonds. Those who find connections between spirituality and art often view art making and appreciation as intensely transformative, sometimes seeing the act of creating art itself as spiritual. The expressive power frequently inherent in works of art can create meaning by providing new perspectives on beauty, death, destruction, and nature; we confront life in all of its forms, including the realities of good and evil. Through these lenses, constructed by the maker and the viewer, humans seek to make sense of their place in the world. However, it is important to state that art is only one of many ways humans search for personal meaning; in my experience, using art for this purpose is natural, life-affirming, and inclusive.

Connecting spirituality and art may not be new, but discussing spirituality in teaching is fairly recent. How do we begin the journey, by first changing our teaching selves? An awakening can occur by acknowledging the nuances of our actions, our speech, and our comments to our colleagues and students. An art activity of this nature allows students to choose a special person, place, or event to express; they reveal what is most sacred or of higher value. This approach first encourages knowledge of the self, while simultaneously looking inwardly and outwardly (Hall 2000) to acquire a sense of grounding. Educators and mentors can set into motion a lifelong practice of teaching as an act of spiritual concern, where students are seen as potential conduits for positive change. Spiritual teachers model this behavior by providing connections and encouraging self-awareness in their students; the arts provide an excellent vehicle for making this happen.

In the field of teacher education, we are mandated by the state to promote professional standards in both methods and content. We are asked to promote reflection about issues of professionalism, but any language about spirituality or important issues in personal development is sorely missing. What could be more important than asking and answering important questions about who we are and what we believe? As we witness continual problems in the world reflected in the classrooms we serve, I cannot think of a more crucial mission than first helping our teachers reach their potential as humans involved in changing humanity, one student at a time. Can we really make this happen in our classrooms? Without the belief that we can promote harmony, respect, and concern for others, teaching seems bland, meaningless, and without purpose.

Advice for Related Disciplines

Art is only one of many ways individuals can choose to express their spirituality, and perhaps artists are fortunate that their mission is sometimes seen as expressing their beliefs in their art. Professional artists do not hold an exclusive position in this expression, and art educators are not in complete agreement about the need for spiritual growth in the curriculum.

However, Kessler (1998–99) finds that many educators feel the urgency to discuss spiritual wellness in light of serious social problems and self-destructive behavior, which is indicative of a "search for connection and meaning and an escape from the pain of not having a genuine source of spiritual fulfillment" (49) in the generation currently in school. This discussion will need to include a serious study of not only how we teach, but also who we are as teachers. According to Palmer (1998), "Teaching, like any truly human activity, emerges from one's inwardness" (2). He also believes that "connections made by good teachers are not in their methods, but in their hearts—meaning heart in the ancient sense, as the place where intellect and emotion and spirit will converge in the human self" (11). I believe that spirituality is an aspect of who we are as educators, waiting to be revealed and modeled in our teaching behavior through our choices for discussion, and through the opportunities we provide for students' expression of their experiences.

A holistic approach to teaching in multiple disciplines, while not a new pedagogical concept, has new meaning when educators focus more on nurturing the spirit, which needs to be encouraged in changing, growing young adults in higher education. A balance between body, mind, and spirit is nonexistent in many school curricula. Miller (2005) argues, "Holism is, literally, a search for wholeness in a culture that limits, suppresses, and denies wholeness" (7). He believes that our problems "are directly related to, if not rooted in…epistemological and spiritual problems…where aesthetic, expressive, and spiritual dimensions are chronically undernourished, if not actively suppressed by schooling" (8). When we approach any subject through a holistic, inclusive, and transformational lens, we can expand our learning beyond our expectations and become leaders in effective education.

More concrete examples of spiritual expression outside of the art curriculum include the use of personal journals, which encourage reflection on growth in self-knowledge in relationship to other as well as one's career. Many contemporary teachers have used technology to encourage self-reflection through Web site assignments that include chat rooms constructed and monitored by professors about special topics in personal and professional development. Visual culture art education is an approach used to deconstruct images in the lives of students in order to understand the underlying meanings of these images and how they challenge students' values. Activities include creating collages by collecting visual images from magazines or creating these advertisements on a computer, re-creating a visual world that more closely fits the life one hopes for in the future. These activities do not belong exclusively to visual art professionals; they require serious reflection and discussion about the meaning of visual images in our lives and can be promoted in any discipline.

Creating a classroom where discussion of spiritual issues is encouraged, after careful distinctions are made between religion and spirituality, will help students gain awareness of their purpose in life. Finding and presenting examples of good leaders in each discipline who frame their lives for the betterment of the world can also help young students understand how each talent they possess can be used for improvement rather than the destruction of our world.

This discussion is relevant in every discipline in every classroom. I would argue that scientists, doctors, researchers, teachers, artists, writers, and engineers need to know their deepest sense of purpose in life and how this purpose is manifested in action. One might call this ethics, but I would argue that while spiritual concerns are inherently present in ethical beliefs, a spiritual approach to life encompasses a sense of awe for the non-material, for the transformation one witnesses in common with other humans. Reaching beyond the superficiality of social behaviors is a spiritual endeavor, and one that is possible for everyone. Activities in the classroom that encourage reflection on how one's inner beliefs are manifested in one's action will provide the necessary vehicle for changing our society.

If educators help young, often unsettled and challenging students take pause and consider the need to develop fully as people with a profound sense of purpose, then progress can be real. It begins with those of us in higher education who can model this way of living. We can then be fully present as teachers, ready to create transformative experiences in our classrooms. In the field of visual arts, as well as all other disciplines, I believe that teaching is more than what we know, it is also about teaching others to find out how they would like to live their lives, and in what kind of world they wish to live.

References

Abbs, P. 2003. *Against the flow: Education, the arts, and postmodern culture*. London: RoutledgeFalmer.

Assagioli, R. 1965. *Psychosynthesis: A manual of principles and techniques*. New York: Hobbs, Dorman & Company.

Campbell, L. 2003. Portraits of visual artist/teachers: Spirituality in art education. Ed.D. diss., University of Illinois at Urbana-Champaign. Abstract in *Dissertation Abstracts International* AAT: 3086029.

Campbell, L. 2005. Spiritual reflective practice in preservice art education. *Studies in Art Education* 47:5169.

Cousins, E. 1996. Preface to *Spirituality and the secular quest*, ed. P. V. Ness. Vol. 22 of *World spirituality: An encyclopedic history of the religious quest*. New York: Crossroads.

Feldman, E. B. 1992. *Varieties of visual experience*. 4th ed. New York: Prentice Hall.

Hall, J. 2000. Art education and spirituality. In *Art Education,* ed. R. Hickman, 11–18. London: Continuum.

Kessler, R. 1998–99. Nourishing students in secular schools. *Educational Leadership* 56:49–52.

Miller, J. P. 2005. Introduction to *Holistic learning and spirituality in education*, ed. J. P. Miller, S. Karsten, D. Denton, D. Orr, and I. Kates. Albany: State University of New York Press.

Palmer, P. 1998. *The courage to teach: Exploring the inner landscape of a teacher's life*. San Francisco: Jossey-Bass.

Wright, A. 2000. *Spirituality in education: Master classes in education series*. London: RoutledgeFalmer.

CHAPTER 10

When Religious Beliefs Conflict with Assigned Readings in Literature

William Jenkins

Scenario

Michael is a kind, soft-spoken, and deeply devout student, around twenty-five years old. He attends a non-denominational Christian college in an urban setting. It is not unusual for classes there to contain students ranging widely in age and preparation, often drawn from a variety of church backgrounds. Quite a few of the students take no part of any Christian tradition, though most of the students who claim any religious commitment are connected to evangelical Protestant churches. Michael was somewhat unique in that his brand of evangelicalism identified the Christian life with rigorous behavioral demands in daily life—such as what sort of entertainment in which he could or could not engage. Rather than fitting into the stereotype of a backwood fundamentalist, however, Michael's spirituality strikes one more as the kind of separatist ethos typically found among groups like the Mennonites.

In this scenario, Michael's religious convictions came into play in an unexpected way in a literature class. Though the course had initially sounded good to him—an introduction to twentieth-century writers of faith in America and England—Michael was increasingly disturbed at what seems to him the un-Christian language and situation of the assigned novels (such as Graham Greene's *The Power and the Glory*). About half way into the semester, Michael was supposed to read *War in Heaven* by Charles Williams, a writer Michael had never heard of but who seemed important in some way, according to me, the professor.

In the introductory lecture on Williams, Michael discovers that early in his life Williams had been a participant in a theosophical group called the Order of the Golden Dawn, an organization that had influenced other writers such as William Butler Yeats. Then, as Michael began reading the novel, he discovered that Williams had tapped into his firsthand experience with this movement. Even though Williams, a putative Christian of some influence, had made an Anglican priest the main character, the novel nevertheless accurately described the various states of mind of those who attempted occultic activity. Michael felt he had to stop reading. He approached me after the second class period devoted to Williams, and, as gently as he could, Michael simply stated that his conscience forbade his reading any more of the book. Michael told me that I could penalize him any way I wished, but he simply could not read a novel that described demonic activity. Taken off guard, I quickly tried to tell Michael that the novel clearly demonstrated by its end that the priest successfully overcomes the antagonists, who were waging a kind of supernatural warfare involving possession of the Holy Grail. It didn't matter to Michael. His vision of reality was such that *any* depiction of a demonic realm, for whatever artistic purposes, deeply disturbed him, and he refused to read the rest of the novel. Always kind and quiet in his demeanor, never abrasive, never proximate to a stereotypical fundamentalist, Michael was willing to accept any grade reduction, but he adamantly stood fast, remaining convinced that reading this work was spiritually harmful to him. Out of a class of ten students, nearly all of whom had some kind of religious commitment, Michael was the only student who refused any assignment, though he made no public display about it.

Analysis of Scenario

Unless a professor shares the particular theological angle of Michael, it is highly likely that the initial reaction he or she might have to this student is repulsion. Even educators who claim a religious identity would probably find Michael's unwillingness to be extreme. Certainly within the highly secularized academy, students like Michael appear not just as obstacles but as enemies in some sense.

Many students annoy literature teachers by being apathetic or indifferent to literary texts or even to reading anything, literary or not. Professors of literature deal with such students regularly, especially in general education classes like composition or world literature. Within an upper-division literature class, however, teachers have at least slightly higher expectations of student interest, even if a student is not majoring in literature but takes the class as an elective. But students who balk at studying works of literature in the way Michael does are rare, and many, if not most, academics would perceive Michael's spirituality as little more than a narrow, even pathological, sectarianism that probably links to an extremely conservative political vision, even though this might not actually be true of the student (e.g., if the student is

Quaker or Mennonite). Few professors would have much patience with a student who so strongly rebels against fulfillment of an assignment. In this case, few would hesitate to assign an "F."

Even within a Christian college, most professors would deem Michael's beliefs retrograde, existing outside of the mainstream of thoughtful theology and devotion. These professors have been socialized into the academic world with its default skepticism and toleration of multiple viewpoints merely by successfully negotiating the requirements for obtaining an advanced degree in the profession. Those requirements rightfully involve honing the critical thinking skills and attitudes necessary for objectively distancing oneself for reading and analyzing all kinds of texts written from all kinds of perspectives, many of them hostile to the professor's own religious beliefs. Even in a religiously oriented college, therefore, professors try to teach this same dispassionate critical reading, even on material ostensibly written by writers of similar religious persuasions. Because of this, Michael would not automatically find a sympathetic ear just because he attends a Christian college. I, for one, would want him to wrestle with imaginative narrative by moving beyond taking it as literal description of reality.

If a professor takes seriously the task of literary education, then he or she will want to move past an initial rejection of Michael, striving to understand his religious vision as unavoidably central to his intellectual, emotional, and social makeup. Certainly writers such as John Milton, John Bunyan, and William Blake demonstrate that strongly held religious views, even idiosyncratic or sectarian ones, do not automatically relegate one to irredeemable ignorance. Thus, trying to draw a student like Michael into a larger arena of thought and aesthetic awareness does not mean one must negate his faith. But getting the student to see is difficult.

Charles Williams is, in the big picture of modern literature, a minor figure. But within the context of this particular course in major authors of the twentieth-century Christian tradition, Williams influenced many writers, including such a master as W. H. Auden. Avoiding a novel by Williams is highly problematic given the purpose of the course. In this particular case, Michael rather surprised me since up to that point in the semester he had not given any visual or vocal sign that he found the reading material objectionable. Taken off guard, I made a quick decision to substitute a work of nonfiction by Williams so Michael would have to gain some exposure to Williams's unique and at times arcane writing style as well as his interesting hybridizing of neo-Medieval and Romantic sensibilities. To avoid forcing Michael to offend his conscience while also requiring him to have at least minimal exposure to Williams's writing, I assigned the book *The Descent of the Dove*, Williams's quirky survey of the history of the church.

As an off-the-cuff decision, the alternative assignment worked well enough in that it drove Michael to read a full-length work by Williams. But in other ways, the alternative was unsatisfying. For one thing, rather than negotiating a work of fiction, Michael read a work of non-fiction. So, even though *Descent of the Dove* exposed Michael to the sometimes peculiar perspective and idiosyncratic vocabulary that are part of Williams's appeal as a writer, the alternative book did not really help Michael connect Williams to the various currents and styles of fiction among the writers covered in the course, which the original assignment had been intended to do. Also, the kind of writing assignment given to Michael differed from what he would have received otherwise. Analyzing a work of fiction demands a kind of reading and writing that analyzing a work of non-fiction does not. Finally, this substitute assignment meant that Michael was on his own since no class time would be devoted to discussing *Descent of the Dove* other than noting it briefly as part of the diverse writing projects that occupied Williams.

When Michael first approached me and stated his objection, I was more embarrassed than dismissive, partly because Michael made his intransigent stand in such a mild-mannered way, and the awkward encounter with him quickly propelled me to the alternative. Since we had just finished a brief introduction to Williams, I was able to draw on a title I knew and I had just touched on in class a few minutes before. However, several possible options either instead of or in addition to a work of non-fiction would probably have helped because these would have been more germane to studying fictional narratives with all the rhetorical and literary demands of fiction. If it were possible to replay this scenario, my first action should have been to set aside embarrassment (or contempt, if that honestly had been my reaction) and tell Michael that the two of us needed to sit down and discuss the problem so we could sort through several possible substitute assignments. This would have given me more time to formulate specific yet sympathetic questions for finding out more precisely the reasons for Michael's resistance and how justifiable those reasons might be. Though a long shot, it is possible that I could prompt Michael to read the novel with a suitable aesthetic distance so that it would not disturb him.

If, after such an interview, I had decided that there is no getting around Michael's balking, a work of fiction by another author more fitting the nature of the class could have been preferable to a work of non-fiction. The decision for this would rest on how badly I wanted Michael to gain exposure to another writer of some influence but who would not prove as offensive, such as Dorothy Sayers. However, I would need to take time to think about this to make sure the substitute work of fiction fit my aims. Even if Michael agreed to this alternative, though, we still have the related problem—Michael would still be on his own because class time would remain devoted to discussing *War in Heaven.* Of course, I could spend office time with him discussing the book, but time constraints really disallow any in-depth coverage this way, and Michael would still miss out on the dynamics of classroom discussion of the Williams novel.

Another possibility that I could have explored in discussion with Michael would be to probe the following alternative assignment that could help him keep track with class discussion so that he would not be left on his own. This assignment would consist of research on the novel itself, even if Michael did not read the actual text. The advantage here is that he might discover that some academics of deep faith and even some pastors and non-academics close to his own practice of religion are quite taken with Williams as a writer. Through research on appreciative readings given by religiously committed scholars, Michael might come to a non-coerced appreciation of Williams's reliability as an important artistic religious visionary.

In formulating these second-chance assignments, I remain aware that they all rely on ideal conditions: I am dealing with one easy-going student in one fairly rare situation, and I actually have the time and energy necessary for negotiations. As long as an encounter like this remains rare, I can easily maintain a positive attitude for dealing with someone like Michael. However, if such encounters increase, I would ultimately have to take action that allows me to maintain some control and demand some rigor without having to redesign assignments for students as they stumble into offensive readings. This probably means I have to put on the syllabus a balanced statement on the limits of substitute assignments or carefully phrase the limits of substitute assignments, such as requiring students to scan the reading material at the first of the semester, produce a written request for substitution if they cannot bring themselves to read one or several texts, and undergo a short interview with me before I allow any student to avoid a specific text.

Advice for Related Situations

The situation with Michael might appear to be nearly stereotypical in its outline: a recalcitrant fundamentalist whose constrictive understanding of art and culture forbids him from being contaminated by the wicked world, including the wicked world of non-sectarian Christianity—in this case, an orthodox if off-beat Anglicanism embodied in the novels of Charles Williams. However, given both the changing demographics and the alterations in educational culture in America, the situation with Michael demands attention, not indifference or hostility. In fact, educators should plan on encountering more classroom situations in which students resist texts and ideas that appear too transgressive.

For instance, though now a tiny portion of the overall population, Muslims are swiftly increasing numerically, through immigration but also through children of naturalized Muslim citizens, and this latter population will only expand in the next few decades. Thus, one can imagine now or soon a situation similar to Michael's, one which seemed remote a decade or so ago except in the largest cities with highly diverse populations, such as Los Angeles or New York. A Muslim girl, to take one plausible example, whose parents are naturalized citizens from Indonesia, refuses to read a novel or short story on grounds similar to Michael's (say, a highly controversial short story like "Brokeback Mountain"). A professor who dismisses such a religiously devout student with a curt "Fine, you get an F" might have to deal not only with irate parents but also with representatives of the Indonesian Muslim Society in America.

Similarly, practitioners of various New Age, neo-pagan, or Buddhist or Hindu spiritualities might find their voices of protest as the number of students who find their identity in these non-Christian spiritualities grows. Even if the number of such students remains relatively low, the mere fact of such diversity will point to the difficulty of singling out fundamentalists of the Protestant Christian tradition for rejection. The irony here seems nearly unavoidable: as multiculturalism continues to influence American pedagogy (and this pedagogical influence extends well into Christian institutions of higher learning), actual, real-life multi-culture in the classrooms could increase friction between students and teachers if the number of students who withhold themselves from some assignments on grounds of conscience goes up even a little.

In a Christian college where institutional identity requires at least some sympathy with a student like Michael, even a professor and Michael's classmates typically see Michael as something of an embarrassing anachronism or theologically and culturally naïve. In a more secular setting, though, it might not be as easy to marginalize someone like Michael as it once was since the putative multicultural commitment will probably have to face recalcitrant religious students of many varieties unless educational policy advances a stringent secularism. This seems unlikely. The Age of Modernity is clearly over in at least one sense: whereas previous generations of scholars took it for granted that spiritual commitments resulted merely from unenlightened presuppositions that a proper education would eradicate, more and more people, academic or not, understand that religion is not going away and it never will. Rather than considering students like Michael as unfortunate victims of psychological or sociological forces beyond their ken, serious educators will recognize their duty to try to educate these students and not simply write them off as invincibly ignorant.

CHAPTER 11

Spirituality and the Discipline of History

Rick Ostrander

Scenario

The syllabus schedule for my course on *American History I: The Founding to the Civil War* called for a lecture on "Slavery and Nineteenth-Century Society." As my early afternoon lecture on the social, economic, and ideological aspects of slavery dragged on, I could see the eyes of my forty-two sophomores begin to glaze over in the stuffy classroom air. Searching for a way to make the events of nearly two centuries ago seem relevant to college students in the twenty-first century, I decided to change tactics. "Of course, given the fact that the system of slavery had been established over a century earlier, one cannot blame nineteenth-century Americans for mistreating and exploiting African-Americans," I declared. "They were simply making the best of what had been handed down to them. And northerners who benefited from cheap cotton goods can't be condemned for doing what they could to make a profit, given the economic conditions of the time."

In the second row, I saw a flicker of interest flash in Jennifer's eyes as she asked, "But if northerners profited from the economic output of slavery by exporting southern cotton to Europe, then they were just as guilty as the southerners who owned the slaves." "That's ridiculous!" Mark exclaimed from the back row. "You can't go back and assign blame to individuals who lived centuries ago—especially to people who didn't even own slaves. They were simply trying to live their lives and support their families like anyone else would do." "But they did so by reaping the benefits of a system that oppressed and exploited other human beings," exclaimed Judy from the third row. "So of course they were guilty—just like we are today when we wear T-shirts with 'Made in the Philippines' labels on them."

Analysis of Scenario

The study of history familiarizes students with social, cultural, and political changes over time and helps them develop the ability to analyze and synthesize data. However, as the record of human experience, history also can provide students with rich sources of spirituality. (For purposes of this chapter, I consider spirituality to be an encounter with questions of ultimate meaning and values that affects the whole person and results in changed attitudes, beliefs, or behaviors. It is often related to a particular religious system, but it can thrive independently of organized religion.) The study of history can help students consider questions about what it means to be human, identify with other humans, and discover what it means to live as responsible moral agents in a complex world. Thus, professors of history can prod students to ponder questions of ultimate meaning even as they focus on the "nuts and bolts" of the course material. The scenario on slavery given above can serve as a useful entry into spirituality in higher education.

One quality that I attempt to encourage when I cover a subject such as slavery is empathy for other human beings. For spiritually mature students, history is not a blame-game in which the goal is to discern the "good guys" from the "bad guys." Students develop both ethical concerns and the ability to see reality through others' eyes and to appreciate their struggles. One way to do this is through primary sources. For example, when covering slavery, a teacher (or a professor) can use firsthand accounts from slaves that describe the sufferings endured by slaves, such as Peter Randolph's *Sketches of a Slave Life*. Primary sources help students move from a rational, distant analysis of the social and economic aspects of slavery to experiencing human suffering firsthand, engaging not only their minds but their hearts in the learning process.

Of course, developing empathy for the sufferings of slaves is not difficult. Empathizing with slaveowners can be more difficult. However, doing so is important if students are to move beyond seeing the world in simple black and white terms. Spiritually mature students combine ethical discernment—even at times indignation at the injustices perpetrated throughout history—with an appreciation of the struggles that individuals face in morally complex situations. In the case of American slavery, one way to develop an awareness of moral complexity is to have students read proslavery arguments and sermons. Doing so accomplishes two purposes.

First, for students from Christian backgrounds, these texts often challenge their presuppositions about how to read a "sacred" text. Southern ministers were extremely wellversed in scripture, and they marshaled biblical texts in both the Old and New Testaments to support their contention that slavery was a divinely ordained institution. For a college student who has grown up being encouraged to interpret the Bible literally, such an encounter with a proslavery writer can be disturbing but enlightening. The student becomes aware of the variety of "literal" meanings that can be derived from a religious text, thus becoming more modest about declaring "what the Bible teaches." Discussing proslavery texts in class helps students become aware of the social and cultural factors that colored nineteenth-century southerners' reading of scripture, and by extension the factors that affect students' own understanding of a text. Such an experience can help students develop toleration of those who hold different religious positions from their own.

Second, reading primary documents from white southerners allows students to appreciate the complex issues and difficulties that the slaveowners themselves faced. What was a slaveowner, whose economic enterprise depended on slave labor, to do about his slaves? Since the typical plantation owner was in debt to coastal merchants who shipped the cotton overseas, simply freeing one's slaves was no easy task. Owning slaves was deeply imbedded in southern economic, political, cultural, and religious life. Furthermore, students are often surprised to discover in the primary sources the affection that slaveowners often displayed for their slaves, and even more amazingly, the affection that slaves often returned to their master and the master's family. Such learning experiences do not eliminate the justifiable moral indignation over the evils of slavery, but they enable students to appreciate the moral complexities that permeate human experience. In the case of American slavery, it helps them appreciate the deep sense of tragedy that lies at the heart of the southern consciousness even today.

Human spirituality involves an encounter with ultimate meaning that may result in reconsideration not only of one's attitudes but also of one's actions. History can challenge students to consider the actions of humans in the past and by extension their own actions and the extent to which their behavior aligns with their moral framework. Of course, the study of the past should not be simply a backdrop for preparing students to be agents of individual and social justice in modern society. Nevertheless, through such topics as slavery, students can be challenged to consider not only the actions of human beings a century ago but how their own actions square with their beliefs. Because slavery is such a stark example of human injustice, it can therefore serve as a useful subject to challenge students to consider their own role as moral agents in society.

Naturally, students see nineteenth-century slavery as morally wrong, just as they tend to oppose modern forms of slavery when confronted with them. But usually the issue seems far removed from their own lives. What is more subtle—and more important—is to help students see themselves as part of a larger web of social and economic networks in which questions of justice and ethical responsibility arise. That is where the opening scenario concerning slavery can be useful. My main purpose in lecturing on the social, economic, and cultural factors surrounding slavery is academic: I want students to understand the basic historical events and issues involved. However, a secondary purpose is to prod students to question how far the ethical web of responsibility surrounding slavery extended. Doing so can lead them to consider their own role in modern social systems.

Obviously, the slaveowners themselves were morally culpable for slavery. Even though nineteenth-century southerners did not create the system, they perpetuated the practice of treating fellow human beings as objects. Moreover, they developed new ideologies to defend slavery and additional slave codes that often made the institution more severe. Many non-slaveowning southerners also played integral roles in the system as slave traders, slave catchers, law enforcement officials, and so on. By going beyond these straightforward cases, however, the educator can generate more vigorous, fruitful discussion. For example, I like to divide students into small groups and give them scenarios such as this:

> You are an editor for the *Richmond Times* and you personally disapprove of slavery. Your newspaper includes advertisements for upcoming slave auctions, and the back page includes notices on escaped slaves. Does this make you morally culpable for slavery, or are you just doing your job as a good businessman? The slave auctions will take place anyway, whether you run the advertisements or not. Moreover, rival newspapers will run the advertisements, and you might lose your job if you refuse to run them.

In class discussions, one can expand the sphere and include northerners, as the opening scenario indicates. What about the New York City merchant who ships, among other products, cotton that was planted, cultivated, harvested, and refined by the hands of slaves? Is he guilty of perpetuating the slave system, or is he simply doing his job as a merchant? Or what about other northerners who were seemingly far removed from the institution of slavery? Did the fact that Indiana farmers purchased cotton products—and did so more cheaply because the cotton was produced two hundred miles away by slaves rather than in India—make them guilty of supporting slavery? Should they have refrained from purchasing American-produced cotton? On what basis do students make such judgments? Questions like these challenge students to move from what may seem to be a straightforward historical issue—southerners were guilty of slavery; northerners fought to end this social evil—and consider the moral complexity of the situation.

Furthermore, such exercises can be done in a variety of historical subjects. Naturally, when I teach about Nazi Germany in a class on Western Civilization, I cover the Holocaust. However, in addition to focusing on the blatant, shocking evil of the concentration camps, I challenge students to consider the extent to which such evil may be embedded in everyday society. So, for example, learning experiences can be produced by having students place themselves in the position of an assembly line worker at a factory that manufactures doors for crematorium ovens; or a quality control engineer at a chemical plant that produces, among other things, Zyklon-B gas for Dachau. What would they do in such a situation? Are they just as guilty for the Holocaust, even if they may not personally support it, or are they just ordinary human beings trapped in a social and economic web that was not of their own making? Such questions yield far more interesting and productive class discussions than asking students what they would have thought of serving as a guard at Auschwitz.

Obviously, such discussions can easily lead to application to students' lives today. We deplore Third World sweatshops that exploit human labor. But does this mean that we should not wear clothes produced in the Philippines? We may disapprove of the disruption of the environment caused by oil drilling. Even so, each morning we start our vehicles and consume fuel in order to drive to work or school. Are we morally guilty, ruining the environment for doing so? Of course, there are no simple answers to these questions, and the purpose of raising them in class is not to enlist students in a particular social reform movement. But such questions, rising from a concrete historical subject and moving to modern social concerns, helps students see the relevance of the past to human spirituality and to consider the extent to which they themselves are responsible moral agents in a complex world. And it helps them develop empathy for people in the past and the present faced with difficult choices.

Our discussion of history so far could lead one to conclude that as far as spirituality is concerned, the study of history is primarily useful as a vehicle for creating a sense of ethical awareness and responsibility. Spirituality, though, is about more than ethics; it is about experiencing transcendence and wrestling with questions of ultimate meaning. In higher education, it means that we not only instruct students' minds, but we also seek to inspire their souls to lead integrated, spiritually fulfilling lives. By presenting examples of exemplary lives, the study of the past can inspire students to seek a deeper sense of their own spirituality. Moreover, a deeper spiritual perspective is often forged in the crucible of human suffering. The study of slavery, therefore, provides a rich field not only for questions of ethical responsibility but also of human perseverance, love, and beauty.

When I teach American slavery, I try to introduce students to individual memoirs such as *A Narrative of the Life of Frederick Douglass.* Douglass's determination to educate himself, his fierce desire for liberty, and his life of service after he escaped from slavery comprise an inspiring example for any modern student facing obstacles to success in life. Moreover, Douglass's deep conviction that his own life had purpose and value—despite his legal status as a piece of property—motivated him to a life of extraordinary achievement.

However, the inspiring examples of slaves who overcame obstacles, such as Douglass and Harriet Tubman, are the easier and more predictable ones. What about the vast majority of slaves who lived, worked, and died in obscurity on southern plantations? Do their lives have anything to teach the modern college student? I believe that they do, for the slaves achieved a spirituality of everyday life and work that can serve as a healthy corrective to modern American middle-class values. College students often seem to believe that spiritual fulfillment comes from acquiring a successful career and material comfort. Most slaves, by contrast, performed mindless drudgery for long hours each day. Yet they infused their work with spiritual meaning, as demonstrated by the Negro spirituals that emerged from their labors. One does not have to share the essentially evangelical Protestant worldview of the slaves to appreciate the extent to which a spiritual outlook on life pervaded and gave meaning to their difficult, monotonous lives. By encountering the daily lives of the slaves and their spiritual worldview—best expressed in songs—students can be challenged to consider the extent to which a spiritually vibrant life does not depend on career and material success.

Furthermore, a look at the individuals involved in American slavery—the slaves, the northern abolitionists, even Abraham Lincoln—can help students consider the larger questions of history and their role in it. Abolitionists such as Theodore Weld and William Lloyd Garrison, for all of their moral outrage over slavery, retained a faith in humanity. They believed that moral conviction could change the minds and hearts of the southerners, and this belief motivated them to lives of sacrifice and commitment to a cause greater than themselves. Abraham Lincoln displayed political pragmatism, a deep sense of the tragic and complex nature of slavery, and a sense that history had a larger purpose to it. This faith led him to oppose slavery while simultaneously displaying charity toward those who fought to defend the southern cause. The trials of the Civil War and Lincoln's own personal tragedies while in office produced in him not only a deep sense of melancholy, but also a spiritual perspective that saw individual events as part of a larger universal process. All of these examples provide rich material for students to ponder as they develop their own spiritual values.

A spiritual perspective on daily life, a devotion to larger purposes, a sense of ethical responsibility in a complex world tempered by empathy for those who differ with them—these are qualities of healthy spirituality that the study of slavery, and history in general, can engender in students.

Advice for Related Situations

The approach to spirituality in the classroom described above is based on the methodology of asking subject-related questions that force students to consider their own attitudes, beliefs, and actions. Usually I do not have a particular truth or "moral of the story" that students should arrive at. Indeed, in the best classes it is difficult to predict where the conversation on history and spirituality will end. Rather, I want students to be moved intellectually and emotionally by a new experience or an encounter with a new idea to consider their own lives in relation to it. Thus understood, spirituality can be incorporated into other disciplines in the humanities.

For example, a course on American literature may include Harriet Beecher Stowe's *Uncle Tom's Cabin*. On one level, the author's portrayal of Uncle Tom as a meek, suffering Christ-like figure in response to slavery may or may not seem attractive to modern readers. However, the novel has other sources of spiritual insight that teachers can present for students' consideration. Concerning the notion of spirituality as empathy for others, Beecher Stowe presents the arch-villain of the novel, Simon Legree, as a transplanted New Englander, not a native southerner. The potential for human evil, she seems to be saying, is a universal human trait, not simply a southern trait. Moreover, the study of literature in the modern academy recognizes that interpretation of the text is inevitably shaped by one's own experience. English professors can therefore encourage students to consider their own spiritual experience and how their spirituality differs from that of Harriet Beecher Stowe or the characters in her novel. Through guiding questions, students who may not share Beecher Stowe's Protestant worldview may still find spiritual insights by reading her novel through a sympathetic lens.

Similarly, a course on American music can address spirituality by considering not only the musical and literary structure of Negro spirituals but also the texts themselves and the experiences that generated them. How did these songs allow slaves to make sense of their situation and place their mundane lives in a larger spiritual context? Why were these particular musical forms used to express the sufferings and hope of the slaves? What emotions and insights do these songs express in those who sing or listen to them today? Obviously, a course on American music should focus on music. As with literature, however, the forms of music cannot be completely understood apart from an awareness of the lived experience of the individuals who developed them. Professors in the classroom, therefore, can introduce students to the experiences, beliefs, and behaviors of the slaves who generated the spirituals. Negro spirituals and the experiences that produced them can thus serve as sources of inspiration and critical insight for modern students.

Comprising academic subjects such as art, history, literature, music, and philosophy, the humanities lie at the center of higher education. At their core, however, the humanities are simply the study of what it means to be human. Since spirituality has always been an essential part of human civilization, educators in the humanities should consider effective, academically appropriate ways to help students nurture and develop their own spirituality.

CHAPTER 12

Recognizing Plurality, Promoting Civility: Religious Pluralism in the Political Science Classroom

Paul Brink

Scenario

"You cannot be serious!" The scorn in her voice was unmistakable. Other students in the room, although probably not surprised by Nicole's position, seemed to be taken aback by her vehemence. "We live in a free society! Using religion in politics can't be allowed! Otherwise you're simply using religion to coerce people!"

Pam, a sophomore political science major, had been attempting to make a case for lifting restrictions on religious discourse in politics. "If someone sincerely believes that the war in Iraq is wrong for religious reasons, how can it be right to say that he has to be quiet, just because we don't like those reasons?"

Nicole was leading the charge against this view. "OK, but then what's to prevent the government from banning gay marriage just because the Pope or the Bible or someone says that it's wrong?"

Pam's brow furrowed. "You're thinking of the worst possible scenario. I'm not talking about theocracy. I'm talking about Martin Luther King. I'm talking about the abolitionists. Religion in politics is a good thing."

"But not always," interrupted Virginia. "You can't only cite the examples you like. If you want to let in Dr. King, you have to let in the Ayatollah. I'm not sure we want to do that." Nicole had apparently found an ally. "There have to be rules and they need to be fair. Otherwise, we're going to have all sorts of religious reasons for things. Besides, how will people talk to each other? Don't we need some sort of common basis for making laws?"

"But who is going to decide what that common basis is going to be?" Pam was quick in her response. "How can you have a common basis that doesn't discriminate? And all this talk about 'letting people in.' How can that be democratic? Who made you a gatekeeper?"

Nicole was almost to her feet when Professor House finally decided to intervene. "Good discussion, folks. We've touched on some fundamental points, and we need to talk about them more carefully if we really want to understand what's at stake here."

Analysis of Scenario

Professor House was quite wise to intervene when he did; enough subjects were raised in this interchange to sustain several classes. Debates concerning the appropriateness of religious expression in politics have become commonplace today—both in the political arena and in the political science classroom. In both arenas, such debates are difficult to navigate, as positions taken reflect not just differences on matters of policy within a neutral context, but also differences concerning the context itself, its character and its goals.

Religious expressions in political science thus pose problems simply by their very plurality. In a sphere of life where public authority judgments concerning controversial matters are expected, political science students are often particularly sensitive about the grounds for these decisions. In their personal lives, students may be quite tolerant of other worldviews, accepting with ease modern liberal versions of "whatever works for you"; however, when competing spiritualities make movements across the private-public divide, students very quickly become concerned. For this reason, handling religious expression in the political science classroom can be particularly tricky, as concerns about freedom and coercion, equality and hierarchy, justice and oppression always lurk in the background. Students may celebrate religious pluralism, but it is also something about which they maintain a vital concern.

In the above scenario, we might follow several strands of thoughts. Nicole's opening salvo, appealing to a commitment to freedom that she hopes her opponents share, is not an atypical approach to responding to the challenge of difference. The difficulty with her argument, of course, is that a strong commitment to freedom will restrict the freedom of those who understand that ideal differently than in her standard liberal account, an argument that Pam began to articulate in her response. Very quickly, conversations along these lines—in classrooms and in legislatures—degenerate, as the limits of liberal toleration rapidly become apparent. The danger in such conversations is that the parties do little more than assert their core beliefs over and over, and with ever greater emphasis. Little hope remains of real understanding and mutual respect in such situations, much less of progress toward persuasion and acceptance; rather, the participants are just as likely to disagree, but in ever greater detail and with ever greater forcefulness. Turning such debate into learning opportunity is a professorial skill not easily acquired.

Nicole's argument is thus a liberal one. The usual liberal solution to religious expressions in politics is generally one of benign toleration: We will tolerate these expressions as they are themselves tolerant. The problem with this view is that it reveals an ignorance of what real faith involves. It turns those expressions into pale reflections of liberal society, which, besides making them a good deal less interesting, is likely to do little to ensure that those other expressions are genuinely heard. Indeed, it is not difficult to see how delegitimizing contributions on the basis of the grounds of arguments might discourage the emergence of genuine classroom dialogue—or a genuine civil politics. On the other hand, the challenge for Nicole is that to do otherwise would undermine her central commitment to a liberal notion of freedom.

Fortunately, the second half of the interchange between Pam and Nicole provides hope that they may avoid that deadlock. By offering a concrete example (of gay marriage), Nicole turns from an expression of principle to a consideration of practice. She hopes that a consideration of what she views as an absurd consequence of Pam's position will make clear her error. However, Pam refuses to take the bait and instead problematizes the choice of examples, setting the stage for Virginia's entrance into the discussion.

Pam's response reveals how the use of examples can be tricky as a rhetorical strategy. It is only too easy for each side in a debate to hold up in support of its view only those examples about which practically everyone is likely to have similar feelings. Nicole warns against theocracy, while Pam appeals to Martin Luther King, Jr. While noting this danger, we can see some progress, however, in that at least both students can agree that *some* religious expressions should be permitted and even be seen as publicly valuable, while others are properly seen as publicly dangerous and perhaps worthy of restriction.

The hard part, of course, is determining the principle by which the two types of contributions should be distinguished. This is the first concern raised by Virginia, in her call for rules that distinguish between "good" and "bad" religious contributions. We can surmise that Nicole and Pam both would have suggestions in this regard, each speaking out of her own perspective, but Virginia's concern is that they be "fair." Fairness can mean different things, but at minimum it would seem to require that the authority—classroom teacher or Supreme Court—be at least impartial, that it not favor one or more perspective above the others.

Virginia's second concern builds upon her first. Is it not necessary when we engage each other with all our religious particularities intact that we meet on some common basis? The question is vital, both for the political leader and the classroom teacher. What is the basis (religious/moral/political/other) for the discussion itself? Is neutrality possible? Can we establish a public philosophy or classroom atmosphere that is itself independent of the many perspectives articulated within it? Virginia is not alone in believing it to be necessary, but determining how we might go about finding or constructing such an independent basis is by no means clear.

Such is Pam's final complaint. Further, she problematizes the "gatekeeping" function that most of the discussion to this point had presumed. Here, she makes clear her essential opposition to Nicole's position. If, for Nicole, freedom is the key value, for Pam, participation is key. The quarrel between liberalism and democracy is by no means new, despite the modern use of the moniker "liberal democracy." Here, Pam's concern is that the liberal preoccupation with freedom not be permitted to override democratic values of participation and equality. Her argument is that if democracies are committed to anything, they must be committed to citizen participation.

Advice for Related Situations

Note that Pam's position is not necessarily or obviously an argument to advance her *own* religious position but rather is concerned more fundamentally with creating the (classroom or constitutional) space where such religious expressions may safely be contributed and genuinely be heard. This is the point that is perhaps most helpful for related situations: for religious expressions to be genuine, all other religions, including the various liberalisms (Deweyian, Rawlsian, Lockean) must be "disestablished." Accepting this disestablishment will be most difficult for liberals such as Nicole. However, it may represent risk as well to other perspectives, especially those who may have had designs of their own about replacing liberalism once it is dethroned. Even so, genuine acceptance of others as equal participants in the educational or civic arenas requires sincere acceptance of the fact of confessional pluralism within those arenas.

The assumption to be overcome here is the belief that what most fundamentally holds our classroom community together is an ideological or doctrinal agreement, whether or not established by the instructor, among all class members concerning the nature of their interaction. Liberals have a special propensity toward this belief, and, for that reason, are apt to be especially alarmed by the extent of societal pluralism. In fact, however, successful college education is sustained by many other things, most of which have little to do with an ideological consensus on educational (or political) fundamentals.

Here's one possibility: the basic pedagogical goal of full student participation in the educational process is more important than a prior agreement concerning the ideological or doctrinal character of that participation. Indeed, we might ask, is not the classroom itself a space in which all students may gain access, regardless of their religious views, race, gender, ethnicity, and all the other distinctions that divide? And if the space is for all, without regard to these divisions, then the primary concern should be one of inclusion, enabling all to participate, without regard to religious divisions, and especially not insisting that participation adopt the form of one particular mode of discourse. The ability of students to speak using whatever reasons they find persuasive should not be restricted.

Once this basic point is established, a number of implications follow. First, there should be no need for a student to be asked to "convert" to another view, or be required to "translate" his or her contributions into more acceptable language that can accompany or substitute for his or her own. Once it has been determined that this is a space where expressions of religious commitment are to be permitted, even welcomed, it should not take long for a general recognition to be reached that no one religious expression is likely to "win out" over the others—pluralism is here to stay, even within the classroom. Second, students should not be asked or required to develop arguments that are somehow independent of all views in the room and therefore "neutral." This can be a temptation for the instructor seeking a secure footing in a situation of diversity; call it "the politics of abstraction," an attempt to create an abstract justification that is independent of any and all religious views and that asks participants to confine their deliberations to those terms.

Can genuine understanding be possible in such an environment? Indeed, can participants in such a conversation possibly hope to come to an agreement on anything? Our ability to answer such questions positively depends upon our willingness to let go of the terms of the debate and to give up our concern to insist on philosophical or doctrinal or spiritual uniformity. Once we have done so, agreement and understanding remain very much in the realm of possibility. This is because it is very possible, even likely, for people to agree on a particular point or conclusion or policy without coming to an agreement on the underlying reasons for that point or conclusion or policy. Participants in classroom discussion and debate, then, can be encouraged to enter into dialogue with all their "convictional particularities" intact, although they cannot demand that others support their conclusions for those same reasons. Happily, there is no reason why this plurality of views cannot be seen as a strength, rather than a weakness, recognizing that religious disagreements need not be seen as a problem to overcome, but rather as signs of widespread support for the classroom enterprise.

However, we must go further, as more questions are to be considered. Beyond considering claims of inclusion, we also should consider obligations that may be entailed concerning the character of that participation. These are the educational virtues that the professor properly seeks to inculcate. And given the sensitivity of these questions in the political arena as well, we may hope that developing these habits in the political science classroom will bear fruit in the civic space as well.

As we consider these obligations, we can do so in terms of two different roles: That of the listener and that of the speaker. In our role of listener, we must be careful not to insist upon certain modes of argument or reasoning as a condition for speaking with us. We are obligated to respect other parties as equal participants in the educational or political process; accordingly we cannot require other participants to borrow a language not their own upon making a contribution. In short, as listeners, we are under an obligation to welcome religious contributions; and, although listeners are under no obligation to agree with these contributions, neither can they be discounted merely because they are different from one's own spiritual foundations. Moreover, listening with respect would seem to imply listening with the goal of engagement—listening to learn from the speaker, to seek points of contact between the speaker's views and one's own, and to discover ways that we might communicate our own views to the speaker.

From the perspective of the speaker, once it is clear that the plurality of religious commitments has been acknowledged, and if we have sought to make a contribution in those terms, we should normally be willing to demonstrate how our particular expression applies to the issue at hand—normally, this will make strategic sense in any case. For example, quotations from the Christian New Testament are certainly permissible in the course of discussion, but speakers will need to take the further step of drawing out the implications of that Scripture to clarify, for example, how it forms their opposition to the war in Iraq. If the speaker does not take the step, he or she will have to accept the possibility that his or her contribution is likely to have little political impact on the decision to be made (although this does not mean it might not have other value).

Note that this is not an obligation to make a religious contribution "secular" or "rational" or "neutral." At most, it is an obligation with respect to the goals of the particular arena of discussion, an obligation to express one's religious views in ways that support the goal of the sphere of education or of political decision-making. The obligations of speaker and listener are thus, in one sense, self-imposed: They are implied by a commitment to the educational process. Again, these obligations are supported by strategic considerations as well. Realizing that listeners are not required to be persuaded by our arguments, in our role as speakers we will normally be motivated to devise communications strategies that will be persuasive. An important task of the college instructor in this environment will be encouraging students to express their confessions politically along the path of learning.

However, we need not see our motivations as entirely strategic. In fact, we can go further: We might also say that the obligations of listener and speaker are imposed by the nature of college education—or of politics—as spheres of normative discourse. The very nature of these spheres of human activity will itself place demands upon participants seeking to make religious contributions; the other participants in that sphere ought not to impose additional demands as a further condition for inclusion.

The fact of inclusion is vitally important, particularly in the sphere of college education. Moving toward inclusion requires placing special emphasis on enabling students and citizens to bring their non-shared, distinctive perspectives into the shared educational space. In the process, we may learn from each other, and we may discover new solutions to old problems; but equally significant, we will be recognizing the value of that person as a responsible student and as a citizen who represents a distinct spiritual community. This recognition is a very great good—both for that person and for us. For political science instructors, the preservation of particularity and the promotion of public civility in this way provides an opportunity to move beyond simply teaching democracy; indeed, it offers the chance to practice in the classroom space an essential component of a truly democratic politics.

CHAPTER 13

Integrating Psychology and Christianity

Bryce E. Fox

Scenario

Brielle sat in horror as the professor finished his lecture on the psychosexual stages of Sigmund Freud's psychoanalytic theory. She could not believe she was sitting in a classroom at a Christian college listening to such ungodly perspectives. After the professor finished quoting Freud's perception of people faced with a cold, ambiguous, and threatening universe as needing to create a comforting illusion, such as an imaginary deity or divine father figure, Brielle could not sit still any longer. She burst out, "How does knowing this help me in any way in my life as a Christian?" She continued, "Why are we studying this garbage? It is obviously not true. I mean, come on, how many of you guys in here lusted after your mother and wanted to kill your father? It is ridiculous. Are we really going to be tested over this?" The professor took a safe response and suggested that Freud is discussed because most of the other psychological theories that emerged after him either built upon his perspectives or reacted against it. He attempted to reassure Brielle by stating that it would be difficult to view other perspectives that oppose Freud's theory without first understanding what Sigmund believed. This explanation seemed to pacify Brielle for the moment. However, as the semester continued Brielle kept finding herself experiencing inner turmoil as she heard about Albert Ellis being a self-proclaimed atheist and William Glasser suggesting that religious circles are sources of excessive criticism that undermine an individual's sense of effectiveness. She could not come to terms with her tuition money being spent to look at the lives and theories of those who do not find God to be relevant to life and emotional health. She e-mailed her professor the following message:

> Dear Professor,
> Do you have any time right away that I can meet with you to talk about the General Psychology class? I am deeply disturbed by your class and what we have been forced to read and listen to in the lectures. How can you call yourself a Christian and teach students who are very impressionable to trust in ideas that are totally, I mean *totally contrary* to everything else this school and the Bible teaches. I need to get

some answers from a "Christian" perspective about the purpose of this course and why I need to know this stuff as soon as possible so I can withdraw and get my money back before the deadline next Friday. Please let me know when I can get an appointment with you before Friday. I hope you're not mad. I like you as a teacher, but I just feel I am dishonoring God by filling my mind with this trash. Thanks. Brielle.

Analysis of Scenario

Before beginning to evaluate the previous situation, it must be stated that the spiritual framework used in the analysis is a Christian perspective. This is not to imply that Christianity defines spirituality or that the Bible is the only context that can be used to assess appropriate responses. This approach was selected due to the ongoing tension between psychology and Christianity that has been present from the establishment of Sigmund Freud's Psychoanalytic Process as a legitimate theory.

Readers will also notice that this chapter is written primarily for professors who teach within Christian institutions. This should not, however, deter professors or students who come with a different spiritual viewpoint from studying the suggestions in this chapter, because the underlying principles can be understood within a broad range of perspectives.

One advantage for students is that they can look through a professor's lens to gain insight into how they can resolve apparent conflicts between the two areas of thought and understand how they might be directed if they ever raise one of these issues in a class.

The idea that psychology and Christianity are incompatible has been around since the establishment of psychoanalytic theory. It should not be surprising that many Christians are repulsed by a number of the conclusions espoused by Freud, especially his focus on infantile sexual desires and his direct attack on religion. Imagine the student who has been raised attending church every time the doors were open, has been a faithful youth group member, and has never been exposed to any psychological theories, hearing for the first time that girls have penis envy, that boys lust after their mother and want to kill their father, and that many of their difficulties in life can be traced back to their toilet training. If the student has Christian parents who have fulfilled their duty to train him or her in the beliefs of the Bible, then these concepts will surely be seen as inconsistent with what he or she has been taught is right and wrong. To lust is ungodly and to harbor hateful feelings toward anyone is spiritually unacceptable. So asking Christian students to spend time and energy learning these perspectives, or worse, entertaining the idea that they may have some validity, may be traumatic.

It may be helpful for students to first look at the general options available in attempting to resolve the issue of integrating psychology and Christianity. Four different approaches can be helpful if professors will encourage their students to evaluate these and attempt to select the model with which they most closely associate. Doing this will lay the foundation for understanding how they plan to approach the more specific aspects of psychology as they emerge throughout the semester.

The following four approaches are labeled differently but are modeled after John Carter's four basic models of integrating Christianity and psychology (1981). The first is the *Opposition* Model. As described at the beginning of this section, there are those on both sides of this argument. On one side, psychology opposes Christianity, and on the other, Christianity opposes psychology. Those that adhere to either of these perspectives do not believe that psychology and Christianity can coexist. They argue that irreconcilable differences make it impossible to integrate the two schools of thought. Those operating from the "psychology opposes Christianity" group believe that Christianity is detrimental to emotional health and should not be a part of the helping process. On my first day in the first graduate psychology class I ever took, the professor entered the room and after making sure we were all in the right place proceeded to make this comment: "If you think that there is any room for God in psychology you are wrong. And if you have come to this incorrect conclusion, then you are probably in the wrong class." She obviously taught from the Opposition Model. I also worked for a hospital in Indianapolis, Indiana, where this philosophy prevailed as well. Bibles were not allowed in the lobby, and prayer or talk about God was not allowed in the counseling process.

Those coming from the "Christianity opposes psychology" perspective believe that the Word of God is sufficient for all emotional needs. These individuals believe that emotional problems are always the result of sin. Therefore, if the sin issue can be dealt with, the emotional problem can be eliminated. Psychology is seen as the ultimate in heresy since it is viewed as using humanistic methods to deceive individuals into feeling they are OK, even though the real issue of sin continues to exist in their life. I witnessed a preacher speaking from this perspective while I was sitting on the front row of a church on a Sunday morning. This old-time preacher, who knew me well, stood on the platform and pounded his fist on the pulpit, stared down at me and yelled, "We don't need counselors. We need God." It was clear from his perspective that a simple prayer is all that is necessary to deal with any and all emotional problems. Professors should be aware that some Christian students may initially follow this model. Throughout the semester this may change for some students as they begin to see those psychological principles that are compatible with the Bible. However, it is possible that some students will continue to use this model as their frame of reference regardless of what material is presented or what evidence is provided. As frustrating as it might be for some professors, it is important to understand that the professor's job is not to get students to follow a particular model, but to provide enough information for them to make an informed decision.

The second option is the *Uncritical Integration* Model. Those who follow this approach find it easy to integrate and uncritically accept the claims of both psychology and Christianity. These individuals believe that the perspectives of both schools of thought are basically the same and if there are differences it is just a matter of terminology. What one would call "sin" the other would call "depression." These people can use one or both approaches to dealing with an emotional problem. Whichever approach works is acceptable. Most individuals who operate from this perspective are probably not critical thinkers. These individuals can hear a good argument and simply say, "Well, that sounds reasonable to me" without ever seeking any other proof.

The third option is the *Both, And* Model. Like the perspective of the Opposition Model, these individuals also do not see psychology and Christianity as integrated. Unlike those who subscribe to the first approach, these individuals see value in both perspectives but believe that both should be kept separate. It is not an opposition to integration but a belief that emotional problems should be dealt with by a counselor, psychologist, or psychiatrist; and spiritual issues should be dealt with by a pastor. This may seem like an attractive option on the surface and may actually be the chosen option for some students; however, it must be remembered that this is a very strict perspective. It is believed that the two never mix; they are completely separate. A deeper look would typically conclude that both psychology and Christianity address similar aspects of humanity. The Bible offers direction and perspectives on both behavior and thinking as does psychology. It seems improbable that there is never a place where they cross over or where both could address the same issue.

The final approach is the *Integrating* Model. This approach believes psychology and Christianity can be successfully integrated. The underlying philosophy of this approach is that "all truth is God's truth." In other words, just because someone is not a Christian does not mean that he or she does not have the opportunity to discover truth. God is the author of truth wherever it is found. Therefore, if something is true, there should be no discrepancy between Christianity and psychology concerning the conclusions. If there is a discrepancy, then the problem is due to the way the research was conducted or the way the data were interpreted or the way a certain passage of scripture was interpreted. If the discrepancy cannot be resolved, then scripture is presumed to take precedent. The freedom of this model is that truth can be freely sought without compromising the authority of scripture.

These four models offer an opportunity for students to begin to unwrap their thoughts about Christianity, psychology, and the processes of learning as it relates to how information from often competing schools of thought can be integrated into an individual's life and practice. Even though the four models are helpful in general terms of thinking about integration, professors will still have to respond to specific questions and concerns raised in their classes. Following are suggestions a professor could use to help Brielle understand different ways to resolve her educational conflict. Three principles that emerge are beneficial under any learning circumstance but will be explained with a specific focus on the scenario.

The *first principle* with which students need to come to terms is that just because a theory is presented in class does not mean that they must believe it. Some students enter college classrooms a little intimidated by all the Ph.D.s and level of scholarship, assuming that whatever the professor says is meant to be taken as fact and applied to their lives. They may not understand how to use critical thinking skills to discern how the material is supposed to be used. Professors may want to explain to students within the first week how to interact with the material to understand the theory, to be open to evaluate the truth of the theory and to determine what Christians can apply to their own lives. This may be more critical for freshmen but can still be a helpful reminder to other students as well. Depending on how important a faculty member thinks this may be for students and how much time he/she thinks is needed in preparing students for the material, John Wesley's Quadrilateral can be a helpful guide. Wesley said that information should be filtered through four different measures in searching for truth. These four areas of evaluation are scripture, tradition, reason, and experience. As was stated earlier, the concept of males lusting after their mother and wanting to kill their father does not fit with Scripture. It could be argued that the concept of original sin may fit in very general terms, but the idea that original sin is manifested in infantile lust would be a stretch. In terms of looking at tradition, as it relates to the church, infantile lust would not fit with that either. It may be that students may not find this idea even reasonable from their own experiences; however, a deeper look at how others may come to this conclusion may shed some light on the concept. For example, it is well known that a mother is typically the first love object for a boy. It is not uncommon for very young boys to say they are going to marry their mom when they grow up. Today most would understand this in other terms than sexual; but, when you add to this idea that very young boys also often fiddle with their penis in the bath tub when they first begin to discover their penis, it may help students understand how others may have created their hypothesis of infantile lust. It is important at this point to not let the students simply throw all of Freud's theory out because it does not fit the quadrilateral very well. Freud also introduced the concept that the first six years of life are a critical time in an individual's development. This would seem to balance well with scripture, tradition (depending on which era used), reason, and experience. This is just one example of teaching students to evaluate information, to attempt to discover how the conclusions were possibly established, and to select what should be retained for personal use.

The *second principle* that students need to understand is that just because a professor presents ideas in class does not mean either that they are accurate or that the professor's intent is to state them as practical truth. This should be obvious in the field of psychology with all the competing perspectives, but students who are hearing certain ideas for the first time may believe the professor is simply teaching facts to be learned and practiced. When I begin teaching a class in any subject I typically encourage students to feel free to challenge the material. I start by asking if the students believe that an instructor would ever attempt to intentionally try to deceive them. Almost universally the students reject the idea. I then share an experience I had when I was in my doctoral program. In a class entitled "Theories of Psychology" the professor told us that most psychological theories were actually created by women. When she was challenged about this idea she stated that because women had been repressed men got the credit, even though women were actually the brains behind the ideas. I happened to overhear her later that day talking with another younger professor. When the young professor asked her if she really believed that women were behind most psychological theories, she quietly said, "no." I couldn't believe it. I was very frustrated to be purposely deceived because of someone's agenda.

I continue the discussion with the class by stating: if there are professors who would purposefully attempt to deceive you, do you think it is possible that other professors may unintentionally be wrong in the information they present. By this time the response from the students is almost universally, "Of course." This helps give them permission to question the ideas professors present and encourages them to wrestle with all the information that is presented and read in the class. The main point with which to close the conversation is that all professors present varying viewpoints and theories, some of which they agree with and some of which they do not. If students simply see all the information being presented as the professor's true beliefs, then they will continue to struggle in many of their classes. While a professor's agenda or error may need to be part of the discussion, students should be cautious about assuming the information is being presented as the professor's true belief. When Brielle heard the professor present Freud's theory, apparently she assumed it was being presented because the professor believed the theory and wanted the students to believe it as well. A response to Brielle that may have resolved this issue very quickly is to simply state that few people today, even in the field of psychology would come to the same conclusions that Freud did concerning lusting and hate. Also understanding this piece helps put into perspective how psychology has emerged and been responded to throughout history. Giving students permission to challenge the material and understand that a great deal of information is studied in class for a broader purpose then simply presenting facts that are to be regurgitated will help students not feel so offended by material that appears to conflict with their own frame of reference.

The *third principle* with which students need to wrestle, even if they totally disagree with the stated theory, is that those in that particular field do believe it and operate from that frame of reference; consequently, it would be wise to try and understand what they believe and why so as not to be ignorant and ineffective when working or consulting with them. A normal part of the learning process is to engage theories that are contrary to your own, not only to be able to understand the other perspective but also to possibly strengthen your understanding of your own perspective. Christian students who have studied the Bible and may have never had to entertain perspectives that do not support biblical teaching may struggle to understand why they should have to study conflicting theories. It may help them to understand that when missionaries enter a foreign land, part of their preparation is to attempt to thoroughly understand the people, faith, and customs to be effective in engaging and helping those people. This perspective is the same for those practicing psychology. However, in very practical terms in response to the scenario, this principle may not be as useful for Sigmund Freud's theory as for others in psychology because the ideas of lust and hate are not as accepted or used today. The principle, however, is necessary to be able to establish a framework that is functional in a broader scope then just Freud's theory. Professors may have to work patiently with students if they are to be able to help them shift their perspective of learning from only studying concepts with which they agree to attempting to understand a concept in its fullness.

Even though some students are going to have a difficult time with the faith perspectives of many of the theories in psychology, the subject matter of psychology is practical and relevant to many issues of life. Students will find these concepts are also common topics in the Bible, mainly thinking and behavior. Many Christian students are attracted to psychology for this very reason. Providing some clarity as to what aspects of life influence people to act and think in certain ways can assist individuals not only in understanding themselves but also in providing insights about how to help others. This leads to the second biggest reason Christian students often migrate to the field of psychology counseling. Since having a servant's heart and loving your neighbor as yourself is at the root of Christian behavior, discovering ways to practically fulfill these exhortations is very intriguing to those wishing to be competent at fulfilling this calling. If professors can be aware of this, they can help students discover those pieces of the different theories that have Christian principles associated with them. For example, even though many Christian students may not accept the deterministic perspectives of radical behaviorism, most still use several of the principles found in behaviorism in their everyday lives. It is probable that students first exposed to behavioral concepts may be surprised that psychology has provided research and models for how to use rewards and punishment to shape behavioral outcomes. Little did they know that B.F. Skinner laid the groundwork for how many of their Sunday school teachers managed their students. How surprising for them to discover that the ice-cream party that was used to motivate them to read missionary books as a child was grounded in the psychological theory of behaviorism.

The word "humanism" is a negative word in some Christian circles. It implies that humanity is moved to center stage while removing God from the scene altogether. Even the process of "Person-Centered Therapy" developed by Carl Rogers seems to promote this same idea. However, even though humanistic psychology has elevated humanity beyond the Creator, Christian students may confess that when someone has truly listened to them and quietly been present with them during a difficult time in their life, they experienced help and healing. Humanistic psychology seems to have provided a glimpse of what it means to "love our neighbor."

As Christian students begin to explore cognitive psychology, neurological psychology, developmental psychology and other psychological areas of study, they will discover practical applications intermingled within the secular concepts that can be supported biblically and can be very helpful in life and ministry. If professors can assist students in sorting through the material and teach them these simple principles of engaging the theories, they can help those students who might otherwise be put-off to learn critical thinking skills, discernment and to develop a love of learning.

Advice for Related Situations

The four models and in particular the three principles described in this chapter have practical relevance to all professors, regardless if they teach at a secular or sectarian institution. This approach was taken purposefully to allow for broad application both within and outside psychology. Whether the field of study be the natural sciences or education, students will still need to come to an understanding that 1) just because a theory is presented in class does not mean that they must believe it, 2) just because a professor presents material in class does not mean that the information is accurate, or even if the information is *factual*, that the professor intended to state it as practical truth, and 3) even if students totally disagree with the stated theory, if there are those in that particular field who do believe it and operate from that frame of reference then it would be wise to understand what they believe and why, so as not to be ignorant and ineffective when working or consulting with them. These three principles established early on in a semester can save the professor and the students much time and frustration.

Hopefully all professors can be reminded and encouraged through these principles to uphold the integrity of the educational process by assuring students of their freedom to explore the information, question it, and integrate it as they see fit. Therefore, it is strongly suggested that all professors, whether they teach in sectarian institutions or secular institutions, and even if they do not believe in Christianity or spirituality, allow students the liberty to question professors' teachings. Professors also should not ask or pressure students into subscribing to those teachings if they find them intellectually flawed or expect students to abandon their Christian/spiritual beliefs when they are incompatible with theories that either do not support or are antagonistic to the students' Christian/spiritual beliefs. Psychology and Christianity can find areas of harmony and integration, but professors and students alike will need to be free to honestly wrestle with all the available information without fear of consequence.

References

Carter, John. 1981. *Secular and sacred models of psychology and religion.* Grand Rapids, MI: Zondervan Publishing House.

CHAPTER 14

Science and Spirituality

David K. Scott

Scenario

Professor McLeod had just read the results of a survey on the role of spirituality in the lives of today's college students (Astin and Astin 2006). One of the questions addressed the connectedness students felt toward others and to the world around them. She was surprised to learn that 80% of entering students expressed an interest in this connectedness as part of their spirituality to some or to a great extent. A similar percentage reported that they often prayed. Indeed, she was even more surprised to discover that the students expressing the lowest interest in spirituality were generally in the physical sciences, mathematics, and engineering, with computer science usually ranking dead last. This finding surprised Professor McLeod, because she believed that many of the results of modern science reveal deep connections between science and spirituality. Since she was teaching a class on quantum physics the next day, she decided to check the views of her own students.

The next day in class, when Professor McLeod asked students about the relationship between spirituality and science, most of the class subscribed to the independence hypothesis for science and spirituality, characterized by Gould (1999) as "non-overlapping magisteria." Both represented valid domains of human experience; they just have nothing to do with each other. The students were not at all sympathetic when Professor McLeod explained Alfred North Whitehead's perspective that a clash of worldviews is not necessarily indicative of disaster, but frequently of a finer perspective, a deeper understanding of reality that has not yet been uncovered. They stated emphatically, "Science deals with external reality while religion—or spirituality—deals with an interior human experience." They confidently proclaimed, "This division was made clear hundreds of years ago, with the birth of modern science, by the philosophers and scientists who separated mind and matter. Furthermore, it is only a matter of time before science explains all of the interior dimensions of human experience through physical and chemical processes of the brain."

Professor McLeod wondered how her students could compartmentalize their views of science and spirituality in this way and whether it could be destructive in their development. Either they had to accept that their spirituality bore little relation to their intellectual studies or, even worse, they were forced to renounce their faith completely. She surmised that similar tensions drove many people to fundamentalist religions, and perhaps was at the root of terrorism in the world. She decided to digress from her next lecture to discuss the history of the engagement of science and spirituality and to raise the possibility that these subjects were actually deeply entangled. She would suggest that ideas emerging from many recent discoveries in physics, biology, neuroscience, psychology, and health sciences were implicit in many, if not all, of the world's spiritual traditions. She had long kept secret her belief in the emergence of a more integrative view of science and spirituality. A senior colleague had advised her early in her career that such topics were taboo in the academy, and might even violate the constitutional separation of Church and State, but now she felt ready to tackle this important topic. Given widespread political conflicts in the world today, which to some extent stem from the tension between science and religion, Professor McLeod believed that she had a professional responsibility to engage students in a discussion about how to integrate science and religion (spirituality). She would be careful, though, to emphasize that such integration is controversial and by no means accepted by many, or even most scientists, and that new discoveries in science and religion might necessitate different interpretations in the future. In fact, she was confident that all our current knowledge about science and religion might be radically transformed in another 100 years. For example, current versions of string theory, perhaps the best available theory for understanding the structure of the universe, postulate that the universe may be 10-dimensional, rather than 4-dimensional in space and time, but that six dimensions are curled upon themselves (Kabat-Zinn 2006b). "Might it not be possible," Professor McLeod speculated, "that our inner unfurled dimensions might equally transform the landscape of consciousness?"

To Professor McLeod it seemed absurd that conscious life could have evolved by accident in a vast, unconscious universe, devoid of feeling and oblivious to the life it had spawned. In fact, it seemed downright unscientific. She recalled how many of the great scientists and philosophers, such as Copernicus, Newton, and Descartes, were motivated by spiritual and religious ideas. Their original discoveries were charged with intense spiritual significance. They "perceived their breakthroughs as divine illuminations, spiritual awakenings to the true structural grandeur and intellectual beauty of the cosmic order" (Tarnas 2006, 5). Perhaps, she surmised, these scientists had intimations of a deeper level of reality that must be uncovered gradually. The line in Emily Dickinson's poem "Slanted Truth" came to mind: "the truth must dazzle gradually, or every man be blind." On the path towards a deeper and fuller understanding of the cosmos, perhaps the universe is kind to us; we might be overwhelmed and become dysfunctional if too much were revealed too quickly about the ultimate nature of reality.

Analysis of Scenario

In the context of this chapter, spirituality means a sense of connection to the cosmos and to all life within it, as well as a sense of transcendence. This view of spirituality is in opposition to the separation between scientific and spiritual worldviews based on the idea that life evolved by chance in an impartial universe and that, while the evolution of life and the evolution of the universe can be described by science, the two are not connected. The separation is to a large degree the result of the birth of modern science and the Western Enlightenment from the sixteenth century onward. However, its roots extend much farther back in time to the Axial Age, centered around 500 B.C.E. Prior to that period, primal cultures did not separate science and spirituality, art and religion or any other area of human experience. Tarnas (2006, 16) points out, "The primal human being perceives the surrounding natural world as permeated with meaning...whose significance is at once human and cosmic. Spirits are seen in the forest, presences are felt in the wind and the ocean, the river, the mountain. Meaning is recognized in the flight of two eagles across the horizon...in the unfolding cycles of the moon and the sun. The primal world is ensouled." In primal cultures the relationship between an observer and the observed, the subject and the object, is not separated.

Karen Armstrong (2005/2006, 34–37;2006) points out that the decades around 500 B.C.E. witnessed the birth of many of the world's principal religions and spiritual traditions. "And in every single case, the spiritualities that emerged during the Axial Age—Taoism and Confucianism in China, monotheism in Israel, Hinduism, Buddhism and Jainism in India, and Greek rationalism in Europe—began from a conviction that the world was awry." The Axial Age occurred at a time when individualism was just emerging to define humanity, as we now know it. During this period men and women became conscious of their existence, their own nature and their limitations in an unprecedented way. "People who participated in this great transformation were convinced that they were on the brink of a new era and that nothing would ever be the same. They sought change in the deepest reaches of their beings, looked for greater inwardness in their spiritual lives, and tried to become one with a transcendent reality." This transformation led to the separation of spirit and matter with spirit in the ascendant (Turner 1998). While today we often associate this split with science, it actually originated in the world's religious and spiritual traditions.

Now fast forward to the birth of modern science in the sixteenth century. The scientists and philosophers of this time accepted the idea of the separation of matter and spirit but set us on the path—unintentionally—of reversing the priority of the spirit-matter split by ascribing greater importance to matter. This reversal led to alienation of human beings from the cosmos, begun by the Copernican revolution, and resulted in the displacement of human beings to a peripheral position in a vast, impersonal universe with a concomitant disenchantment with the natural world (Tarnas 2006). According to Tarnas, a century later another shift took place with Descartes' *cogito ergo sum*, resulting in the human mind being distinct from the world, and the apprehended world being ultimately the mind's creation. After another century Kant expanded the epistemological consequences to say that all human knowledge was interpretive, affirming that the world is a construct of human thought. Darwin further intensified the alienation in the nineteenth century through emphasizing the relativism of the human being in the flux of evolution. In the twentieth century, Freud first recognized the deep continuity linking the Copernican revolution with the depth psychology revolution. Just as the former event had irrevocably transformed the outer cosmos, so the latter irrevocably transformed the inner cosmos, in each case radically overturning humankind's naïve conviction of its centricity. The Copernicans displaced the earth from the center of the universe to reveal a much larger, unknown cosmos in which the earth was now but a tiny peripheral fragment, while the Freudians displaced the conscious self from the center of the inner universe to reveal the much larger unknown realm of the unconscious. The modern self had to acknowledge that it was not master of its own house, as the confident Cartesian *cogito* had implied, but was rather a peripheral epiphenomenon of far more powerful processes working unfathomed beyond the boundaries of its awareness. This multidimensional alienation has led to cosmological, ontological and epistemological estrangement in a universe without hope and with no room for spirituality or God (Schafer 2006).

However, there are signs that we may be in the midst of a new transformation, moving from modernism and postmodernism to trans-modernism and a more integral worldview. Indeed, Armstrong suggests that we may be entering another Axial Age. If so, then the integration of science and spirituality will be key to this transformation and therefore an important topic to discuss in classes. Having moved from the unexamined integration of the unitive cosmology in primal cultures to the dualism stretching from the Axial Age to the modern era, we may now formulate a new level of integration, built on the deep knowledge acquired in all the separate disciplines, including science and the world's spiritual traditions. The pluralism and multiplicity of worldviews of the postmodern era, all with their separate validity, have set the stage for this transformation with the potential to alleviate the alienation felt by societies everywhere.

In considering how to approach the integration of science and spirituality in the classroom, it is useful to frame a discussion around three ideas with philosophical implications potentially as far reaching as those originating in the sixteenth century. Each is illustrative of an apparent fundamental connectivity and coherence in the universe that is central to a spiritual worldview.

The first idea relates to consciousness. In contrast to the modern worldview of separating subject and object, quantum mechanical theory implies that they are fundamentally entangled, suggesting, according to some interpretations, that consciousness may be necessary for the full manifestation of reality. Prior to observation of an event an infinite potential for possible outcomes exists. Only through the participation of the observer, i.e., through consciousness, does the event crystallize into reality. Consciousness in some form may even have been present at the birth of the universe for the universe to manifest itself, or at least some information content must have been present, possibly inherited from prior universes. In this theory, consciousness is not a chance byproduct of matter in the universe but is an integral constituent of the universe. The entire universe is participatory and coherent.

The second idea that can help integrate science and religion is the anthropic principle, which asserts that many parameters of the universe, for example the strengths of the four fundamental forces and the masses of elementary particles, are finely tuned to make life possible. Even minute variations in these constants would lead to a sterile universe without life. This remarkable observation has several interpretations. Some say the universe is simply a matter of chance; the universe is the way it is and were it not we would not be here to talk about it! A vast mechanical, unconscious universe would play out its lonely existence without observers. However, this chance is estimated to be so remote that most scientists find the explanation unacceptable. Another interpretation is that our universe is simply a local region of a much more vast universe—or possibly of a series of multi-universes evolving over time either in parallel or serially—most of which, if not all, with different parameters that exclude life. According to Randall (2005) many disconnected universes probably exist, but we inhabit one with an incredibly small value of the vacuum energy necessary for life to exist, but the only one apparently allowing structure, including life, to form. In response to this, many scientists are "optimistic" that in time we will discover there is nothing remarkable about the fine-tuning that makes life possible; it will be a consequence of some undiscovered principle. Some conjecture that the "purpose" of the universe is to maximize the number of black holes (Smolin 1998), a constraint that may just happen to coincide with the conditions for life. However, we might ask why this outlook is optimistic. Might it not also be possible that our universe is special in some way with its "design" for life? At least it is worth considering whether the universe, life, consciousness and the fundamental parameters all exist in some participatory, self-consistent, coherent design with some other "purpose." Perhaps that discovery might be more optimistic—and even the greatest discovery in the history of the universe! As Freeman J. Dyson once said, it is as if the universe had to know that we were coming from the first instant of the Big Bang when the fundamental constants were determined. Many other apparent "coincidences" also suggest design, such as space-time being perfectly flat in the absence of matter, implying an equally finely tuned universe in which even one billionth less or more matter would have resulted in a curved space-time (Laszlo 2004). A possible conclusion from these and other apparent coincidences is that the coherent structure is difficult to understand in the absence of any purpose or self-consistent design. Our universe may have crystallized into actuality when consciousness was generated through an exploration of infinite possibilities. Where this consciousness came from is an open question—at least in science. Buddhist philosophers would claim that consciousness is primordial and exists prior to entering the physical event. The complete understanding of these matters may call for all the tools at our disposal, whether from science or spirituality.

These ideas serve as more productive launching point for discussing "intelligent design" in the theory of evolution of the universe rather than in the evolution of life, which is only one component of the entire design. The question of design or chance in the evolution of the *entire* universe remains an open question, whereas biological evolution is better established. The finely tuned constants may be understood in a future theory, but in the meanwhile belief in either the extremes of chance or design is a matter of faith—faith in science or faith in religion. A wise approach is to keep an open mind, not rejecting *a priori* the spiritually connected and coherent universe implicit in the world's spiritual traditions for hundreds and even thousands of years.

The third idea that can be used as evidence for coherence between mind and matter, between cosmos and psyche, comes from mathematical theorems created as elegant models which then often find an application even hundreds of years later in a new theory of the universe, seemingly implying a connection between the structure of the mind and the structure of the universe (Polkinghorne 2002). An example is certain theorems of Euler developed over 200 years ago, which now find an application in modern string theory of the universe. An older example is the abstract shapes of conic sections in Greek geometry, which then found application in the motions of the planets.

All three ideas point to a very different model of the universe from what we are accustomed. Bohm (2002) has proposed a holographic theory in which information about the entire universe is embedded in each and every component of the universe and vice versa. He refers to an implicate order in the universe, ultimately requiring that the universe has to be understood as a single, undivided whole. According to this theory, the uncertainty principle is simply a principle of unavoidable ignorance with epistemological rather than ontological significance. At a deep level of reality, everything may be determined (Polkinghorne 2006). This idea, if correct, has enormous significance beyond science, such as notions of free will (Merali 2006). An extraordinary and ancient description of a holographic reality is also to be found in a Hindu Sutra describing the heaven of Indra where there is said to be a network of pearls so arranged that if you look at one you see all the others reflected in it. In the same way each object in the world is not merely itself but involves every other object, and in fact is in every other object (Eliot 1954, 6). We have to marvel from where that remarkable insight, now discovered in some scientific theories, appeared from thousands of years ago. In a speech at Independence Hall, Havel (1994) drew an analogy with the Gaia hypothesis, according to which we are parts of a greater whole in the world. Havel says that these principles of wholeness are not new, that we have long suspected and long projected into sometimes forgotten myths. Moreover, he asserts, these principles are no more than archetypes that have lain dormant within us, making us aware that encoded in all religions are integral parts of mysterious entities that are higher than us but part of us.

What if the world of appearances is not totally wrong? Could it be there may be objects at multiple levels of reality? If we penetrate through and look at the universe with a holographic system, we arrive at a different reality, one that can explain things that have hitherto remained inexplicable: synchronicity as an apparently meaningful coincidence of events, such as the strange coincidences in the fundamental constants of the universe and the requirements for life.

If we believe in this interpretation, our relationship to the universe, to the world and to each other could change radically for the better (Apffel-Marglin 2006; Barad 2006). For those who question whether such abstract ideas have any relevance to everyday experience, we need only remind ourselves that the theories leading to separation and fragmentation were equally abstract hundreds of years ago but have nevertheless succeeded in generating a worldview separating the human being from the cosmos and from each other. The practical outcome has been that our universe and world are seen in a utilitarian way that has shaped human motivation in relation to the environment, to the persecution of anyone and anything we regard as separate. If everything is connected, we might more easily adopt a more global outlook. Of course, many might argue that the nature of reality at the quantum level has little to do with our macroscopic world. However, then we have to ask where the quantum reality disappears. Recent experiments show that macroscopic phenomena may also exhibit non-locality, appearing in two places simultaneously, or be influenced by merely observing them (Naik et al. 2006).

Related Situations

Since scientists are often considered the least likely to accept a spiritual dimension to their quest, the evidence for a connection in the light of modern discoveries may be a powerful catalyst for engaging other disciplines, which are *a priori* better disposed to a dialogue. One approach to connecting science with other disciplines uses the Kantian Big Three—the knowledge areas of science, art and religion, or equivalently science, humanities, and spirituality—which are central to all cultures and societies throughout human history (Wilber 1998). In the spirit of the analysis in the previous section, it may well be that the three knowledge spheres are akin to three languages, each projecting an understanding of reality, the ultimate understanding of which may require a new language. Our discussion here attempts to show a path forward, integrating the best insights and research from all disciplines—the essence of an integral worldview and a goal worthy of education at all levels everywhere.

A promising gateway to this integral worldview may be opening through research on meditation and contemplative practice in various fields—law, education, health care, and many others (Bush 2006; Kabat-Zinn 2006a; Lutz et al. 2004). Research on long-term meditators shows that their mental training involves a temporal, integrative mechanism in the brain, as well as a heightened capacity for compassion. It appears that we have a built-in integrative capacity, which is not well developed in most of us, but which may be enhanced through contemplative practice. Great spiritual leaders have a deeper understanding of this potential, but it is latent in all of us. Imagine the transformative power of discovering that a better developed spiritual sense might enhance the integrative and caring capacities we have always sought in all of education (Goleman 2006).

Sarath (2003) quotes testimonies from students engaged in meditation at the University of Michigan that suggest a wide range of benefits, from relieving stress to listening more carefully to each other, learning to clear the mind and focusing better on doing our jobs, and to enhancing our ability to remain calm in difficult situations. There is also evidence that meditation can promote a profound connecting link between different cultures, running sharply counter to prevailing postmodern tendencies that reject such transcendent connections. Sarath goes on to say that, ironically, the academic world—due to the necessity of extricating contemplative practice from overtly religious practice—may be poised to play a leadership role in restoring to religious practice the unifying aspects of this important domain of human experience. Meditation and contemplative practice may be thought of as simply extending the continuum of what constitutes education from more quantifiable, external kinds of knowledge (often regarded as the territory of science, the intellect and, indeed, of all academic knowledge) to those that are more interior (often regarded as the territory of spirituality) and abstract, but no less important to students' overall development. These developments suggest a growing interest in the relationship between spirituality and science as well as other disciplines. Not only have the discoveries in science generated this interest, but also the methods of science validate spirituality as a way of experiencing reality.

Mathematics is yet another point of contact for the integration of science and religion (spirituality). As we mentioned earlier, mathematics, an abstract creation of the human mind, is well accepted as a valid way of knowing in science and has, as we have seen, the remarkable capacity to explain the structure of the universe. The idea of mathematics as a spiritual activity has a long lineage from Pythagoras and Plato to Newton, Einstein, and, in modern times, Stephen Hawking (McFarlane 1995). Given this accepted expansion of the scientific way of knowing that has little connection with materialistic reality, it would be unscientific—as Professor McLeod conjectured while she was preparing to discuss science and spirituality with students—to reject out of hand the possibility of this third way of knowing, the path of spiritual insight and contemplative practice. Far from denying spirituality as a force in the universe and in human experience, science can pave the way for an expanded and integrative view of reality. The European Idealist philosophers in the eighteenth and nineteenth centuries wanted to bridge the diverging positions of empiricism and idealism, and they attempted to unite subject and object by ascribing all power to reason as the source of reality. The Idealist program may now be pursued afresh, based on theories of quantum reality, which seem to infer that fundamentally reality is mind-like (Schafer 2006). In a mind-like reality, expanding human spiritual powers seems natural to the evolution of the universe and our actions should contribute to enhancing this reality (Polkinghorne 2006).

Tarnas in his recent book, *Cosmos and Psyche: Intimations of a New World View*, quotes Sir James Frazer in *The Golden Bough*, written over a century ago. His words are also appropriate to end this essay. "In the last analysis magic, religion, and science are nothing but theories of thought and as science has supplanted its predecessors, so it may hereafter be itself superseded by some more perfect thought—the dreams of magic may one day be the waking realities of science" (Tarnas 2006, 492).

References

Apffel-Marglin, F. 2006. Private communication.

Armstrong, K. 2005–2006. A new axial age: *What is enlightenment (interview with Jessica Remischer)?* December–February, 34–37.

———. 2006. *The great transformation: The beginning of our religious traditions.* New York/Toronto: Alfred A. Knopf.

Astin, A. W., and H. S. Astin. 2006. *The spiritual life of college students: A national study of college students' search for meaning and purpose,* and *Spirituality of the professoriate: A national study of faculty beliefs, attitudes and behaviors.* http://www.spirituality.ucla.edu (accessed September 10, 2006).

Barad, K. 2006. *Meeting the universe halfway: Quantum physics and the entanglement of matter and meaning.* Durham, NC: Duke University Press.

Bohm, D. 2002. *Wholeness and the implicate order.* London/New York: Routledge.

Bush, M. http://www.contemplativemind.org (accessed September 10, 2006).

Eliot, C. 1954. *Hinduism and Buddhism: An historical sketch in three volumes.* New York: Barnes and Noble.

Goleman, D. 2006. *Social intelligence: The new science of human relationships.* New York: Bantam Press.

Gould, S. 1999. Non-overlapping magisteria: *Special issue of Skeptical Inquiry on science and religion.* July–August:55–61.

Havel, V. 1994. *The need for transcendence in the postmodern world.* Speech given at Independence Hall, Philadelphia. http://www.mindfully.org (accessed September 10, 2006).

Kabat-Zinn, J. 2006a. *Coming to our senses: Healing ourselves and the world through mindfulness.* New York: Hyperion.

———. 2006b. Wherever you go, there you are: Living your life as if it really matters. In *Integrative learning and action: A call to wholeness,* ed. S. M. Awbrey, D. Dana, V. M. Miller, P. Robinson, M. M. Ryan, and D. K. Scott, 157–172. New York: Peter Lang.

Laszlo, E. 2004. *Science and the akashic field: An integral theory of everything.* Rochester, VT: Inner Traditions.

Lutz, A., L. L. Greischer, N. B. Rawlings, M. Ricard, and R. Davidson. 2004. Long-term meditators self-induce high-amplitude gamma synchrony during mental practice. *PNAS* 101(46):16369–16373.

McFarlane, T. J. 1995. *The spiritual function of mathematics and the philosophy of Franklin Merrell-Wolff.* http://www.integralscience.org/sacredscience (accessed September 10, 2006).

Merali, Z. 2006. Free will—you only think you have it. *New Scientist* 6 May 2007:8.

Naik, A., O. Buu, M. D. LaHaye, A. D. Armour, A. A. Clerk, M. P. Biencowe, and K. L. Schwab. 2006. *Nature* 443(7108):193–195.

Polkinghorne, J. 2002. The new physics and opportunities for ontological initiatives. *International Conference on Foundations of the Ontological Quest—Prospects for the New Millennium, Rome, Vatican City.* http://www.pul.it/CD%20IRAFS'02/index.htm (accessed September 10, 2006).

———. 2006. *Exploring reality: The intertwining of science and religion.* New Haven, CT: Yale University Press.

Randall, L. 2005. *Warped passages: Unraveling the mysteries of the universe's hidden dimensions.* New York: HarperCollins.

Sarath, E. 2003. Meditation in higher education: The next wave? *Innovative Higher Education* 27(4):215–233.
Schafer, L. 2006. Quantum reality and the consciousness of the universe. *Zygon: Journal of Religion and Science* 41(3):505.
Smolin, L. 1998. *The life of the cosmos.* New York/Oxford: Oxford University Press.
Sorokin, P. 1992. *The crisis of our age.* Oxford: Oneworld.
Tarnas, R. 2006. *Cosmos and psyche: Intimations of a new worldview.* New York: Viking Adult Press.
Turner, H. 1998. *The roots of science: An investigative journey through the world's religions.* New Zealand: The DeepSight Trust.
Wilber, K. 1998. *The marriage of sense and soul; Integrating science and religion.* New York: Random House.

Acknowledgment

I wish to thank Theodore Slovin for his many insights and suggestions on science and spirituality, particularly when we were teaching a course on this topic, and also my colleagues in the Community for Integrative Learning and Action (The CILA Project) for their development of an integrative worldview. And finally I acknowledge the support, advice, and guidance of my spouse, Kathleen L. Scott.

CHAPTER 15

Religion and Spirituality in the Practice of Health Care

Allen Pelletier

Scenario

A resident physician[1] in our clinic came to me to discuss a problem he was having with one of our patients, Mr. Hadeed, a middle-aged insulin-dependent diabetic. His diabetes appeared to be poorly controlled, and he was experiencing wild fluctuations in blood sugar level, from dangerously low to dangerously high. Mr. Hadeed insisted he was taking insulin twice daily, exactly as prescribed. The medical resident wondered if Mr. Hadeed was being completely honest with us. Was he skipping insulin doses, then taking too much or not adhering to the carefully scripted diabetic diet we had provided? Our resident physician was concerned and frustrated at the same time. He thought Mr. Hadeed was a "non-compliant patient," one who does not or will not stick to a prescribed course of medical treatment.

Several attempts at adjusting Mr. Hadeed's insulin regimen had failed. I suggested that our resident schedule Mr. Hadeed for a visit with our diabetic educator (a clinical pharmacist). During the course of this interview, the nature of the problem became suddenly obvious. Mr. Hadeed was a devout Muslim and was observing traditional Islamic religious practices during the period of Ramadan. This annual cycle during the Islamic religious year is often (somewhat erroneously) referred to as the "fast of Ramadan." This is a period of heightened and intense spiritual commitment for the devout Muslim. It includes both a time of fasting (during daylight hours, when both food and water are proscribed) and feasting (after sunset, when the faithful gather to celebrate with communal meals where they eat to their hearts' content).

Mr. Hadeed was indeed giving himself insulin twice daily. His daytime fasts led to dangerously low blood sugars, since he was administering insulin without food. The evening feasts led to precisely the opposite result, since his insulin intake was now inadequate to handle the glucose load of his large

---

[1] "Resident physician" refers to a doctor (usually with an M.D. or D.O. degree) who is in a period of specified post-graduate training, leading to certification in a particular medical field.

meal. Once we realized this, we instructed Mr. Hadeed how to adjust his insulin regimen, and his blood sugar became much better controlled. He also appreciated the fact that we respected his religious practice, since no other physician had done so before.

Analysis of Scenario

Spirituality is notoriously difficult to define. For my purposes, spirituality can be broadly defined as the experience of transcendence, both intrapersonal (development of the self) and connection to God or a higher power outside the self (Coyle 2002). Religion has been distinguished somewhat from spirituality. Religion is the more formal pattern of beliefs, codified observances and practices that express spirituality. Spirituality is usually thought of in highly individualistic terms. Religion is, one might say, the outward and visible practice of an inner spirituality. As such, religion includes the communal dimension: relationships, family, and often (although not always) membership or some formal connection with an institution that expresses a particular set of beliefs.

Religious and spiritual commitments held by individuals, their families, or even a whole community, can have a major role in health and health-care decision-making. Individuals bring prior spiritual and religious commitments into our offices and hospitals. My contention is that physicians, nurses, and allied health-care professionals in North America, at least, are trained in ways of thinking about health that tend to exclude and marginalize the spiritual and religious dimension of human experience.

The "biomedical model" of health and disease still shapes the training of most health-care professionals in North America. The fundamental assumption is that health can largely (if not exclusively) be understood in the language and terminology of biochemistry, anatomy, physiology, and genetics. Disordered biochemistry or physiology is the basis of disease. The task of the clinician is to intervene to restore a "normal" (disease-free) state produced by pathologic processes. This approach is scientific, empiric, and disease centered.

I will not disagree that the rigorous application of the scientific method to health care has served us well in many ways. Few, I think, have any desire to return to the pre-antibiotic era, or the horrors of surgery or dental work without anesthesia. Nevertheless, I argue that the training and practice of most health professionals in North America focuses heavily on science and technology in the medical encounter, to the extent that other modes of understanding and relating to the human experience of wellness, health, and illness are generally ignored. In our preoccupation with the analytic and the rational aspect of the medical encounter, we can miss "seeing" and knowing, relating with and deeply understanding, the person who is right in front of us. Wordsworth maintained that we "murder to dissect." We have dissected science and technology away from faith and mystery. We pay the price in truncated medical encounters that fail to address the whole person.

The role of the health professional is, of course, to arrive at a correct diagnosis and to develop the plan of treatment accordingly. There is nothing inherently wrong with setting achievable numeric goals, whether that is a goal for weight loss, a target for blood pressure control, or a target for blood sugar. Furthermore, none of the assumptions of biomedicine inherently *exclude* factors related to behavior (diet, exercise, motivating the patient to perform the onerous task of monitoring the glucose in his or her blood). So what is the problem here?

To explain the scenario that opened this chapter, I believe we must begin by understanding some of the ways that typically define (and thereby limit) interactions with patients. Health-care professionals tend to focus on technique and manipulation of numbers (the biomedical paradigm) and exclude matters of the spirit. They rarely ask, "What could faith or religious practice possibly have to do with _____ (diabetes, heart failure, arthritis, etc.)?"

The failure to take Mr. Hadeed's religious practice into account had not been a calculated or malicious decision. Rather, it was simply a failure to recognize that religious practice can have something to do with health and health care. This blind spot locked the practitioner into a set of assumptions about the clinical situation, from which followed certain logical (but entirely incorrect!) conclusions about what to do to "fix" the problem.

The medical resident focused on defining success or failure in terms of blood glucose numbers. Following the logic of the biomedical model, achieving success should be a matter of applying science and following correct technique. The medical resident had done his part by diagnosing and defining a treatment plan. He had instructed the patient in proper technique. Therefore, failure to achieve the goal must be the fault of the patient.

Besides being incorrect, this false conclusion could have resulted in a tragic breakdown of the doctor-patient relationship in mistrust and suspicion on both sides. The health-care provider assumed Mr. Hadeed was ignoring sound advice and was being less than honest when reporting adherence to recommended diet and insulin treatment. Eventually Mr. Hadeed would become aware of being labeled as a "difficult" patient, or worse, subtly accused of being a liar. The latter would be an especially egregious insult to a devout Muslim, who prizes truth telling as a high virtue. Equally disastrous, Mr. Hadeed's blood glucose fluctuations could have caused severe medical complications. By focusing intently on the goal of blood sugar control, we missed the goal. The paradox is that our focus narrowed our vision, preventing us from accomplishing the very thing we sought to achieve.

This was a treatment failure, but one that is really only understandable in light of allegiance to a model of understanding health that all too often ends up reducing the health-care encounter to mere technique. We failed to see the person, with his prior religious and spiritual commitments. We not only missed achieving the goal of good patient care but also risked destroying the doctor-patient relationship.

Once Mr. Hadeed's religious practices were brought out into the open, we took a step toward recovering the person behind the label "diabetes." We were able to tailor a treatment regimen that both respected his religious commitment and achieved the goal of better blood-sugar control.

Advice for Related Situations

Several salient lessons emerge out of this scenario. The first is simple yet profound. We must train ourselves first, then our health-care students, to look beyond the biomedical model to see the whole person. The power of the biomedical model is that it undeniably gives us powerful and precise tools for analysis of disease states such as diabetes. However, when we focus our attention only on lab tests, X-ray studies, numbers and technique, we tend to forget that the person in front of us is more than a set of numbers. Sometimes, simply stepping back and observing the whole context places things in their proper relationship and focus. I often remind my students: "Remember that we treat people, not lab values."

The practice of medicine is fundamentally a relational art that historically was understood to require specific moral, spiritual, and even religious commitments from the practitioner (Cameron 1992). The Hippocratic Oath, on which the entire Western tradition of health care has been built, implicitly recognizes the spiritual and religious commitments of both the person/patient and the person/health provider. Health and religious commitment were never seen as separate or in competition with each other. The one can and does affect the other.

The second lesson is to remember that the person in our office or hospital bed does not exist in a vacuum. He or she lives in a network of family, friends and community. This "biopsychosocial" model of health and health care at least takes social relationships into account and so is an improvement on the biomedical paradigm. But even this does not go quite far enough. Persons come into our offices and hospitals with all sorts of personal values, including spiritual and religious convictions. They do not check these beliefs at the front desk, so to speak, as so much excess baggage that is not to be brought into the medical encounter. Spiritual and religious beliefs are translated into practices that can directly influence health and health status.

A number of studies demonstrate a positive correlation between religious observance and health (Koenig 2002). Patients who attend religious services on a regular basis are less likely to use tobacco or abuse alcohol, for example. Some religious beliefs may promote unhealthy behavior. For example, fatalism, the idea that I can do nothing to control my destiny, may lead to harmful health practices, such as neglect of immunizations or other preventative health measures.

Here are just a few examples where knowledge of the patients' spiritual beliefs and religious practice may be of great practical importance: the Muslim patient who observes Ramadan (the scenario we have discussed); the Jehovah's Witness, who will likely have deeply held scruples about accepting a blood transfusion; the patient who for religious or spiritual reasons adopts a vegetarian or vegan diet, and who may need vitamin or mineral supplements. In addition, it is important to know about a patient's wishes for end of life care and to help a patient struggle with difficult issues such as placing an aged parent in nursing home care.

Knowing a patient's particular faith commitment provides insight into family and community resources. For example, patients may look to a religious leader for advice with a difficult medical decision. They may want their provider to know this, or even to discuss the pros and cons of a particular medical decision with their spiritual authority. Patients may want a chaplain, pastor, priest, or imam notified when they are in the hospital. All of these things can immeasurably strengthen the bond between patient and provider and provide additional sources of support for patient care.

Many patients indicate they are open to praying with a provider. This is a sensitive and highly individual matter, beyond the scope of this discussion.

However, many patients do want their provider to pray with them, especially during a difficult or painful illness, when a loved one is seriously ill, or when the medical prognosis is not good.

Health-care providers need not feel threatened or uncomfortable with addressing spirituality and religion in the health-care setting. With a little training and practice, spiritual and religious values can be assessed in a non-intrusive and sensitive manner. After all, health-care professionals learn to collect all kinds of sensitive and potentially embarrassing information from patients. We routinely inquire about the status of personal relationships, sexual activity, and practices, divorce, alcohol use, illicit substance use, depression, abuse, and domestic violence. It is not any more difficult or embarrassing to include a survey of the patient's spiritual and religious commitments than it is to collect this other information.

Many instruments are available to help health professionals quickly and efficiently survey spiritual beliefs and religious practices that may affect health. One of the simplest is a self-administered questionnaire that the patient completes on his or her first visit to a medical office or hospital facility. During an interview, the provider may incorporate a brief "spiritual history" or "spiritual inventory" as part of their routine. A number of approaches have been suggested (Anandarajah and Hight 2002; Maugans 1996; Pulchaski and Romer 2003).

It is also important to realize that we do not practice medicine in isolation. Most medical offices, and all hospitals certainly, rely on a multidisciplinary, team approach to health care. In the scenario, a clinical pharmacist, not a physician, realized the importance of religious practice in understanding the patient's poorly controlled diabetes. If a provider genuinely feels unqualified to approach matters of spirituality and religion in the health-care setting, then at least he or she can partner with other health professionals or chaplains to help here.

Finally, I maintain that we need a model of health care that recognizes people as more than the sum of their biology, genetic make up, or even social interactions. Such a model is being developed. This new philosophy (some would say, rather, the recovery of ancient wisdom about health) has been called "integral medicine," "integrative medicine," or "patient-centered health care." It is not always entirely clear what these terms mean. Some proponents use the term to mean a blend of Western biomedicine with Eastern mysticism; others advocate openness to a wide variety of "alternative" medical treatments ranging from herbal medications to manipulative therapies, such as acupuncture or reflexology.

The paradigm I am advancing might be defined as the intentional and conscious practice of "bio-psycho-social-spiritual-religious personal awareness" in all health-care encounters. The term is ungainly, and certainly not euphonious. You can call it whatever you like. The term merely describes the approach to health care I am advocating, and that is what matters.

The point here is to recognize that each component part (the biological, the self, the social, the spiritual and the religious, the whole person) has its proper place in medical care. This model does not force an "either/or" approach but rather sees each of the component parts as distinguishable, yet related and interconnected. This is a "perspectival" approach to health and health care. Each part serves as one "perspective" or lens through which the practitioner may focus the counter. Each encounter with a patient will emphasize one or perhaps several of these perspectives, depending on the circumstances, yet that perspective is never divorced from the whole. With my colleague John McCall, I have described an approach to teaching this model in a state medical school (Pelletier and McCall 2005).

If we treat the whole person, we can avoid the pitfalls I believe limit the biomedical and biopsychosocial models of health as presently taught and practiced. We can begin to develop a more deeply relational style of health care that treats the biological, social, personal, and religious dimensions of persons with appropriate seriousness and proper balance. I believe this model (whatever it is ultimately called) will restore rich and deeply meaningful relationships with our patients. It may even help us in the health professions to recover our own humanity and "calling" to our noble art and to pass this on to the next generation of health-care providers.

References

Anandarajah, G., and E. Hight. 2002. Spirituality and medical practice: Using the HOPE questions as a practical tool for spiritual assessment. *American Family Physician* 63:81–89.

Cameron, N. G. de S. 1992. *The new medicine: Life and death after Hippocrates.* Wheaton, IL: Crossway Books.

Coyle, J. 2002. Spirituality and health: towards a framework. *Journal of Advanced Nursing* 37(6):594.

Koenig, H. G. 2002. *Spirituality in patient care: Why, how, when, and what.* West Conshohocken, PA: Templeton Foundation Press.

Maugans, T. A. 1996. The SPIRITual history. *Archives of Family Medicine* 5:111.

Pelletier, A. L., and J. W. McCall. 2005. A modular curriculum for integrating spirituality and health care. In *Spirituality in Higher Education. New Directions for Teaching and Learning,* no. 104, eds. S. L. Hoppe and B. W. Speck, 51–58. San Francisco: Jossey-Bass.

Puchalski, C. M., and A. L. Romer. 2003. Taking a spiritual history allows clinicians to understand patients more fully. *Journal of Palliative Medicine* 3(1):129–137.

CHAPTER 16

The Strident Duet

Moses L. Pava

Scenario

I entered Avi's grade into the computer system with the other 75 grades from last semester three weeks ago. Now, Avi was the first person I saw as I returned to campus for the first time in a month for the new spring semester. With a grim and serious look, he told me he was surprised and very disappointed at the "low" grade I had given him. He almost never gets lower than an A–, and he certainly didn't expect this kind of a grade, a B+, in business ethics. "It's so subjective," he said, adding that "It was nothing like the finance courses I usually ace!"

Avi was careful to explain to me that he is not like some of the other students who might go to the Dean to complain about a low grade. "That's just not my way," or so he told me, anyway. However, he needed to talk to me about the grade right away. As I took off my winter coat and boots, I thought to myself, "oh boy, let the games begin."

I told Avi that I would be happy to talk to him, but we needed to set up some ground rules. First, we would limit our discussion to 10 minutes (if we need more time, we could continue the conversation the next week). Second, no negotiation about the grade. I explained that if I made a calculation error I would be happy to change it, but if it's a judgment call, "I just don't negotiate," I repeated. I had read his paper twice and had given his grade a good deal of thought (or at least as much thought as any of the other 75 grades). Third, I would be happy to explain to him what I felt the strengths and weaknesses were in his final paper, and I would encourage him to point out his own views. Avi agreed to the ground rules with a hesitant nod in my direction, but I was certain his sole goal was to get me to change the grade.

I was angry about what I interpreted as his veiled threat to go to the Dean, but I tried to put those feelings away. I began by telling him that, first of all, a B+ is a good grade. He selected an interesting situation to write about, and he did a good job describing what happened. The reason he didn't get an A, though, was that he didn't analyze his defining moment in a sufficiently systematic or deep way. The assignment had been to describe and analyze an ethical situation that had an important impact on his life. Avi chose an interesting episode that had occurred a few month earlier at a job interview. He did a great job describing what happened to him, and he even did a good job talking about his feelings both during and after the interview. All the while, though, his thoughts and observations remained on the surface. He seemingly refused, or was just unable, to truly examine the roots and implications of his own dilemma.

Part of the assignment was to talk about how the dilemma might help him in the future, but in Avi's case, although I didn't put it in these precise terms to him, he seemed to be uninterested in learning anything new about himself. Avi ignored everything but the most peripheral and obvious effects of his decision. As I discussed his performance in the class, I was torn as his teacher between my obligation as to be as honest as I possibly could and my obligation to encourage his future growth and curiosity. The more honest I was, the more accurate I was, and the more accurate I was, the better I would be able to explain (defend) why I gave him a B+ and not an A.

But, my goal was not just to defend my grading system, it was also to encourage Avi to better understand and analyze his own motivations in the future. I began the ethics class on day one by noting that one of the reasons we study ethics is to learn how to understand our past behavior better in order to improve future behavior. I knew the more brutal I was in describing the limitations of his paper, the less he would listen. How to find a balance? Enough truth to justify giving him the lower grade, but not enough truth to discourage him from ever thinking about these issues again.

Avi disagreed with my interpretation, claiming that he had done everything that I had asked him to and more. Again, he reminded me that "I'm just not the kind of student who goes to the Dean ... that's just not an option for me!" He emphasized how he did not get his paper off of the Internet, but had done all the work himself. "Wouldn't you please reconsider the grade?" he asked again. I mockingly laughed and said to myself, "Because you didn't cheat on a business ethics paper, you want me to give you an A?"

I looked at the clock and told him that our self-imposed time limit was just about up. It sounded like we would need to continue our conversation next week, but I did remind him, that the only point in meeting would be to better understand each other. "I don't negotiate grades with students," I said one last time. I thanked him for his feedback and told him that what I took from our conversation was that in the future I would try to be a little more careful in how I worded the assignments. Perhaps, I wasn't as clear about what I had wanted from students as I thought I was. As Avi began to gather his belongings together, he quickly wiped away a tiny tear that had somehow escaped from this supremely confident student.

Analysis of Scenario

I had suspected all semester that Avi was really only interested in his grades and would have gladly stopped coming to class if I had promised him an A. But Avi is a good kid. He's smart, ambitious, and he did come to class displaying good leadership skills during his group project. I have little doubt that he will enjoy a successful and financially rewarding career in finance.

In making Avi cry, what have I really accomplished? I tried to contain my anger at his strategically-placed Dean remarks—at least that's how I imagined them, but, to tell the truth, those feelings clearly drove me to adopt a "professional tone" with him. By the end of our conversation, I did feel empathy for him, but I felt stuck—my hands were tied (had I tied them myself?). I thought about my own run-ins with teachers over the years—I don't think I ever won one of those contests either.

As I reflect back, on what was happening between us, it seems almost as if we were singing some kind of strident duet—the louder he proclaimed he would not go to the Dean, the louder I responded by telling him I don't negotiate grades. We were both talking, but neither one of us was talking to the other one. Grades are an incredibly powerful stick with which to beat students, but why would any teacher want to beat his students?

I'm hired and paid to be Avi's teacher. Somehow, though, in my office, on that day, I became his antagonist and not his teacher. Perhaps I had been too tough on Avi. Maybe I was judging him on a different scale from other students in the class? Maybe he really did deserve an A? You know what, business ethics really is much more subjective than finance. I have my doubts, and Avi seemed to sense this, but fortunately for me he's not going to go to the Dean, at least not yet.

In my self-doubt, my thoughts turned to spirituality. To my mind the word spirituality most usefully describes a quality of everyday experience. An experience of integrity and connection. A feeling of being at home everywhere in this vast universe. It is a going home to a place that you've never been before. It is this-worldly and not other-worldly. This experience can be associated with many kinds of practical and prosaic aims, activities, and projects, especially, in my view, teaching undergraduates business ethics. This is why I believe my meeting with Avi had provided me a unique opportunity to experience spirituality. Unfortunately, in the end, it was a botched opportunity.

Martin Buber once wrote that "The world is not comprehensible but it is embraceable; through the embracing of one of its beings" (2006). This is the kind of profound and natural spirituality to which I aspire, but, as this scenario illustrates, sometimes fail at.

Were I given the opportunity to do this over, how might I change things to improve the outcome? I believe that there are several practices one can adopt in order to experience spirituality. These include acceptance, commitment, reasonable choice, mindful action, and dialogue. In the case at hand, I believe that the practice of dialogue is most relevant.

In dialogue, there is a flow of meaning among the participants. A dialogue is not the same thing as a discussion or a debate. In dialogue everyone is committed to making meaning together. To participate in a dialogue requires one to listen to another, to respect one another, to suspend one's own beliefs and to let go of one's judgments, and to express one's unique voice. In dialogue, we move beyond toleration and argumentation into a place where we feel comfortable reflecting about our own thoughts and attachments. There is a mutual recognition that this not about you or me, but it is about us. In dialogue we are accountable to one another and we are responsible for one another. Dialogue is not just about identifying a set of facts. Dialogue is about emotions. How do we feel about each other? In dialogue, I must be true to my anger, fear, joy, sadness, and love, just as I must respect the full spectrum of your emotions.

Dialogue is also about identity. The very point of dialogue might be thought of as trying to figure out what it means to be us. Dialogue demands openness, honesty, and imagination. In a real dialogue, I might suddenly take your point of view and you can take mine because we both realize that our talk is not really about promoting our own views. As I begin to see things as you see them, my own view is altered.

So, if I was given another chance with Avi, I would try to listen better, respect him more, and suspend my own judgments. As I re-read my own description of this scenario, I see myself as defensive and full of suspicion. Rather than going out to embrace Avi, as Buber (2006) would suggest, I see myself as withdrawing and building a wall around myself. Avi never really threatened to go to the Dean; I drew that conclusion. He may very well have agreed with my initial ground rules, but I assumed he only wanted me to change his grade. I assumed Avi was uninterested in learning anything new about himself, but this was a completely unwarranted assumption. My goal, I asserted, was not just to defend my grading system, it was also to encourage Avi to better understand and analyze his own motivations in the future. But, how true is this?

As important as all of these issues are, however, I believe the most important question I need to ask myself is whether or not I truly expressed my own unique voice in this situation. As I experienced this situation I truly was torn between my dual obligations of being as honest as I possibly could and encouraging his future growth and curiosity. Now, though, with the aid of 20–20 hindsight, I see this perceived trade-off between honesty and encouragement as an artifact of my own fear. I should have been more open and honest with Avi about the limitations of his paper in order to encourage his growth and development. My inability to own and express my beliefs about business ethics was a major cause of our inability to communicate with one another. Deep change does not begin by changing the other, but by changing one's self first. This to me is the real lesson of our strident duet.

Advice for Related Scenarios

We often assume that there is a trade-off between integrity and connection. I can be more honest and authentic, but only if I move away from you. Alternatively, I can move closer to you, but only by compromising my own integrity and sense of self. Spiritual opportunities are those situations that allow us to enhance both integrity and connection simultaneously. I failed to frame my encounter with Avi in spiritual terms and viewed it exclusively as business as usual ("oh boy, let the games begin").

The conclusion I draw from all of this is that every situation we face is potentially spiritual. The question we have to ask ourselves is do we have the imagination to see it this way? In addition, do we have the courage to seize the infinite opportunities our already rich and complex lives offer us?

Rabbi Nachman of Bratslav, one of the most famous Hasidic Rabbis, once said that "the whole world is a narrow bridge, and the most important thing is not to fear" (Levin 2004). This kind of a bridge is an apt metaphor for dialogue and the spirituality to which it leads. There is a deep fear in joining together with others and our dialogues should openly recognize this fact. But, I think, we should be even more afraid of standing alone, singly. Dialogue is the bridge that connects us and this is exactly why it is so essential to spirituality and the blending of integrity and integration.

References

Buber, M. n.d. Thinkexist.com. http://en.thinkexist.com/quotes/with/keyword/ comprehensible/ (accessed April 5, 2006).

Levin, M. 2004. *The whole world is a narrow bridge*. http://72.203.104/search/-cache;:tjGb87QUTMJ:beth-torah.org/Sermons/Yiskor%25 (accessed April 5, 2006).

CHAPTER 17

Integrating Spirituality in Education Courses

Larry D. Burton
Constance C. Nwosu

Scenario

Monday, 4:27 p.m. Janet gathers her course materials around her in an arc on the desk. She opens *Models of Teaching* (Joyce, Weil, and Calhoun 2004) and contemplates how she will conclude her three-week unit of instruction on inductive thinking methods. She silently prays for guidance as she constructs the lesson. Her main goal for this lesson is to see how she might help her students probe their deeply held beliefs about education and see how these beliefs relate to their spirituality. For Janet, spirituality concerns one's relationship with the supernatural. She views spirituality as the core dimension of a person's life. Her aim in teaching is to help her students align all dimensions of their lives, including the professional, with their spiritual core.

Since it is ten weeks into the semester, she has already led her students, all in their final year of secondary education, through multiple learning experiences focused on two different teaching strategies: cooperative learning and role play. They are proficient at using both of these strategies as well as inductive thinking methods and have demonstrated emerging teaching skills with them as well. After tomorrow's class the students will be engaged in a three-week field experience. Janet wants to conclude these ten weeks with a meaningful synthesis of the learning she has been trying to foster.

Since this general methods course for secondary education focuses on the process of teaching and learning, Janet sometimes feels a tension surrounding the "content" of this course. Strictly speaking, the content of her course is the process of teaching. But Janet wants her students to think beyond the "how to" of teaching methods. She wants her students to explore spiritual implications of using specific teaching methods.

She thinks one final role play experience will help accomplish those goals. Her first task is to create a problem situation that will catch her students' interest. She has little problem generating ideas for this lesson launch; she simply relies on her personal experience as a high school English teacher, and, more recently as supervisor of student teachers. After several minutes of writing and revising, she is satisfied with her work. The problem situation reads like this:

> Javier Mendez is a young, enthusiastic high school teacher. He invests a great deal of his time and money into his students. One day after school Mrs. Wilson appears to discuss her daughter's experiences in Mr. Mendez's class. Javier is surprised when Mrs. Wilson says, "Why do you teach teenagers to cheat in class? All I hear about your class is how students can work together and they have fun playing in class. School is supposed to be hard work!"

Next, Janet crafts questions to prompt her students' thinking as they analyze this situation. She settles on two broad questions: "How would you describe the basic problem in this situation?" and "What are the possible sources of conflict in this situation?" These two questions will "force" her students to tap into their critical thinking skills and will help them understand how to confront issues and find resolutions. Janet recognizes the ability to think critically and resolve issues will help her students work toward the alignment of their spirituality and their professional actions.

As the majority of students will be watching and only a few students will enact each scene, Janet decides on roles to assign the observers. Since she wants to connect this role play lesson closely to the content of her course, she chooses two primary roles. Half of the class will focus on "Mr. Mendez" during the enactment and observe how effective he is in communicating his reasons for his instructional choices. The other half of the class will focus on the enactments in general and try to identify additional issues or sources of conflict as they arise as well as propose scenes for further enactments. Janet wraps up the planning for her role play lesson by creating additional questions for use in discussing each enactment and for helping the students generalize their learning at the conclusion of the lesson.

Tuesday, 10:00 a.m., Janet uses a computer projector to display the problem situation she crafted yesterday. As the students read the situation, several chuckle and Clarisse remarks under her breath, "That happened in my high school."

Since they are familiar with the role play process, the lesson starts quickly. The students list three possible sources of conflict in the situation: differences in level of education, miscommunication between school and home, and stereotypical perceptions toward schooling. The class suggests two or three locations for the initial confrontation but settles on the idea of having the action begin in the hallway outside of the principal's office. Kareem volunteers to play the role of Mr. Mendez while Clarisse volunteers to play Mrs. Wilson. A third student, Jackie, volunteers to play the role of the principal "just in case" the principal is needed. While the actors prepare for their first enactment, Janet gives the observers their assigned tasks.

First Enactment, 10:08 a.m. As with many role play lessons, the first enactment is fairly superficial as the actors begin to create a character and act from that perspective. Janet stops action after about 90 seconds for the first discussion. She asks the students who were focused on Mr. Mendez to share their observations. The observers report that Mr. Mendez seemed to be defensive in his responses and unsure in his defense of what happened in his classroom. The second set of observers suggest three alternate enactments or re-enactments, and the class finally decides to re-enact the same scene with Mr. Mendez applying the principle of "seeking first to understand" (Covey 1992, 45).

Second Enactment, 10:14 a.m. As the second enactment unfolds, Mr. Mendez tries to listen more than speak. The few times he speaks, he asks clarifying questions of Mrs. Wilson. After about three minutes of action, Janet closes the enactment and asks for feedback from the observers. The first group of observers were pleased that Mr. Mendez did not appear as defensive in this enactment but were disappointed that he found no opportunity to explain his instructional choices. The second group of observers indicates that the enactment ended with what seemed like a "victory" for Mrs. Wilson since she had been able to make all of her points, while Mr. Mendez had been able to make none of his. They think this lack of clarity in communication will lead to future conflict. The class decides Mr. Mendez should work toward a "win-win" solution in the next enactment. Janet asks for two new volunteers to play the parts of Mr. Mendez and Mrs. Wilson.

Third Enactment, 10:23 a.m. The new actors try to incorporate the suggestions from the class as they re-enact the scene. After listening to Mrs. Wilson for about one minute, Mr. Mendez thanks her for coming to him to discuss her concerns and suggests they move their discussion to his classroom where he will be able to show her examples of the kinds of work he assigns to his students. As the two actors begin to "walk" toward Mr. Mendez's classroom, Janet breaks the action.

She turns to the rest of the class, "Does this action help the characters move toward a win-win resolution of the conflict? Why or why not?" The students discuss their ideas with a partner and report back to the entire class. Most members of the class view the movement of the discussion to the classroom as a positive move. After this short discussion Janet allows action to resume.

After another minute of action the conversation between Mr. Mendez and Mrs. Wilson begins to resemble that in the first enactment. Janet ends the enactment and starts the class's discussion. The observers watching Mr. Mendez believe he is still having a hard time expressing his reasons for his instructional decisions. Janet asks, "How about you? Can you give some good reasons for methods you are planning to use during your field experience next week?" She then asks the students to form groups of four and identify what they think are the core educational beliefs of each character in the role play. She allows five minutes for this discussion. The class decides they want to restart the enactment at the point the players entered the teacher's classroom. A female student volunteers to play the teacher's role, so Mr. Mendez becomes Ms. Mendez.

Fourth Enactment, 10:33 a.m. As action begins for the fourth enactment, Ms. Mendez asks Mrs. Wilson a question, "Do you believe that students learn best when the teacher is up front and in charge?" This leads into a discussion of both characters' beliefs about what makes a good school and leads to positive student learning outcomes. Janet lets this enactment reach its natural conclusion. During the discussion session students seem to be satisfied that the last enactment was realistic and a positive solution to a potentially negative situation. They identify three principles that they think led to the positive resolution of the situation: seeking to understand the other, searching for a win-win resolution, and explaining educational practices on the basis of beliefs about education.

Generalization of Principles, 10:45 a.m. To transition to the final portion of her role play lesson, Janet asks the students to identify other situations in their personal or professional lives where these three principles might be important. Students discuss the question in groups of four before responding. They generate the following ideas: in dealing with teaching colleagues, in job interviews, in relationships with educational administrators, or in parenting.

Janet now poses her final question prompts to the students. This is what she has been working toward throughout the entire semester. She projects it on the screen so all can see it clearly, "What are your deeply held beliefs about education? Where do those beliefs come from? What teaching processes are best aligned with your belief system? Which teaching processes are opposed to your educational beliefs?" Janet knows that individuals' professional and life decisions tend to be shaped by their core beliefs, which are based on their spirituality. Therefore, these questions are intended to help her students discover their deeply held beliefs and where they come from.

Then Janet tells the class, "This is your final examination. You will write a five-page paper answering these questions. Start with the ideas you have already expressed at the beginning of the semester in your educational philosophy paper and move on from there. Identify your beliefs and their sources. For example, do you believe all children can learn? If so, where does that belief come from? Next clearly identify any teaching processes you feel you can use to support your beliefs and which teaching processes you cannot use because of your educational beliefs. Remember the lessons we learned today from Mr. Mendez and Mrs. Wilson. Be sure to clearly communicate your beliefs and explain your reasoning. Your paper will be due on the last day of class."

Analysis of Scenario

Analysis of the scenario above reveals Janet's approaches to the integration of spirituality in her class. It also discloses her reasons for using such approaches. The first approach Janet employs to integrate spirituality in her class is the pedagogical approach (Nwosu 1999; Burton and Nwosu 2003; Lawrence, Burton, and Nwosu 2005). The pedagogical approach to infusing spirituality in higher education helps students unearth things in their lives without placing the responsibility of labeling or telling on the teacher. A teacher who uses this approach to integrate spirituality in her class purposefully plans instruction she believes will help students confront issues with spiritual implications and help them inspect their daily decision-making processes within the context of their spiritual lives. We see this happen throughout the scenario above. We also notice that Janet spends time outside of class planning. Her focus is on designing learning experiences in such a way that her students will grow academically and spiritually.

In a pedagogical approach, spiritual concerns and issues are infused into the class by using teaching strategies that enhance the learning experience: students are engaged in the learning experience; they are led to think critically and make decisions; they work together to help one another; and they usually enjoy the process as well. In this approach, the teacher does not assume the role of "knowledge repository." Therefore she does not monopolize all the class time "pouring" her knowledge "into the students." Rather, she designs learning experiences that force students to look beyond the immediate and seek the underlying principles, beliefs, values, and reasons in their lives and in their world.

As Janet plans her class sessions, she tries to be very clear about the learning outcomes she wants her students to demonstrate at the end of the lesson. Then she chooses methods from her teaching repertoire that will help promote the type of learning she desires. For example, in the scenario above, Janet chose to use role play because research supports its ability to help students develop decision-making skills and interpersonal problem-solving skills, to consciously examine their personal values and beliefs, and to reflectively analyze these values and beliefs (Joyce, Weil, and Calhoun 2004; Shaftel 1967).

Likewise Janet chose to use discussion in cooperative groups because it provides the opportunity for *all* students to respond to the question posed by the teacher. In the traditional question-answer process only one or two students typically respond to the teacher's questions while the rest of the class may or may not be engaged. Since Janet allows all students to briefly discuss each question she asks and then usually follows this by having a few students share their responses with the full class, she devotes more time to the question-answer process than do some teachers. As a result she takes care to craft questions that are vital to the success of her lesson and usually only asks questions that require higher-level thinking by her students.

Janet's students continue to struggle with the issues they confront and how to resolve them. Rather than telling them what to do and how to approach the situation, Janet uses questions to push their thinking beyond the surface level. Questions force them to think about what they are doing and why they are doing it. Questions lead them to make decisions that affect life beyond this class period, beyond this day, and beyond this life.

By using this approach, Janet is able to equip her students with processes, principles, and skills that they can use in all of their lives' experiences—the ability to think critically, make meaningful choices, and solve problems—all in a manner that is consistent with their individually held beliefs. She is able to help her students examine or re-examine their beliefs, philosophies, and where they spring from. Integration of spirituality in learning works best when students are led to make such discoveries rather than when they are told.

Janet's choice of the pedagogical approach springs from her spiritual beliefs about the nature of her students and her role as a teacher. She believes that her students are created in the image of the Eternal and therefore have the potential, the responsibility, and the freedom to learn, to think critically, to create, and to make decisions. She believes her students need to develop the ability to become thinkers who make wise choices that are of eternal consequence. Since Janet believes her students are responsible for their own actions and their own learning, she does not spend much class time presenting material the students have already been assigned to read or research on their own. Rather she uses class time to clarify, refine, and extend her students' understanding of their assigned readings.

The pedagogical approach to integration of spirituality in the classroom is not the only approach Janet uses. She also implements the attitudinal approach and the ethical approach (Holmes 1987). The attitudinal approach focuses on the attitude of the teacher, the student, and the institution toward integration of spirituality in learning. In the scenario presented above, Janet implements the attitudinal approach first by being professional about her job. She takes the profession of teaching seriously and spends quality time contemplating, preparing, and planning ahead. She understands that she has been called to teach students, not courses. She believes her teaching is spiritual work; therefore, she prays for wisdom about what and how to teach. She knows that as a teacher she is "the living link in the epistemological chain" (Palmer 1993, 29). Therefore, she is aware she could be the only vehicle the Eternal has to help her students achieve their purpose.

In addition, Janet practices reflective teaching. In the scenario, we see how she kept "a pad of paper nearby to jot down ideas, questions, and needed materials for class the next day." She models to her students what a role play lesson plan looks like by preparing one and distributing it to them. She spends time to create a problem-solving exercise that will accomplish her goal for her students, and she "crafts" some questions ahead of time to help push her goal. And, just before the class, she reviews again to ensure that everything is in place.

Furthermore, Janet shows respects to her students not only by greeting them, but also by affording them the opportunity to express themselves; and, she listens to them and works with them. Holmes (1987) observes that "the first task of integration is at the personal level of attitude and motivation" (49). A teacher's attitude towards learning is the "most single factor" (50). Rather than tying spirituality to content or subject matter, a teacher can express spirituality in how he or she relates to students, in how students are treated, and in how they are shown respect.

The third approach to integrating spirituality that Janet uses in the scenario is the ethical approach. Ethical issues come up in every aspect of college life. Ethics is an important aspect for teachers as they are constantly faced with decisions that carry moral implications. The scenario Janet presents in her role play lesson confronts her students with ethical issues. Rather than discuss or "tell" her students about these issues and how to resolve them, she immerses them in a scenario that makes it possible for them to see how they could resolve the problem. The scenario also enables them to unearth their core spiritual beliefs and how they relate to their chosen profession. Holmes (1987) argues that teachers do not teach morals, one aspect of spirituality, only by making factual statements; neither do they have to be pompous or dogmatic. He suggests they can teach morals by creating a system of evaluation that runs through the entire pattern of their courses, in the way they select topics to teach, in the way they state their assumptions at the beginning of classes, and in the readings and papers they assign students.

Advice for Related Disciplines

Integrating spirituality in the classroom is complex and therefore requires approaches that will help both the teacher and the students explore their beliefs and the implications of their beliefs. This type of exploration requires dialogue in an environment in which the teacher does not impose his/her beliefs on the students or indoctrinate them. The three approaches to integrating spirituality exemplified by Janet in the scenario are transferable across disciplines within higher education, but the implementation of the pedagogical approach needs perhaps a bit more explanation for professors in other fields.

This scenario provides a glimpse of one day in Janet's classroom. Not all days look like this day. Her instruction is varied from day to day and depends upon the learning goals selected for a particular lesson. Likewise, professors' classes in other disciplines would look differently and would vary from day to day. Some learning goals, such as mastery of basic knowledge and skills needed to pass external examinations, are easily met through assigned readings that are reinforced by lecture, laboratories, or mastery approaches. Other learning goals require "uncoverage" or in-depth investigation (Wiggins and McTighe 2005). Deciding which content is worthy of "uncoverage" is the responsibility of the professor. "Uncoverage" typically requires additional time and alternative pedagogical approaches to foster meaningful learning in the classrooms.

References

Burton, L., and C. Nwosu. 2003. Student perceptions of the integration of faith, learning, and practice in an educational methods course. *Journal of Research on Christian Education* 12(2):101–135.

Covey, S. 1992. *The seven habits of highly effective people: Principle-centered leadership.* Fireside ed. New York: Simon & Schuster.

Holmes, A. F. 1987. *The idea of a Christian college.* Grand Rapids, MI: Eerdmans.

Joyce, B., M. Weil, and E. Calhoun. 2004. *Models of teaching.* 6th ed. Boston: Allyn and Bacon.

Lawrence, T. A., L. D. Burton, and C. C. Nwosu,. 2005. Refocusing on the *learning* in "Integration of faith and learning." *Journal of Research on Christian Education* 14 (1):17–50.

Nwosu, C. C. 1999. Integration of faith and learning in Christian higher education: Professional development of teachers and classroom implementation. Ph.D. diss., Andrews University, Berrien Spring, MI.

Palmer, P. 1993. *To know as we are known: Education as a spiritual journey.* San Francisco: Harper.

Shaftel, F., and G. Shaftel. 1967. *Role-playing for social values: Decision-making in the social studies.* Englewood Cliffs, NJ: Prentice-Hall.

Wiggins, G., and J. McTighe. 2005. *Understanding by design.* 2nd ed. Alexandria, VA: Association for Supervision and Curriculum Development.

PART THREE

Practice in Student Affairs

CHAPTER 18

Campus Ministries

Keith Garner

Scenarios

Having grown up in a family with strong faith, Steve had not encountered much opposition to this faith until he reached the campus of State University. In his first semester, Steve is confronted by fellow students' lifestyles that are contrary to how he believed. As a Human Studies major, Steve is also confronted with many philosophical beliefs and ideas that run counter to what he believes. With so many voices speaking against what he believes, Steve becomes desperate and begins to feel isolated. Then Steve meets Jill, an upper-class student involved in a campus ministry. As Steve begins to attend the campus ministry meetings with Jill, he finds friends with whom he has much in common. Steve also finds a friend in Bruce, the campus minister. Bruce becomes a great resource for Steve to ask questions of and bounce ideas off of.

As an international student, Anna wants to experience as much of American culture as possible. Having grown up in a country where the state religion was heavily enforced, she is looking for a non-threatening place to learn about Christianity. Anna gets involved with conversational English classes offered at an on-campus Christian organization. Here she finds a friend in her conversation partner, Katie, who not only helps Anna with her English but also becomes a good friend. Katie helps Anna navigate campus life and life in America in general. As they become more comfortable with each other, Anna begins to ask questions about Katie's faith. Katie invites Anna home with her on several weekends and at holidays. Through their friendship Anna not only learns much about Christianity and life in America, but her English also improves greatly. In addition, Katie learns about Anna's beliefs and life in her country. Both girls gain new insight and appreciation for the other's culture.

Analysis of Scenarios

In the previous scenarios, the reader finds two students from very different backgrounds who are both looking for a voice on campus that can help them understand faith and how that faith can fit in on the American campus. A study done by UCLA (Astin et al. 2004) found that the majority of students surveyed see spirituality as important in their college experience. The findings state, "Despite the fact that considerable numbers of students are 'searching for meaning and purpose in life' (75%) and discussing spirituality with friends (78%), more than half (56%) say that their professors never provide opportunity to discuss the meaning and purpose of life" (6). If students are not able to have these discussions in the classroom, then where on campus are they to find a place for these discussions? One vital resource may be found in campus ministries. These religious-based organizations are often staffed with educated theologians or at least devoted, mature people of faith. The ministries are places where students and even faculty and staff can come to have dialog about spiritual issues. Whether the student is a person with a strong faith or one who is seeking, campus ministries can provide a place for students to get answers they may not be finding in the classroom.

In scenario one, Steve's situation is similar to many students who come to campus. Steve has grown up in a faith-based home but has a need to make his faith his own. Steve, like countless other students in similar situations, can go many directions. One is to give in to the pressures from peers around him and abandon the morals and faith with which he has grown up. This may lead Steve to the party scene, destructive sexual relationships, and other derailing experiences. Many students who follow this path end up in despair. For some, a crisis will lead them back to their faith and moral beliefs; many others will not return. In my experience, many students who abandon their faith and follow the path described above will end up either failing at school or dropping out. In Steve's case, the spiritual and moral input he found from professors and peers was mostly counter to his beliefs. In many cases on the campus, the only voice a student hears from a professor is one opposed to religion and spirituality. Even faculty with strong faith are often reluctant to share their faith in the classroom. In contrast, the campus ministry can provide vital support for the student and student affairs staff, creating a place where students can go and openly discuss faith and ask questions. This is especially true when the depth of despair reaches the point that students no longer want to go on living. While university counselors can help with psychological problems, many will not enter the realm of spirituality and use its potential to help a student move from suicidal thoughts to a life of meaning and purpose.

In the case of Steve and students like him, campus ministry can assist with the university's goal of student retention and student contentment on campus. In the UCLA study (Astin et al. 2004), students involved in religious activity showed on average higher grade trends than expected and a higher level of satisfaction with their overall college experience than expected. Consequently, if student affairs personnel and campus ministries can become partners, their collaboration can have a positive effect on the student.

In scenario two Anna comes to America wanting to experience American culture and explore other beliefs. Anna, like many internationals who study in the States, is in need of a support system. Some campuses have more resources than others for internationals, and campus ministries are often especially fertile ground for programs aimed at meeting the needs of international students. Through such programs, students like Katie and Anna are brought together. When friendships form, students have firsthand opportunities to learn about other cultures and beliefs. Thus, campus ministries can work in partnership with international affairs offices on the local campus to help add a personal touch to American campus life. Beyond just helping students make connections, campus ministries can reach out to international students in many ways. Since many international students have a great need to improve their spoken English skills, conversational English classes are a common and helpful first step and do not require a great deal of training for a campus ministry to begin. Basically the campus ministry just needs to have willing students who will spend an hour or more a week with an international student talking and helping him or her learn to pronounce words properly. Most campuses have resources to help international students with written English skills but need available English speaking students for conversation partners. Campus ministries can fill this void with little or no costs.

Campus ministries can partner with the campus staff to help meet the needs of internationals in many other ways. When students arrive in the country, they will need help learning where and how to shop. Even Wal-Mart can be a bit overwhelming for students from other countries. Cooking may also be a challenge when their native foods are not available or at least not commonplace. Campus ministries can assist students in locating people in the community who are from the students' native countries, or they might help students find online sources for the foods they are familiar with.

Another area where campus ministries can be helpful is connecting internationals with American families. This can be done by establishing an adopt-a-student program through local churches with the help of the campus minister or by connecting American students with internationals so that the internationals can go home with an American student on some weekends and holidays. As with Anna, students who have opportunities to spend time in American homes find a rich treasure trove for mining cultural differences and religious beliefs. The goal is not necessarily to persuade foreign students to change their beliefs, but to expose them to other viewpoints while encouraging both American students and international students to think critically about beliefs.

Other ideas include setting up travel opportunities, cultural exchange opportunities, thesis defense parties and Bible studies designed to explain Christian beliefs to students from other religions and backgrounds. Taking international students on a trip to explore local areas of interest, national and state parks, or other areas they may never have experienced is a great way to build relationships. Particularly in the quiet of nature, openings are often found for serious discussions on spiritual issues. Likewise, cultural exchange events are a great way to get American students to think outside themselves and to experience perspectives they might otherwise never consider. In a different setting, thesis defense parties give internationals in graduate programs a place to practice defending their thesis in English before they stand before an often-intimidating committee. These parties are best if they can involve American students who are studying or at least have knowledge of the field that is being discussed.

In most of the scenes in the previous paragraph, a campus minister may learn a great deal more than he or she ever dreamed by hosting these parties. Offering a non-threatening discussion of Christian beliefs can be a great way to have dialogue about your faith with international students. It can also be a mechanism for examining or reaffirming (or sometimes changing) beliefs of all who participate. The leaders of these groups need to be knowledgeable, sensitive and not overzealous. If not handled properly, these groups can be more detrimental than helpful in building relationships with international students. These ideas are just the beginning in a discussion of how the campus and campus ministries can partner together to help international students have a growing and positive experience in America. An international student who has had a positive experience in the States can be the best ambassador the United States and a campus could ask for.

According to Paulson (2003), many schools are doing away with their chaplaincies. Spirituality has become such a sensitive terrain, Paulson says, that even religions-based colleges are often reluctant to delve too deeply into the realm of the spirit. Many other schools across the country are doing away with their Bible Chairs, an organization that brought campus ministries together with the campus for dialogue and cooperation. These campuses try to isolate campus ministries in an attempt to control spiritual input on the campus or to decrease liability for controversial discussions. Instead of seeing campus ministries as a threat, those involved in student affairs should seek to befriend campus ministries in an attempt to gain their assistance in the quest to help students in their spiritual lives.

While secular institutions are often precluded from engaging students in an in-depth analysis of personal beliefs about spirituality, those institutions can ensure students have such options through support of campus ministries. In addition to the areas mentioned above, partnerships can be formed in other contexts. Campus ministries can often be a great resource for local service projects, such as working with ministry-based homeless shelters, crisis intervention groups and local missions. Through service to others, students can find meaning in life, which is often considered the outcome of spiritual quests. Travel opportunity is another area where campus ministries can help student affairs assist students with their search for meaning. Many campus ministries offer summer, Christmas and spring break mission opportunities. These mission trips often take students all over the globe, greatly affecting their college experience as well as strengthening their faith. Providing opportunities for students to see the value of helping others through international mission trips guides them toward a life of servant leadership. Most campus ministers intuitively practice servant leadership, and they lead students to emulate this style of leadership not only by creating opportunities for students to serve but also by demonstrating in their own roles that the leader must first be a servant before he can lead. This involves listening intently to students without being quick to insert the minister's own opinions and beliefs. It requires accepting and empathizing with students whose beliefs may differ from the campus minister's own faith. Students should be encouraged to conceptualize their own beliefs and then examine them critically, rather than being told their beliefs are wrong. A campus leader who is committed to the growth of students will lead them not through direction but through the example he or she sets as they build community and serve the students.

Campus ministries can also be a great support to student affairs in countering drug and alcohol abuse on campus. Recognizing that addiction often follows substance abuse because of genetic makeup, campus ministers can supplement student affairs' interventions through acceptance and support of students who are struggling with issues that drive them toward alcohol or drugs. Often, guilt is a factor that must be examined. While counselors and other student affairs personnel in secular institutions often cannot guide students toward a religious or spiritual approach to forgiveness of self, campus ministers have no such prohibition. Consequently, they can help students see that blaming themselves is harmful and that forgiveness or absolution can allow self-respect to exist simultaneously with imperfection.

Times of crisis, both locally and nationally, illustrate another opportunity for campus ministries to be a resource. The death of a student or faculty can open the door for campus ministries to work with campus administration to aid students who are dealing with tragedy. During times of national and even international crisis, campus ministries can be a resource. After Hurricane Katrina, many campus ministries responded locally to aid evacuees and then took trips to help with the cleanup and recovery. The summer after the tsunami in Asia, many campus ministries organized trips to the affected regions to offer aid. These types of responses give concerned students an opportunity to get involved that might not be present through other means. Through that involvement, the search for meaning—the quest for spirituality—often makes great strides.

Many campus ministries have great resources for developing student leaders. Many of these resources can also be utilized by secular groups too. One example is Campus Crusade for Christ's Web site, LeaderU.com. Using this tool, a local campus minister may be a good resource to aid in developing student government leaders and other key students on campus, helping them work through ethical issues they face in the decisions they must make. Campus ministers can accomplish this by empowering students to take responsibility for their actions after having gone through a process of self-examination. As students move toward leadership roles, they should be guided through questions such as "Who am I?", "What do I believe in?", and "What do I stand for?" Campus ministers can assist students as they try to identify the things that drive them and the things that give them satisfaction, while simultaneously guiding them toward ethical behavior through discussions about values. Students must work their way toward a recognition that behaviors are markers of beliefs and values and that consistency is essential for credible leadership.

With a little communication, campus ministries and student affairs can work together to help students navigate their college experience and explore their spiritual lives. Even campus ministers who have themselves been out of college for only a few years often need to be reminded that student perspectives should be considered and valued. Likewise, having found purpose and meaning in life does not mean that the path taken is the only one that can lead to spiritual awakening. Reading books such as the ones suggested and talking to students with an open mind and heart are essential if students are to see campus ministries not only as safe havens for interacting with others who share their beliefs but also as places where all questions can be asked without fear of being called a heretic. Beliefs and values, like meaning and purpose, are not finite and unquestionable—they should be open to discussion and debate. Those beliefs that are sound and wellfounded can survive questioning and analysis.

Two resources that might be of interest to both the campus staff and the campus minister are: *Chris Chrisman Goes to College* by James Sire (1993) and *Letters from the College Front* by Doug and Ron Hutchcraft (1993). Both books are written from a student perspective and can provide insight into the discussion of the role of spirituality in the life of the student.

Advice for Related Situations

Student Affairs is not the only area of campus with which campus ministries can partner. Because campus ministers differ in their expertise and areas of interest, it is impossible to lay out every area where a campus ministry may be involved. However, some examples of areas on campus that might benefit from a relationship with campus ministries are history, languages, arts, music, drama, speech, athletics, recreation, ethics, science, education, social sciences, and human development and family studies. If a campus minister is a trained theologian, he or she will most likely have a background and insight into history from a religious perspective. This person can be a resource to teach or guest lecture in history classes or to speak at special campus events. Some other trained theologians may have significant knowledge of biblical languages and could teach or lecture in a Greek or Hebrew class. Other campus ministers may have served as missionaries in a foreign country and may speak any number of languages. These ministers could tutor students or help provide cultural training in language classes. Many campus ministries have groups involved in the arts, music, and drama. These groups could partner with a department to put on events for the campus. Many campus ministers are trained or at least have experience in the area of public speaking. These ministers can act as tutors or guest teachers in a speech department. Athletic and recreation departments on campuses often host camps and other activities for children and youths, in the community. Campus ministries can provide caring and reliable student help for these events. Although campus ministers cannot use non-campus ministry forums to advance their own religious beliefs, they can use them to meet and get to know students who may later seek them or their organizations out for spiritual guidance.

Campus ministers can be a source of insight for those in the area of ethics, science, education, social sciences, and human development and family studies. In each of these disciplines a campus minister and students involved in a campus ministry can be a resource for discussions of religion's role. For instance, in the area of ethics a campus minister can aid in the discussion of faith and ethical issues such as euthanasia, abortion, capital punishment, and many others. In the area of science, some campus ministers may be well versed to discuss creation versus evolution. Again, a word of caution is required. Presenting a one-sided view when multiple perspectives clearly exist can be dangerous. Campus ministers, especially in secular institutions, must be cognizant of campus backlash and/or legal ramifications if they are dogmatic in their presentations. The goal is not to use a classroom as a forum for preaching or evangelizing; the goal is to expand students' horizons and their critical examination of truth.

In the field of education a campus minister may be well suited to aid in areas such as teaching styles, religion's role in education, and opportunities for teaching in private religious schools. In the area of social sciences, campus ministries can aid in the discussion of and actively engaging in areas of social concern. Many campus ministers have education and experience in areas of counseling that could be a resource to human studies and family studies departments. In all of the preceding examples, campus ministries and the campus minister can be a resource to the campus.

Again, it must be noted that, especially in secular institutions, a campus minister must not insert his or her beliefs in an inappropriate venue. The role must be to help students critically analyze beliefs and values—not direct them toward one particular religion.

Many different campus ministry groups are found throughout the country, some specific to local campuses, others on multiple campuses throughout the country. Following is a list of contact information for national ministries I am aware of:

- Baptist Collegiate Ministry, formerly BSU (http://www.student.org/)
- Campus Crusade for Christ, a non-denominational, international campus ministry (http://www.campuscrusadeforchrist.com/locator/index.php)
- Chi Alpha Campus Ministry (http://www.chialpha.com/)
- Episcopal Student Center (http://ecusa.anglican.org/)
- InterVarsity Christian Fellowship, a non-denominational international campus ministry (http://www.intervarsity.org/)
- Navigators, a non-denominational, international campus ministry (http://home.navigators.org/us/collegiate/index.cfm)
- Catholic Campus Ministry Association (http://ccmanet.org)
- Wesley Foundation, a national student ministry associated with the United Methodist Church (http://www.gbhem.org/asp/campusMin.asp)

Campus ministries exist to engage the campus community. Such engagement can best be accomplished through a strong working relationship with student affairs, campus administration and the campus at large, producing benefits for everyone involved but most importantly for the individual students served. The search for spirituality can take many paths, and campus ministries can provide maps to places where meaning and purpose can be explored with interaction and support.

References

Astin, A. W., H. S. Astin, J. A. Lindholm, A. N. Bryant, S. Calderone, and K. Szelenyi. 2004. Spirituality in higher education: A national study of college students' search for meaning and purpose, summary of selected findings (2000–2003). Higher Education Research Institute, University of California, Los Angeles. www.spirituality.ucla.edu/results/index.html (accessed January 21, 2006).

Hutchcraft, R., and D. Hutchcraft. 1993. *Letters from the college front.* Grand Rapids, MI: Baker Books.

Paulson, A. 2003. Religious upsurge brings culture clash to college campuses. *The Christian Science Monitor,* December 10. www.csmonitor.com/2003/1210/p01s03-ussc.html (accessed January 12, 2006).

Sire, J. W. 1993. *Christ Chrisman goes to college.* Downers Grove, IL: InterVarsity Press.

CHAPTER 19

Practice in Student Affairs: Counseling

Elliott Ingersoll
Karsten Siebert

Professional organizations like the American Psychological Association and the American Counseling Association generally agree, as does the literature in mental health, that religious and spiritual concerns are integral parts of the human experience that should be attended to in a counseling relationship. However, the often interchangeably used terms "religion" and "spirituality" represent two distinct concepts with, albeit considerable overlap, distinct concerns. In this chapter we will refer to spirituality as an inner attitude that yearns for meaning and relationship with a higher power, while religion refers to a framework, heavily influenced by culture, through which spirituality is expressed. (For a detailed discussion of the myriad ways of defining these concepts see Ingersoll 1994.)

The following case study highlights some of the religious and spiritual concerns that may be encountered in a college counseling setting. Within the framework of the counseling process, the client addresses his presenting problem by moving from an introjected religious perspective to a more reflective spiritual perspective.

Scenario

Jacob, a 20-year-old Caucasian undergraduate, came to the college counseling center with the presenting problem of ambiguity related to his major and ultimately a career. At the time of that first session he was a psychology major but uncertain about whether or not he wanted to pursue graduate training which is a prerequisite to work in the field. As is often the case, after two sessions of career counseling he expressed concerns that he labeled "the real problem" that he wanted to talk about. This "real problem" had to do with his girlfriend and their relationship. He and Amber had been dating since they began college two years ago. They met in their second week of classes and had what he described as a passionate, intense relationship. After a session discussing the relationship, Jacob's "concern" was not clear. Getting up to leave at the end of the fourth session Jacob noted that his concerns were really about their sex life. We began the fifth session on this topic and it was the focus of the remainder of the therapeutic relationship (ten more sessions).

Jacob wanted me to understand that he was raised in a very "moral" household. When asked to describe what "moral" meant in this context he described a traditional, conservative protestant Christian upbringing where sex was never directly discussed but only alluded to pejoratively as something related to marriage. While Jacob loved his family, he purposely chose a college 2,000 miles away from them because he experienced their religious choices to be stifling and wanted to find out who he was apart from family.

Jacob had decided at age 18 that he did not agree with his parents' and sister's religious worldview. He had done a great deal of reading on religions and came to reject his family's understanding of Jesus as the only incarnation of God, the teachings of his church about heaven and hell, and his church's habit of concretely interpreting the Bible. He had read with great interest several Eastern and Western mystics who talked about ecstatic experiences that were mystical in nature and in particular Matthew Fox's "creation spirituality," which interprets the mystics to affirm the natural world and incarnate existence. This led back to his relationship with Amber and their sex life. Jacob said this was the first sexual relationship for both of them. They had been sexually active for six months and practiced birth control. Amber was raised in a more secular household but told Jacob her parents tended to shelter her and her brother. After a general discussion of their relationship, the end of the session was upon us again; as Jacob rose to leave he asked "Is it normal for people to enjoy hurting each other during sex?" I commented on his habit of introducing rich and complex topics at the end of the session. After quickly screening for whether serious harm was being alluded to (it did not appear to be), I asked him to prepare for the next session some thoughts on what he meant by "hurt each other" and "normal."

Jacob was late for our next session and visibly uncomfortable. We explored the nature of his discomfort, some of which was related to his family background and his religious socialization, and some of which was general to talking about sex. Jacob shared that his sex life with Amber was so good it really had turned him against any religion that would try to limit his sexual expression. He was wrestling with not having a great deal of sexual experience, what is "normal" and how that related to his relationship with Amber. Jacob opened up about how he and Amber liked to "hurt each other." This seemed to revolve around sex play like biting, spanking, and what he described as "athletic" types of intercourse. Perhaps the most telling aspect was

Jacob's description of his state following sex. He described a profound sense of peace that in some cases carried through several days and helped him engage other people more positively, less cynically.

Analysis of the Scenario

There seemed to be three primary issues in Jacob's case. The first was how to negotiate and contextualize sexual activities with one's partner and how each couple negotiates what is "normal" within the broad parameters of human sexual ability and preference. The second issue was attacks of guilt and anxiety related to how his family would interpret his sexual activity. He stated on several occasions that these attacks "just come over me" then vanish. He recalled many of the sermons he sat through as a child that emphasized the devil's infinite ways to trick the wayward spirit into sin—the pleasures of the flesh being the most common. While cognitively he claimed not to believe this, emotionally he seemed uncertain as to what he believed. If he had truly rejected his family's religion, why did he still suffer from guilt about his sexual relationship?

The third issue was related to what Jacob described as ecstatic moments during and after sex that he and Amber shared. In these moments, they shared feelings of "oneness" that felt like some of the mystical experiences he had read about. He wondered if sexuality could actually be a spiritual experience or a pathway to the Divine?

The important principles in working with the case of Jacob are psychotherapeutic, religious, and spiritual. Jacob's bewilderment with regard to the normality of his expression of sexuality was easily assuaged. There is little dispute that intimacy between consenting adults that is neither physically, mentally nor emotionally harmful, as was the case between Jacob and Amber, can be considered a normal expression of human sexuality. However, there is a vast difference in opinion what constitutes a moral expression of human sexuality. As Jacob was struggling to normalize his sexuality from a biological as well as a religious/moral perspective, he may have benefited from bibliotherapy on sexual ethics. He may have been surprised to find out that his family's version of sexual ethics is not the only interpretation of the Bible. As Spong (1990) puts it, "sex outside of marriage can be holy and life giving under some circumstances, but it can also be evil and life diminishing under other circumstances" (215).

Jacob's main psychotherapeutic issues were related to a felt dissonance between his cognition and his emotions and his desire for, if not integration, at least resolution of this dissonance. This is important because, as Festinger (1957) described, without support and guidance people who are suffering from a state of dissonance will likely take the path of least resistance to decreasing it, even if that path departs from their sense of what is right. All approaches to counseling and psychotherapy assist clients with such dissonance by making what is overwhelmingly subjective an object of awareness. This is nicely described by Freud's (1964) summary of therapy as a process ending in the realization of "Where it was, there I shall become" (80). In Jacob's case the "it" was the anxiety "attacks" that "just came over him." The idea here is that what Jacob was experiencing as "it" was really a part of himself (a part of his "I"), and one aim of counseling was to help him rediscover and re-own this disowned aspect of self.

The part of himself that he was pushing out of awareness, turning into a third-person "it," was his religious upbringing. In exploring this with Jacob, he was surprised to recall that it was not all negative. In fact, it provided him a great sense of security, especially in childhood. It is a natural cycle of human psychological development to distance oneself from recent identifications so that one can stabilize in newer identifications (Kegan 1982). For example, Jacob had distanced himself from the religion of his childhood in order to explore and stabilize his newly blossoming identity as a young adult. The key here is that an individual eventually needs to re-own those previous identifications—they cannot be kept at a distance forever because, although they are usually remnants of the past, they also contain a good deal of the individual's abilities and potentials. For Jacob, the family and religious experience of childhood contained his potential for healthy relationships and community. He could not access these potentials without making peace with the religious "package" they happened to come wrapped in.

According to Barbour (1997), "anthropologists and sociologists have portrayed the functional role of religion in binding individuals in social groups and in preserving the social order" (267). Moreover, religion teaches individuals to internalize the group's expectations. Given Jacob's childhood experience of family and religion, it can be presumed that his view of the world and his place in this world were basically defined by a Judeo-Christian cosmology. In distancing himself from the religion of his family, Jacob's membership in the social groups of his adolescence as well as his entire cosmology has become questionable, if not obliterated. Consequently Jacob was confronted with what Yalom (1980) terms "ultimate concerns": he was facing the freedom, the isolation and potentially the meaninglessness of his own life, a classic existential crisis.

The substance of Jacob's psychotherapeutic work, therefore, had to focus on the discovery and exploration of his authentic self: Who am I, apart from my family and Amber? Which parts of my self are pushed out of awareness? How do I arrive at values and how do I make meaning? Or to frame it in terms of quite diverse schools of thought: helping Jacob to identify the schemas and underlying assumptions that influence his thoughts and feelings (Cognitive Therapy); helping Jacob to identify his introjects and making contact with his emotions (Gestalt); or helping Jacob to rely on his organismic valuing process instead of introjected parental conditions of worth (Rogerian).

Addressing the spiritual issues of Jacob's case requires a description (as opposed to definition) of the nature of spirituality that a counselor can use in the sessions. There are quite a few such descriptions, some of them pretending to be definitions, which for counseling purposes can be summarized in four general categories. These four descriptions (Wilber 2004) include spirituality as a line of development, spirituality as a level of development, spirituality as a temporary state experience, and spirituality as a particular attitude. We will outline these four definitions and discuss their relevance to Jacob's case.

Spirituality can be summarized as its own line of development that people traverse over the course of their lives. This description elucidates how spiritual worldviews change as individuals grow similar to Fowler's (1981) work on faith development. From this perspective, Jacob was moving from concrete definitions of spirituality provided by his family of origin's religious practice, to defining for himself what spirituality meant. The second description is spirituality as the highest levels in any given line of development. While this did not play a prominent role in Jacob's case, it refers to the fact that the upper levels of any line of development (including sexual development) more and more closely approximate spiritual in their reflection of a mystical union of sorts. In sexuality these levels are the aim of Eastern Tantric and some Western magical (or "magickal") practices.

The third description of spirituality as a temporary state experience did apply to Jacob's case. Clearly he was reporting temporary states correlated with sexual activity that he interpreted as ecstatic and mystical. With regard to the feelings of oneness, I had suggested that Jacob read psychologist Jenny

Wade's (2004) book *Transcendent Sex* as it details interviews with people who felt they had mystical experiences during sex. Jacob found this to be akin to Robinson Crusoe seeing the "footprint in the sand" and supplied some validation that what he was experiencing was not isolated or "weird." It also helped him see that his chosen major of psychology was not mute on this subject, which increased his excitement for graduate-level study.

The final description of spirituality as an attitude seemed related to Jacob's case in the sense that his sexual experiences appeared to positively affect his outlook and interactions with others, sometimes for days at a time. Some developmentalists may attribute this to the limerance stage of a young adult relationship, the stage where romantic love infuses all daily activities with a positive quality. Existentialists on the other hand may interpret this as a result of Jacob defending against his existential anxiety. The ecstatic "fusion" with Amber gives Jacob the illusion of oneness (avoidance of his existential isolation) and the illusion of infinity (avoidance to face the ultimate concern death). However, these rationalizations would seem to be selling the client's experience short in light of how we are describing spirituality. If spirituality can be an attitude that one cultivates toward everyday life (and the psychological literature supports this), then we must consider taking Jacob at his word regarding how his sex life affected his daily experience.

Advice for Related Situations

Perhaps the most important advice for related situations has to do with the person of the counselor. In counseling, spirituality has been described as a component of the human experience that, while it may be expressed and nurtured through particular religious institutions, does not require those institutions for its expression or development (Turner et al. 1995). Counselors aiming to address religious or spiritual issues in counseling must make their own assumptions about spirituality an object of awareness and then compare these to the way spirituality is presented in the literature (starting with the four descriptions offered here). In self-exploration and supervision, counselors should explore at least the following four areas:

- Their subjective beliefs and experiences of what is spiritual and how they define that. The experiences are far more important than beliefs in this sense.

- Behaviors that counselors engage in as a part of their religious or spiritual practice. Counselors without a chosen religious or spiritual practice may find it difficult to work effectively in this area.
- Counselors should understand both their own and their client's cultural backgrounds related to spirituality and the "cultures" of the institutions they are working in.
- Counselors should know any guidelines existing in the institutions they work in related to addressing spirituality in counseling sessions.

A final word on ethics in counseling clients with spiritual issues: Therapists must be aware of their own beliefs and should ask themselves if they can maintain objectivity and avoid countertransference. Welfel (2002) suggests therapists must be honest with themselves about strong convictions or negative emotional reactions that might influence the counseling relationship as well as the chosen interventions. She recommends that if a particular client issue is a strong trigger for the therapist, a referral might be the safest choice.

The therapeutic relationship between client and counselor creates unique challenges and opportunities to address religious and spiritual issues. Nonetheless, some of the principles espoused in the case of Jacob can be transferred to the work of faculty and staff around campus. While students may not explicitly express spiritual or religious concerns, many students are confronted with some kind of dissonance between their faith tradition or spiritual development and the religious and spiritual realities on campus: a sexually conservative student like Jacob being confronted with the reality of an boisterous sex life on campus, a born-again Christian student challenged by a secular institution eager to enforce the separation of church and state, a Pagan student dealing with a perceived dominance of Christian values, or the student of any faith tradition for the first time confronted with fundamentally different ways of making meaning of spirituality and religion.

In an environment where religious or spiritual differences may not be visible, how might, for instance, an art professor use the subject of art to discuss spirituality with a student like Jacob? How might a professor in political science help students consider their particular issues vis-à-vis political concerns about laws related to human relationships or marriage? How might a philosophy professor stir a student like Jacob to consider spirituality regarding obligations, promises, and duties? While each of these scenarios presents with distinct problems and every student is faced with a unique set of issues, the most important guidance for faculty and staff mirrors the advice for counselors: spirituality must be made an object of awareness, first for faculty and staff and equally important for students. The above-mentioned four areas of awareness can be employed to guide instructors' self-exploration and to facilitate classroom discussions. A meaningful discussion of this enormous subject additionally demands a common language. How do we define religion, spirituality, the Divine? Finally, given the emotional response often attached to spirituality and religion, it is important to create a safe environment for classroom discussion. Therefore, notwithstanding the instructors' own convictions, no faith tradition must be granted priority. If a particular subject is a strong trigger for an instructor, analogous to the recommendations for counselors, an outside speaker might be the best option for a classroom discussion of this topic.

In Jacob's case, the primary resolution came about in making both the positive and negative aspects of his family's religion an object of awareness as well as his conclusion that he was unlikely to reach an omniscient endpoint with regard to the meaning of life or the meaning of what is spiritual. In the course of the three months we explored this in counseling, he came to accept that spiritual development, and spiritual maturity, require an ability to tolerate ambiguity, engage life, and revise one's conclusions as new experiences unfold. Perhaps Jacob summarized it best when he said the spiritual journey was like stepping off a cliff every day with great faith and great doubt—great faith that the journey can be trusted and great doubt that one can ever fully predict what this means in a given life.

References

Barbour, I. G. 1997. *Religion and science: Historical and contemporary issues.* New York: HarperSanfrancisco.

Festinger, L. 1957. *A theory of cognitive dissonance.* Stanford, CA: Stanford University Press.

Fowler, J. 1981. *Stages of faith: The psychology of human development and the quest for meaning.* San Francisco: Harper and Row.

Freud, S. 1964. *New introductory lectures on psychoanalysis: Standard edition, Vol. 22.* London: Hogarth.

Ingersoll, R. E. 1994. Spirituality, religion, and counseling: Dimensions and relationships. *Counseling and Values* 38(2):98-102.

Kegan, R. 1982. *The evolving self: Problem and process in human development.* Cambridge, MA: Harvard University Press.

Spong, J. S. 1990. *Living in sin: A bishop rethinks human sexuality.* New York: HarperSanFrancisco.

Turner, R. P., D. Lukoff, R. T. Barnhouse, and F. G. Lu. 1995. Religious or spiritual problem: A culturally sensitive diagnostic category in the DSM-IV. *Journal of Nervous and Mental Disease* 183:435–444.

Wade, J. 2004. *Transcendent sex: When lovemaking opens the veil.* New York: Paraview.

Welfel, E. R. 2002. *Ethics in counseling and psychotherapy: Standards, research, and emerging issues.* 2nd ed. Pacific Grove, CA: Brooks/Cole.

Wilber, K. 2004. *Integral psychology: Consciousness, spirit, psychology, therapy.* Boston: Shambhala.

Yalom, I. D. 1980. *Existential psychotherapy.* New York: Basic Books.

CHAPTER 20

Spirituality and Leadership Development in Student Affairs

Diane Berty

Scenario

Timothy, a student in my upper-division leadership class, approached me as I was gathering my books and papers and walked with me as I returned to the office. As we arrived at my office, he asked me if I had a few minutes.

A junior from a small farming community in west Tennessee, Timothy is a first-generation student who has lived in the same small town all of his life. Coming to our comprehensive, regional four-year institution was a major move for Timothy. His family wanted him to attend the local junior college and transfer to a four-year institution closer to home. Timothy, in his first of many decisions that would serve to clarify his values and thereby strengthen his spiritual journey, saw opportunities for personal growth when making his decision to attend Austin Peay State University.

The classroom discussion, this dreary mid-October afternoon, focused on leading with integrity and ethical purpose and included an exercise designed to challenge perception and acceptance of self and others. Timothy, throughout the lecture, was attentive and engaged, asking appropriate questions and providing thoughtful comment. However, during the exercise, "Archie Bunker's Neighborhood," (n.d.) I could tell Timothy was struggling. His struggle was a direct result of his participation in the exercise. Timothy did not yet have the capacity to take on the perspective, much less acceptance, of a gay man, as was required by his role in the exercise.

As I sat in my office and looked into Timothy's eyes, I saw confusion, dismay, and conflict. He said, "I've been approached by Matt (the vice president of the Gay/Straight Alliance, an organization representing the gay, lesbian, bisexual, transgender, questioning, and straight-supportive community), who asked me to talk with the Administration about establishing a Center for the gay community. I realized during *Archie Bunker's Neighborhood* that I *can't* do it. I know as SGA President I have to represent all students but does that mean that I, Timothy, have to carry his proposal forward?"

Analysis of Scenario

Timothy like so many of the students with whom I work and teach in my role as a senior administrator in student affairs, is conflicted by his struggle to lead while remaining true to his perceptions of what it means to be a moral man as defined by his background and upbringing. He explains, "My church tells me that homosexuality is sin, point blank! I believe homosexuality is wrong."

The study of leadership creates opportunities for students to question and seek answers to their purpose in life while determining how that purpose affects those they choose to lead. For this chapter, I am using the Relational Leadership Model definition of leadership published in *Exploring Leadership: For College Students Who Want to Make a Difference* (1998) by Komives, Lucas, and McMahon: "Leadership is a relational process of people together attempting to accomplish change or make a difference to benefit the common good" (31). Inherent in this definition is the essence of spirituality: "the need to center and strengthen inner well-being and to maintain a sense of balance so as to effectively and ethically make an impact on our environment" (Matusak 1997, 35). By struggling to gain insight into who he is, Timothy examines his spirituality, striving for balance as he faces day to day leadership decisions.

If student affairs professionals are to help students like Timothy develop their spirituality while strengthening their inner well-being, maintaining a sense of ethical balance, and developing their leadership potential, we must intentionally link theory to practice. Cuyjet and Newman (1999) argue that the student affairs professional, in understanding student development theories, also must deliberately create conditions in a variety of campus settings that augment student learning and personal development. It is imperative, as leadership educators, that we involve ourselves in teaching students how to be exceptional learners; how to think critically to solve complex problems; and how to transfer learned skills from one situation to another. Students must be engaged in active-learning processes that result in reflection, letting them relate the learning to similar experiences and transfer the learning to their everyday lives. In other words, we must design curricular and co-curricular learning opportunities that challenge and support students as they strive to reach their fullest potential. I, like many other practitioners, am continually astonished at our students' lack of understanding and resistance to self-empowerment. Although numerous student development and leadership theories can assist us in designing curricular and co-curricular experiences that foster in students the innate desire to create meaning in their lives, the Relational Leadership Model lends itself to practical application.

The Relational Leadership Model is comprised of five elements: inclusion, empowerment, ethics, purposefulness, and process-orientation. These five elements provide opportunities for students to assess various aspects of self; to understand and appreciate themselves in a leadership role; and to assess, measure, and respond to the needs of others while seeking to effectively and ethically make an impact on their environment to effect change for the common good.

The Model defines inclusiveness as "understanding, valuing, and actively engaging diversity in views, approaches, styles, and aspects of individuality…" (Komives, Lucas, and McMahon 1998, 73). My discussion with Timothy affirmed that he was comfortable and effective in including others. He recognized that when he interacted with people different from him there were differences he found difficult to understand, much less accept, homosexuality being one of those. He did voice an intellectual understanding that his inability to move beyond tolerance limited his ability to bring about change for the common good. His spirituality was in conflict with his external behavior as he was oblivious to the fact that he regarded homosexuals as not valueless, but of less value.

Empowerment recognizes that everyone has something to contribute. The empowering leader, according to the Model, understands that opportunities of growth and development for others are necessary and important and that contributions of others are to be solicited and valued (Komives, Lucas, and McMahon 1998). When I questioned Timothy as to how he had attempted to maintain a sense of inner balance when in turmoil concerning moral decisions, he immediately described how he *always* solicited and valued the contributions of others. He further attested that power, information, and decision making are to be willingly shared among all. Timothy said, "Blair, the SGA vice president and a friend, aggressively challenges me when I allow my Christian upbringing and background to influence what I insist we are to be doing as SGA leaders."

The Model asks ethical leaders to be grounded in their beliefs, values, and principles, meaning to be worthy of trust and of good character. Being ethical also requires leaders to confront unethical practices and to act in congruence with their own principles. Being ethical allows leaders to know that they did the right thing, even if the goal was not accomplished, because they did not sacrifice their integrity (Komives, Lucas, and McMahon 1998). I asked Timothy, "If you fail to bring the Gay/Straight Alliance's request forward to the administration, will the Senate question your integrity and authenticity as the President?" With confusion and sadness that I attribute to the need to strengthen and center his sense of spiritual well-being, Timothy said, "Yes!"

Being purposeful and process-oriented, according to the Relationship Leadership Theory, requires that the leader has a vision and the willingness and ability to share that vision. "When they [the leader and members] design and implement ethical, inclusive, empowering processes, groups can trust the processes to take them through difficult times, resolve ambiguous tasks, and be assured that together they will be better than they might be individually" (Komives, Lucas, and McMahon 1998, 94–95). As we talked, it was evident that Timothy cognitively knew that SGA should bring the request for the Center forward, stating, "I know the senators would challenge me and would argue that we have no choice." He clearly understood that his desire to get his own way biased the organization's vision and therefore limited possible outcomes. With defeat, Timothy looked at me and said, "Tell me how I can serve as president and represent the students and not take the proposal forward. You have to tell me what to do!"

This Model, through its interrelated elements, reminds each of us that "the spiritual journey of transformation, spirit, and intellectual wonder is an everyday occurrence" (Manning 2001, 32). Student affairs professionals are obligated to lead our students on the journey through which they create meaning in their lives. We accomplish this through our day-to-day contact with our students, our delivery of programs and services, and our collaboration with others in the academy. I am convinced, as discussed by Matusak (1997), that the spiritual aspects of leadership are not about manipulating the external environment as Timothy so unknowingly wanted but are about the personal growth and clarification of values that lead to inner strength, allowing students to transcend their own personal boundaries to support and serve others.

Timothy's spiritual leadership journey with me began during his freshmen orientation and continues beyond graduation. When Timothy demanded that I tell him what to do I looked at him and said, "Timothy, I can't do that!" He said, "I know." I reminded Timothy of the discussion we had on our first day of class when the definitions of leadership were debated. I asked, "Do you remember what we discussed differentiated the ethical and/or moral leader from the unethical and/or immoral leader?" He stared at me with a bewildered look and then I saw the transformation, "I know, intent!" Timothy then went on to talk through how he, Timothy, would not be morally supporting homosexuality as he, the SGA President, acted with ethical integrity in supporting his constituents and taking the proposal forward. Timothy and I had many more conversations throughout his academic career. Upon graduation he affirmed for himself that he had achieved a balanced life of spirituality and action that improved his own quality of life while contributing to the common good of SGA and the university community as a whole. I sincerely believe Timothy has taken advantage of the leadership theoretical framework through which he has achieved a centered and strengthened spirituality so as to effectively and ethically make an impact.

Advice for Related Situations

Student affairs professionals, as leadership educators, are instrumental in guiding students through the journey that begins at freshmen orientation and continues through graduation. The Relational Leadership Model's five elements provide a road map for students' leadership journey and necessitate for them an exploration of their spirituality. A comprehensive leadership program that embraces spiritual maturity, whether delivered inside or outside the formal classroom, can be developed by aligning its goals and objectives within the Model's five elements. Minimally, a program should address goals and objectives for each element.

Whether working with freshmen and transfers at orientation; training student orientation leaders, resident assistants, peer educators, programming board members, student organization executive officers, student judicial board members, or student employees in my office; or teaching students in my leadership development class, I have similar goals and objectives. I want the learning outcomes for leadership development, enhanced by spirituality, to include but not be limited to:

- a high level of participation from all so everyone is exposed to ideas, values, and mores that are different from those that they hold;
- self-assessment, specifically as related to values clarification;
- an exploration of how spirituality—a reflection of one's inner strength—affects one's leadership;
- an understanding of the concepts of authority and power and how these reflect one's spirituality;
- a demonstration of adaptability and flexibility in modifying one's leader in given situations without compromising one's values;

- an understanding and application of effective communication skills to reflect honesty, integrity, and respect; and
- the ability to identify leadership issues, their connection to one's spirituality and their cause and effect for the whole.

By accomplishing these learning outcomes, the student leader will have addressed each of the elements of the Relational Leadership Model and will have a better understanding of their spirituality.

We must remember, however, effective spirituality and leadership development is more than teaching students skills that enable them to manipulate others and/or their environments. We must provide students with direction that allows them to arrive at their own decisions through meaning making, a reliance on their inner self or, simply put, their spirituality. This can be accomplished by first providing an opportunity for students to gain an understanding of what a value is and how values guide their behavior and influence their interaction with others. I would recommend the use of a values clarification exercise such as Rokeach's Instrumental and End Values (Rokeach 1979), which allows students to see how their espoused values affect their decisions and actions. Spiritual leadership dictates that students be reminded a value is a value only if it consistently guides their decisions and actions.

In addition, *Archie Bunkers Neighborhood* may be used to move students to a point of recognition of how their values define the self. The activity provides a combination of circumstances that forces students to assume stereotypical roles. In this activity students are not aware of their assumed role until such time that behaviors and actions of others provide clues to their status and worth. Students participating in this activity will find, just as Timothy discovered, often they are not prepared to take on the perspective, much less acceptance, of others.

After having students participate in values clarification exercises and activities, I have found that processing of thoughts and feelings is a must. To move students to an understanding of the impact of their spirituality on their leadership practice, it is necessary for the student affairs practitioner to lead an open and safe discussion. This discussion must include an examination of how the students' values guide their behavior, how those values influence their interactions with others, and subsequently how each affects the leaders' decisions and actions. After this discussion I often use situational case studies that have practical application to the students' current roles, such as orientation leaders. The outcome of the use of case study analysis is the students' recognition that there may be more than one right way and that "my way" is not necessarily the "only way."

For students, inner strength will be developed as they strive for congruence between their spirituality, their values, and their external behavior. Congruence will then result in an external behavior that reflects their spirituality (inner strength) and values so they can claim the peace and balanced perspective that Matusak describes. It is only when students achieve congruence that they experience Timothy's "Ah ha" moment, a moment that we want for all of our students.

References

Archie Bunker's Neighborhood. n.d. ResidentAssistant.com. http://www.residentassistant.com/reslifepro/ArchieBunker'sNeighborhoodExercise.html (accessed October 24, 2006).

Benfari, R. C. 1999. *Understanding and Changing Your Management Style*. San Francisco: Jossey-Bass.

Cuyjet, M. J., and L. L. Newman. 1999. Learning and development from theory to practice. In *Enhancing student learning: Setting the campus context*, eds. F. K. Stage, L. W. Watson, and M. Terrell, 59–76. Lanham, MD: University Press of America.

Komives, S. R., N. Lucas, and T. R. McMahon. 1998. *Exploring leadership: For college students who want to make a difference*. San Francisco: Jossey-Bass.

Manning, K. 2001. Infusing soul into student affairs: Organizational theory and models. In *The Implications of Student Spirituality for Student Affairs Practice*: New Directions for Student Services, no. 95, ed. M. A. Jablonski, 27–36. San Francisco: Jossey-Bass.

Matusak, L. R. 1997. *Finding your voice, learning to lead...anywhere you want to make a difference*. San Francisco: Jossey-Bass.

Parks, S. 2000. *Big questions, worthy dreams: Mentoring young adults in their search for meaning, purpose, and faith*. San Francisco: Jossey-Bass.

Rokeach, M. 1979. *Understanding human values*, New York: The Free Press.

CHAPTER 21

Fostering Student Spiritual Development through Selected Student Affairs Practices

David M. Eberhardt
Jon C. Dalton

Scenario

Annie Jones was a busy, high-achieving student in high school, popular with both her peers and teachers. She was a leader in numerous school activities, fairly active in her religious youth group, and found much reward through community service projects in which her family participated. She also worked in her family's small business several afternoons each week. Her academic success, solid friendships, religious experiences, civic service, and ability to balance a demanding schedule gave her a strong sense of self-confidence and purpose as she prepared for college during the fall term of her senior year. Amid her preparation, Annie often expressed to friends and family members how she looked forward to college life with much anticipation, as she expected to study biology and enter a career in the medical field.

In January of her senior year, however, Annie's aunt was diagnosed with cancer, which progressed very rapidly and eventually led to her death early in the summer. Annie had enjoyed a close relationship with this particular aunt as she grew up, and in the months prior to her death, Annie began to struggle with deep personal questions about her aunt's painful circumstances and the meaning and purpose of her own life. This struggle led to many conversations with her dying aunt in which they talked about finding meaning in life, how to live peacefully during difficult situations, and why tragic events like terminal illnesses happen to people, especially early in life. Annie had never considered these topics so intensely, and her aunt's quick passing only increased Annie's difficulty in resolving these challenging issues and events. As she grieved through the remainder of the summer, Annie periodically reflected on her aunt's death and the unsettling awareness it had raised about her own life's purpose and future.

Although saddened, Annie continued with her plans to enter college about five hours from home, leaving the immediate comfort of her family and friends. As she is now settling into living in her residence hall and beginning classes, Annie has become busy with the normal activities of a new student. Amidst this hectic schedule, though, she is discovering that the search for answers about her meaning and purpose in life, provoked by the events of the summer, are becoming more persistent and pressing issues in her mind.

Analysis of Scenario

Although not every new student arrives on campus with recent tragedies in his or her past, Annie represents a relatively typical undergraduate who might be found in any public or private, faith-based or non-sectarian college or university. The historic mission of these higher education institutions, particularly within their student affairs divisions, has revolved around the holistic development of students. Traditionally, holistic development has been understood to include emotional, intellectual, social, interpersonal, moral, and physical growth and maturity. More recently, however, spiritual development has also gained attention as a significant dimension of college students' overall growth. Findings from the Spirituality in Higher Education project (Higher Education Research Institute [HERI] 2004) support this focus on spiritual development, indicating that many students enter college like Annie, interested in spirituality and engaging in a spiritual quest, even if they do not understand or articulate their search within a spiritual context. Therefore, as we focus on Annie throughout this chapter, we believe that she exemplifies many students on our campuses. We also contend that the developmental approaches we discuss in this chapter represent important potential steps that institutions may take in creating holistic educational environments that are conducive to student spiritual development, and that they apply not only to our fictional Annie, but to a great many of her peers as well.

Before exploring Annie's particular struggle in the context of different student affairs practices, it is important to consider the meaning of spirituality, particularly as it applies to the learning and development of college students. The term *spirituality* has a wide range of meanings and uses, so it is essential that we be clear in how we conceive and utilize the term. We use spirituality broadly to refer to students' inner search for meaning and purpose in their lives. This definition emphasizes three important characteristics worth highlighting. First, the domain of spirituality is internal, focused on individuals' inner lives. Second, spirituality usually takes the form of a personal search or quest, involving such activities as reflection, meditation, and contemplation. Third, the objective of a spiritual search or quest is to discover ultimate meaning and purpose for an individual's life, to consider profound questions, and to develop a meaningful philosophy that guides an individual's life (Chickering, Dalton, and Stamm 2006; HERI 2004). Thus, when we speak of spirituality in reference to college students, we refer to the process by which they engage in thoughtful and personal reflection about their beliefs, values, and deep concerns, so that they may clarify and commit to the genuine meanings and purposes they discover for their lives.

Spirituality shares aspects with religion in this definition, but it is important to note that these concepts also represent different phenomena in the lives of students. Spirituality certainly can be religious in form and often is expressed within that context, but it is not always religious in nature. Religion incorporates a specific faith tradition, with sacred symbols, rituals, beliefs, and behaviors, through which spirituality may be manifested. Spirituality is more private and inward in expression, taking on a multitude of forms of belief and behavior through individual exploration. With fewer external expectations or observances, spirituality is often viewed by students as less confining and restrictive in terms of personal beliefs and behaviors. Spirituality should not be regarded as anti-religious, but simply as a more open and personal form of soul-searching in which students seek to develop their own beliefs and understandings.

Returning now to the scenario of Annie Jones as she begins college struggling to understand life's purpose and wrestling with difficult questions, her first significant opportunities to find support for her spiritual development could possibly occur in her initial days on campus during student orientation and her first-year experience course. These programs are primarily intended to facilitate the successful transition of new students into their college or university environment, but Annie may find that some of the events and exercises involved in these programs also encourage her to continue her reflections and questioning from the summer. Through orientation and the first-year experience course, Annie would likely find herself grouped together with other new students, led by one or two current student leaders as well as instructors, each of whom is meant to help guide her through important learning moments in her entrance to college life. During orientation meetings and class sessions, these facilitators will create opportunities for discussion of numerous topics, including study skills, student services, responsible behaviors, and other topics. These discussion leaders might also encourage new students to discuss their purpose for being in college. While most first-year students, including Annie, would likely focus initially on practical goals such as career preparation, discussion leaders could use such opportunities to challenge students to think deeper and more broadly about why they are in college, what they hope to gain from their collegiate experience, and how college can become a time of personal exploration and discovery of their deepest beliefs, goals, and aspirations. The first-year experience teachers might encourage students to keep a journal in which they reflect on their learning and their emerging ideas. They can also pose questions about personal values and dreams for students to consider through their journal writing. Through such conversations and exercises, Annie would have occasions to examine more deeply her goals and purpose in life and connect these to her current life and involvements in college. These reflective moments would offer Annie the chance to pause amid her increasingly busy life and consider what she wants her college experience to encompass. The outcome of these occasions would likely be that Annie deepens her awareness of purpose in her own life, becomes more attuned to and intentional in her search for understanding, and begins to seek the invaluable opportunities college offers for spiritual and overall personal development.

The campus residence hall where Annie lives provides a powerful setting for socializing and learning to be independent, but it also affords another potentially meaningful opportunity for Annie's spiritual growth. The housing professionals who oversee Annie's living area have many opportunities to work with their resident assistants to create experiences that encourage all residents to reflect on their purpose and meaning in life, as part of the many other social and developmental programs they typically offer. Such activities might include inviting faculty and student affairs personnel to speak and lead relevant discussions in residence halls or having resident assistants use a self-discovery resource, like one of the many books of conversation-starter questions, to generate discussions about personal values, spiritual beliefs, and similar concepts. A specific example might involve a late-night pizza party where Annie's resident assistant asks her and her hall mates to respond to statements like, "At the end of my life, I most want to be remembered for…" or, "At the end of my time in college, what do I most want my friends to miss about me?" In addition, Annie's residential staff could post attention-grabbing flyers throughout the hall with meaningful quotes, thoughtful questions, and reminders to pause and reflect on their experiences. These simple projects would help create an environment in which Annie and her peers feel encouraged to talk about these issues on their own, an activity that the Spirituality in Higher Education project (HERI 2004) has discovered is fairly common and comfortable for undergraduates. The residential living department could also reserve and furnish a particular lobby or room to serve as a quiet and comfortable space for personal reflection and meditation, something often difficult to find in active, community living arrangements. Surrounded by efforts such as these, Annie would find opportunities to continue her personal quest within an educational environment deliberately designed to promote spiritual development. Rather than ponder big questions and concerns by herself, Annie could use the conversations with peers to explore her own thoughts and also learn what other students think, gaining new insights from them. Annie's rising motivation to seek meaning in life and the pressing questions in her mind would find channels to follow through these measures, while she also learned to be an active member of her residential community.

Annie's search for purpose and meaning is also likely to lead her to the student union and student activities programs. As the campus "living room" for students, student unions usually provide the relaxed and informal setting that are important for students' inner search. Although little if any space is usually provided in campus commons for quiet places, student unions might designate space for individual reflection and even group meditative exercises, along with exterior gardens or relatively secluded courtyards that lend themselves to such activities. These spaces would be particularly beneficial to Annie and her peers when they feel the need to escape from their residence halls or seek brief quiet periods, and also would be helpful to her peers who commute to campus daily. Additionally, as Annie gains more awareness about her own inward journey and continues to wrestle with challenging questions, she may look for specific activities she believes will support her growth, and thus may consider several religiously affiliated or spiritually oriented organizations. Providing space for these organizations so that Annie and her fellow undergraduate seekers can attend group events represents an important service offered by student unions. Offering assistance to the leaders of these groups in promoting themselves, publicizing their activities, and developing their student leadership potential is another significant way that student activities offices enhance the environment in which college students like Annie continue their spiritual growth. Similar to the residential living department, these efforts by the student union and student activities professionals provide a social context in which students develop interpersonally and spiritually. Their programs would likely appeal to Annie and permit her to continue her spiritual journey by exploring various settings where she can find connections to others who feel similar to her, and where she can identify groups that match and meet her spiritual needs.

Annie's spiritual quest may lead her to valuable resources in the wellness programs of both the campus health and recreation centers, as well. They support this growth by helping her to take care of herself physically, so that she can attend to her mind and spirit more effectively. The campus recreation center may offer classes on yoga, relaxation, meditation, or other discipline-oriented exercises that have been found to benefit students' mental and emotional health. When Annie goes to the fitness center to exercise with her friends, she would likely see these programs advertised. Although she may have never attempted such activities before, in focusing on her spiritual search more intentionally she may decide to see if they benefit her sense of purpose and direction in life. In these classes, the instructors would lead students to learn new principles of quieting their mind, calming their spirits, and discovering new insights through reflection. Participating in these activities would possibly spur Annie to increased depth and awareness, as she seeks to understand herself and the deep questions she sometimes encounters. When Annie visits the health center for any medical issues, she may find further concern from the service personnel for her overall well-being, including her spiritual health. When health center doctors and nurses see particular students often, and notice a pattern of illness or sense they are engaged in possibly dangerous behaviors, they may question students about the stressors that are influencing their life, including religious or spiritual struggles. The Spirituality in Higher Education project (HERI 2004) has found that students in the midst of religious questioning and uncertainty sometimes display risky behaviors, such as drinking heavily. Annie's responses to their questions might lead them to refer her to the counseling center or other appropriate resources that would ultimately contribute to her spiritual quest for understanding and her growing sense of purpose and meaning in life.

Career Services represents another essential area, sometimes linked with student affairs divisions, where Annie would likely find her quest for purpose and meaning strengthened. Like many of her peers, Annie begins her collegiate experience already aimed toward an eventual professional career, with her interest lying in the medical field. As she questions her life's purpose, however, she may find herself less certain of her future direction. Her past ideals of wanting to help heal ill people and similar thoughts may not bring her the same sense of purpose she felt when preparing for college. Instead, Annie's journey may lead her to discover other personal motivations and to seek other career routes. When she visits her institution's career center with these types of questions, the personnel there can challenge and support her search process in various ways. Through assessments they offer and programs they publicize for all students, the career center staff could urge Annie to try to discover her passions by thinking about what touches her deeply and by encouraging her to explore potential areas of interest throughout college. For example, they may encourage her to take sociology and political science courses along with biology classes based on her responses to an interest inventory, and could help set up volunteer opportunities or internships at particular service agencies or hospitals. Through the combination of academic and practical experiences during college, Annie may find herself deeply affected by people who are hurting medically but also discover her greatest reward comes from being involved in public policy work related to health care. Though much different from becoming a medical service practitioner, Annie would find a sense of vocation that propels and sustains her much more intensely, giving her a true sense of calling and deeper purpose in both her academic and future professional work. The result for Annie will be greater spiritual development while in college, and most likely a more satisfying and productive career.

Volunteering to help others through community service activities can provide additional rich opportunities for Annie's self-examination and reflection. Annie may decide to help raise money for disaster relief, tutor children in after-school programs, help build homes for people in need, or select from the dozens of other service programs that college and university campuses tend to sponsor through their civic engagement offices. Through participating in these activities, Annie would likely find opportunities to see the problems and struggles that others encounter and these experiences may help her to reflect on her own values and commitments. The campus leaders for these programs could actively encourage such reflection by providing opportunities to discuss volunteer experiences. Whether on extended service trips during school breaks or in simple debriefing sessions after a long day's work, facilitators can challenge students to think about what they learned from their involvement, and how that learning shapes their approach to their academic and personal lives. In these moments, Annie's spiritual quest would likely undergo additional growth, as she finds deeper meaning in her life goals and develops these goals into personal commitments.

As Annie continues her spiritual quest throughout college, she would likely discover that numerous other experiences and learning opportunities provided by student affairs divisions would influence her as she interacts with them. For example, campus speaker series and performance programs might expose Annie to new ideas, ideals, and artistic expressions that enrich and broaden her experience. Living-learning programs that bridge the divide between academic affairs and student affairs through residential living, campus compacts or values creeds included in diverse areas' programs, and Greek life efforts to reinvigorate their social organizations' values could also help establish environments that foster Annie's spiritual growth. In these and many other unique and special programs, Annie's search for meaning and her profound questioning would encounter intentional campus efforts that would challenge her to grow spiritually, while supporting her as she continues along her journey of self-discovery.

Advice for Related Situations

Having covered numerous areas of practice within student affairs, we now turn our attention briefly to the academic dimension of colleges and universities where students such as Annie can also find guidance and support for their spiritual quest. Research has shown that faculty-student relationships hold substantial influence in students' lives, particularly in the way they understand the world and their place within it. This relationship develops both within the classroom and in interactions beyond it, offering faculty a valuable opportunity to stimulate students' spiritual development.

One of the ways students often seek to deepen their spirituality is by taking classes that deal with human values and moral issues. Annie may choose to take courses in philosophy, literature, sociology, psychology, religion, and various other disciplines, along with the classes she must complete for her general education and major requirements. In all of these courses, both general and specifically themed, faculty members often require readings and foster discussions about profound questions similar to those that Annie contemplates. They may also discuss historical figures and literary characters who wrestled with difficult issues or underwent similar searches for meaning and purpose. Through papers and projects, instructors might allow students to research and write about related topics, encouraging them to develop their own ideas about purpose in life and facilitating their search for deeper awareness and knowledge. In these readings, discussions, and assignments, Annie would observe what diverse authors have written, hear what other students think, and have her ideas challenged by professors' questions. These activities would provide Annie time and space to continue her quest, by both broadening her knowledge and processing her thoughts further. She would find herself progressing deeper and gaining more understanding of the major questions in her life, which would also likely motivate her toward greater engagement with her academics.

Outside the formal classroom setting, Annie could find support for her spiritual journey through her personal conversations with professors, as well. When faculty members invite students to come by their offices to discuss their coursework, they can allow that time to expand into opportunities to continue class discussions, as well as express interest in their students' collegiate experience. Simple questions such as, "What did you think about the author's argument that we discussed today," may initiate conversations that powerfully facilitate students' understanding and awareness of both class materials and their own thinking. Similarly, basic requests like, "Tell me how your other classes are going," or "Tell me how your first semester is going so far," may elicit responses that provide faculty members the chance to encourage and support students as they move forward in their spiritual quest. When Annie visits professors about her coursework, these types of questions would permit her to talk about her background and emerging ideas in more personal discussions, avoiding any concerns or embarrassment she may feel by speaking up in class. Those interactions would ultimately provide a comfortable space for Annie, in which she can discuss the big issues that she ponders periodically and possibly find mentors and supporters for her quest.

Along with student affairs, the other administrative areas of higher education institutions can provide additional support for students such as Annie to advance in their spiritual development. As noted earlier, residence halls and student unions can provide quiet and safe places for students to explore their life purpose and reflect on their diverse experiences. If isolated, reflective spaces do not already exist in these areas, then campus planners can ensure that appropriate renovation projects and new buildings include these types of rooms in the future. In addition, many college students are employed in campus work-study jobs, where they are supervised by diverse college personnel. In training these supervisors, the financial affairs area can emphasize the types of development that students are experiencing, including their spiritual growth. If these personnel begin to sense any troubling issues for their student workers, they can encourage the students to utilize the resources available to them, such as the counseling center or campus ministries area. In this way, if Annie were working in the library, the development office, academic affairs, or other administrative areas, she would find herself supported by those around her. In addition, as she builds relationships with them, she may eventually share her background and current struggles and find other mentors or guides similar to her professors.

Throughout this chapter we have discussed a fictitious college student in Annie Jones, but as discussed previously, she exemplifies a growing number of students currently enrolled in American colleges and universities who are engaged in spiritual search. Many undergraduates may not express the same active and sometimes deliberate search that Annie does in our scenario, but they are still young people undergoing a process of identity development that involves a spiritual quest for meaning, purpose, and understanding. Whether they eagerly pursue that quest or simply respond to the opportunities presented to them, students need educational environments that encourage and support their spiritual growth. When the types of activities and programs discussed in this chapter are provided on campus, students are more likely to find themselves participating in a spiritually oriented learning community that inspires and motivates their quest in the context of their overall growth. Students feel valued and safe to explore in such an environment, because they know that campus educators want them to progress through their journey. The common result for students is greater holistic development, as well as much stronger commitment of themselves to their deepest values, ideals, and dreams.

References

Chickering, A., J. Dalton, and L. Stamm. 2006. *Encouraging authenticity and spirituality in higher education.* San Francisco: Jossey-Bass.

Higher Education Research Institute. 2004. *The spiritual life of college students: A national study of college students' search for meaning and purpose.* Los Angeles: Author.

PART FOUR

Directions for Future Research

CHAPTER 22

Spirituality in Higher Education: Directions for Future Research

Bruce W. Speck
Sherry L. Hoppe

In this chapter, we discuss directions for future research by dividing research into two components, theory and praxis. Because praxis arises from theory, even when praxis is derived from an inchoate theoretical position, we recognize the undeniable relationship between classroom pedagogy and the theory that underlies that pedagogy. Thus, we begin with suggestions for research related to theoretical concerns regarding spirituality/religion and call for a sharper focus on a cluster of terms—spirituality, pluralism, and tolerance—so that the study of spirituality can be open to investigation.

Theoretical Issues

We begin with the term *spirituality*, but we recognize that all three terms are interwoven, and all three are in need of sharper definitions. Although various authors of books and articles on spirituality seem content to define spirituality in nebulous terms, clear definition is the beginning of reasonable discourse. If those engaged in dialogue cannot with reasonable precision define spirituality, the odds of the speakers making informed judgments about spirituality are low. Indeed, the odds of engaging those skeptical about spirituality as a legitimate topic for investigation in the academy are extremely low. We pause here to make sure that our use of *reasonable* is not mistaken as a code word for a positivist epistemology. By using reasonable we are not eliminating the need for, what is often referred to in the literature on spirituality, a holistic approach to human development. We are simply acknowledging the importance of reason in discourse and seeking to establish grounds for investigating spirituality. Reason cannot, in our view, be the arbiter that eliminates essential paradoxes or antinomies, but reason is vital in evaluating truth claims. We affirm, therefore, that the intellect in concert with the complex whole person cannot be eliminated from any academic discussion of spirituality. We have noted above that definitions of spirituality often suffer from vagueness. In fact, though, despite the various and sundry definitions of spirituality, the insistent claim is that "spirituality is not religion," so spirituality, one might suppose, can be defined in terms of what it is not. However, the attempt to define spirituality in opposition to religion can be perceived as making religion a foil. Take Tisdell's (2001) definition of spirituality, which is emblematic: "spirituality is not the same as religion; religion is an organized community of faith that has written codes of regulatory behavior, whereas spirituality is more about one's personal belief and experience of a higher power or higher purpose" (3). If spirituality is about inwardness, then by comparison, religion is about outwardness. But that means, logically, that spirituality is personal, and religion is not personal. If religion is about written codes that regulate behavior, spirituality is not about codes that regulate behavior. Logically, spiritually would not address ethics. If spirituality is about an individual's belief and experience of a higher power and purpose, religion cannot also be about those things. Clearly, however, such distinctions don't hold. In fact, because spirituality is "neither religious nor secular, it is a hybrid of the two" (Schaper 2000, A56).

As a hybrid, spirituality is difficult to define and analyze. It certainly can't be defined exclusively in terms antithetical to religion because for some, spirituality becomes a substitute for religion, which may be no more than ersatz religion. However, who can tell, when the definition of spirituality is so pliable? Spirituality, as defined in antithesis to religion, appears to create common ground because of its ambiguity, thus allowing for personal interpretations, but as Hicks (2003) warns, "...the claim that 'spirituality creates common ground' cannot be readily established without undertaking more work at least to address the philosophical and theological difficulties of the term and its definitional components. Authors who make broad and sweeping claims about spirituality should clarify the connections and coherence of their account" (56). Despite commonalities in spiritual experiences, all spiritual journeys do not lead to the same destination. Spiritual journeys have different forks, detouring some toward one religion and some toward another, and still others to non-religious experiences. Commonality in spiritual experiences thus does not provide the needed clarification. Those who are serious about engaging the academy in a genuine academic discussion of spirituality should tackle the problem of defining spirituality so that it can be discussed rationally. (If spirituality is genuinely an American backdoor to Eastern religions and philosophies, and thus an attack on Western ways of thinking, then *rationality*, as we are using the term, can be discounted, even disregarded. However, the relinquishment of rationality creates what we think are insuperable problems to creating a dialogue about spirituality in the academy.)

Perhaps multiple definitions of spirituality are appropriate, but definitions that hinge upon personal preference, as though such preference can be universal, do a great disservice to any serious consideration of spirituality as a valid academic topic. Empirical studies might be useful in helping to define spirituality, but if the studies do no more than determine what people think spirituality is, it would appear, given the literature on spirituality, that we already know the multiple definitions people hold (Beaudoin 1998; Fuller 2001; Roof 1993; Roof and McKinney 1985). In short, the definitional problem regarding spirituality is the greatest difficulty theorists face in attempting to develop a viable research program for investigating spirituality.

Another major difficulty in conducting research about spirituality is the philosophical problem of pluralism. As Wolfe (2002) notes, pluralism raises "the question of whether human beings are better off attempting to maximize one particular good to the best of their ability or trying to live with diverse, sometimes mutually exclusive, goods, even if the cost of doing so is the inability to maximize any of them" (22). However, theoretically, pluralism in the literature on spirituality generally does not recognize the validity of the problem Wolfe cites because pluralism is assumed to allow "diverse, sometimes mutually exclusive, goods" as the only viable philosophical approach. Again, this assumed philosophical approach puts spirituality at odds with religion because religion is seen as maximizing one particular good, faith in and obedience to God, as superior to all other goods, whatever they may be. However, the claims made in the name of spirituality about goods often assume the validity of a particular worldview without thoroughly vetting that worldview. As Glanzer (2003) confirms, though, "We all bring to bear a conceptual framework to our inquiries" (3), and simply *assuming* the validity of a conceptual framework—a worldview—is not the same a defining, carefully explaining, and defending the validity of the worldview.

Our reading of the literature on spirituality suggests that pluralism, along with spirituality and tolerance, are terms prized even when readers are not adequately apprised of their precise meaning. A more rigorous philosophical approach to pluralism is needed, and Nash's (2001) claim about the inherent tensions of genuine pluralism should be heeded: "Pluralism in a democracy will always create difficulties, because in the interest of consistency and fairness, even those who would seek to destroy the notion of pluralism, and democracy along with it, have an 'inviolable' right to exist" (38). Nash's claim can be helpful so that simplistic notions about unitary pluralism (or spirituality or tolerance) are tempered with the reality of genuine differences being maintained.

A more critical evaluation of pluralism is also needed for tolerance, the handmaiden of pluralism. Given that pluralism, as commonly defined in the literature on spirituality, denies the validity of maximizing one particular good, tolerance becomes no more than acceptance of that single view of pluralism. In fact, "tolerance can only be a virtue if we think the other person, whose viewpoint we're supposed to tolerate, is mistaken. That is to say, if we do not believe one viewpoint is better than another, then to ask us to be tolerant of other viewpoints makes no sense. For to tolerate another's viewpoint implies that this other person has a right to his or her viewpoint despite the fact that others may think it is wrong" (Speck 1998, 77), which echoes Nash's claim. Wakefield (2002) gets at this problem of tolerance by saying, "Nel Noddings, in *Dialogue between Believers and Unbelievers*, suggests believers and unbelievers may unite intellectually and even grow together, yet the idealism of faith communities and the realism of intellectual communities often generate friction while traveling down the same road. Christianity's mandate to confront and transform culture is surely at the heart of interfaith conflict. The Judeo-Christian tradition teaches social responsibility, condemnation of immorality, and cultural transformation" (90). Wakefield goes on to describe events at Berry College, a Christian school, that raised issues about interfaith tolerance, and stresses the need to move beyond tolerance to hospitality: "Tolerance often carries the connotation of dislike or disagreement—'I don't agree, but I'll tolerate you.' Few of us wish to be objects of toleration. Hospitality suggests friendly respect for guest and host alike. More importantly, hospitality emphasizes tact, sensitivity and polite acceptance without conformity" (98).

Of course the crux of Wakefield's argument is "polite acceptance without conformity," which surely needs thorough explication. Is the distinction a matter of intellectually acknowledging civilly that the position another holds is wrong but the other still has a right to hold to that position? If so, what is the difference between tolerance and "polite acceptance without conformity"? In other words, what affective result is Wakefield encouraging that leaves intact a person's belief in the other's error while allowing civility? Furthermore, how is that affective result different from what can be attained by practicing tolerance?

In sum, more theoretical work needs to be done to clarify a cluster of terms—spirituality, pluralism, and tolerance—that are central to discussions about religion and spirituality. Empirical studies might be useful in providing data to establish more precise meanings. However, we readily admit that topics trading in metaphysics cannot be reduced to definitions that disregard paradoxes, antinomies, and mysteries. Ultimate concerns in ontology we think, by definition, press beyond the limits of reason without denying the viability of reason in reaching limits.

Practice Issues

We move somewhat reluctantly to a discussion of praxis because the theoretical work we recommend should be the foundation for pedagogical research. Without the results of theory in hand, questions about pedagogy are difficult to frame because the theory will help guide pedagogical research. Nevertheless, we recognize the symbiotic relationship between theory and praxis, acknowledging that praxis can raise questions that theory can help explain, so we provide tentative suggestions for pedagogical research.

To begin, we return to Glanzer's observation that "We all bring to bear a conceptual framework to our inquiries." Regarding spirituality, we affirm that the ethics of spirituality, the kind of conduct that follows from a person's spirituality, is linked to a worldview. Although not calling them worldviews, Urmson (1988) provides a succinct summary of the goals of life that can help frame our discussion of praxis in spirituality: "The three types of life commonly put forward as candidates for supremacy are the life of sensual pleasure, the life of involvement in the affairs of one's country and the life of theoretical contemplation. The first of these is the aim of a mere animal; the other two must include activity involving the use of reason, either practical or theoretical" (19). What exactly does Urmson's position have to do with spirituality, especially since Urmson says nothing about ultimate concerns?

First, Urmson allows for the possibility of hedonism, although he relates it to "the aim of a mere animal," thus disqualifying hedonism as a proper goal in life. The literature on spirituality says as much. And here's how that works. Spirituality is most often defined in individualistic terms, but those who promote spirituality clearly do not want just any individualistic agenda, so to guard against hedonism, spirituality is couched in positive values. The individual, for example, is seeking wholeness, a higher power, transcendence, and/or connectedness. Those terms are sufficiently abstract to allow for a range of behaviors, but we can't recall any place in the literature in which the range of behaviors allows for looting, raping, and killing, much less the tamer excesses that characterize hedonism. Indeed, the individual is allowed latitude in seeking for a greater good, whatever that may be within the limits of positive values, but the individual greater good is generally seen in the second and third types of life Urmson cites. Thus, the life of involvement in one's country is certainly the life of civic engagement and can (often *must*) be broadened to include the world community, whether that community is at a person's backdoor knocking for admittance or in a distant geographical location. Civic engagement, typified in the literature on service-learning, as we have noted elsewhere (Speck and Hoppe 2004) can take various political paths. Just as, under our discussion of theory, we stressed the need for precision in definitions and a critical distance that allows for solid critique of one's position, so we repeat those requirements when the praxis of spirituality turns to civic engagement.

In addition, the problem of community will have to be addressed. How can individual spirituality, which depends on personal preferences, give rise to any legitimate notion of community? We have noted that the literature redeems personal preference in spirituality by insisting on some positive result, including community building. But that rhetorical move should be based on a reasonable case for community building. To what extent should professors and students engage in community activity to promote their own and others' spirituality? Is spirituality indistinct from a particular philosophical approach, such as Marxism, in community building, and if it is indistinct, what is the value of associating spirituality with Marxism, for instance? In general, what is the relationship between political activity and spirituality? Should professors try to produce spiritual Republicans, spiritual Democrats, or spiritual independents? What should students believe about their spirituality vis-à-vis social activism?

In addition, what are students expected to do when they engage their spirituality in community building? Would an internship at the New York Stock Exchange be considered a spiritual activity, especially when such an internship is designed to prepare students to work as stock brokers? What are the limits, if there are limits, on what students can do to develop, explore, and use their spirituality in activities sanctioned by the professor, but accomplished outside the class?

Inside the classroom, what should professors do to explore spirituality? Although this volume offers examples of what might be done in classrooms to investigate spirituality, the paucity of examples, and the virtual absence of examples in some disciplines, suggests that much work needs to be done to provide models for the uses of spirituality in the classroom, especially as they relate to community building. The preponderance of literature on spirituality within academic disciplines is found in the healing sciences, the visual arts, management, and the social sciences. When compiling the bibliography for Chapter 1 and in seeking authors for the chapters both on theory and practice in the disciplines for this book, we found countless articles on spirituality in health-care fields. Likewise, plentiful articles were located on spirituality in the arts—especially the visual arts. Surprisingly, we did not find many articles on spirituality and music, which have had connections for centuries. Perhaps the connections are so old that the demarcation between the two is seamless, leading researchers to believe no new outcomes might be found. Some disciplines, like English and history, also have natural and thematic connections, both in religion and in the broader notion of spirituality, but few articles relate research examining those connections and how they contribute to the disciplines. In the discipline of business, management and leadership articles describe numerous ways to lead with spirit, but most fail to address how non-management workers' spirituality affects daily work life.

In the social sciences, psychology stands apart from other disciplines in the preponderance of research on religious and spiritual nuances in humankind. In recent years, political scientists have shown a renewed interest in religion and spirituality, and undoubtedly myriad researchers will focus on the influence of religion on terrorism and other twenty-first-century crises. Such research will be critical in mapping out strategies to detect and deter terrorism. We must seek first to understand before we can deal with those who believe their religion supersedes all other beliefs and who feel compelled to use dogmatic tenets as the basis for acts seemingly devoid of any kind of spirituality.

In other areas of social science, including sociology and social work, we uncovered little research on how these disciplines relate to spirituality or religion. While undoubtedly these disciplines include such concepts, we put them forth as needing more definitive research. Likewise for education, an area where one would expect to find extensive research. Teachers cannot teach in a vacuum; they teach whole persons, many of whom are struggling with their own spirituality or spirituality in a larger sense. Research is needed on how teachers are dealing with these issues. In Health and Physical Education, where one might expect to find research on holistic approaches to life and living, those approaches rarely addressed the spiritual dimension. Spirituality research is beginning to evolve in biology, with new theories on where spirituality might reside in the brain. Could spirituality be physical as well as otherworldly? Further research on this topic will be forthcoming, and we hope it will be fruitful. Other disciplines where spirituality studies are limited include communication, theater, and international education.

In other parts of the university, more research is needed on how experiences outside the classroom can support a student's spiritual growth. Clearly, student affairs professionals believe they provide an invaluable service to students that both complements and enhances the classroom experience. One particular area that has potential is in "learning communities," which are designed for spillovers from the classroom into residence hall life and university life in general. Research is needed on how learning communities might be used to help students examine their spirituality and search for purpose and meaning in their lives across the campus. Yet only the naïve believe that student affairs and academic affairs work hand-in-hand on most campuses. Although cooperative efforts exist between those two divisions, student affairs professionals often believe that they can offer much more to professors in helping them promote student learning. So questions about the relationship between community building in student affairs as it relates to community building in academic affairs could precipitate activities between the two units regarding the development of student spirituality.

We think the third type of life Urmson cites, the life of theoretical contemplation, should be central to the purpose of the academy, but, ironically, such a life has little appeal to most students, and, perhaps, to some faculty. However, the literature on spirituality, in many ways, endorses this life, especially by focusing on the individualistic nature of spirituality linked to ultimate concerns. The juxtaposition of spirituality with individualistic preferences has the force of cutting the individual off from history, in part, because history is the domain of religion, especially the monotheistic religions. So what could be a rich source of materials for stimulating theoretical contemplation—works of philosophy, history, literature, for example—are effectively minimized because grand narratives are replaced by individual narratives. In addition, the intellectual effort required to interact profitably with the body of works that traces the footsteps of Western and world culture is not given much credence in the literature on spirituality, because whatever effort is required to develop one's spirituality is directed toward introspection and outward action. It appears, therefore, that a very fruitful area of research is the role of theoretical contemplation as it relates to spirituality. We think the research possibilities for such an undertaking would be attractive to many faculty and would be a bridge for introducing spirituality to students.

Conclusion

Nord and Haynes (1998) have observed that "no hard and fast lines can be drawn between spirituality, traditional religion, and those functional 'secular' religions that shape the thinking and lives of so many people" (3–4). Perhaps they have pinpointed an essential premise concerning research about spirituality. If so, the dichotomy between spirituality and religion, which we believe is forced, would have to be replaced by a much more sophisticated understanding of spiritual concerns.

Can research on a topic as personal as spirituality be productive and profitable? We believe it can not only be that but also rewarding. The students who come to our colleges and universities are seeking not only knowledge but also truth. They seek knowledge outside themselves and within themselves. As educators, we have an obligation to guide them in both quests. However, is the academy open to *any* exploration of spirituality? Astin and Astin (1999) provide evidence that the faculty they interviewed "were able and willing to speak openly about the role of either 'spirituality' or 'meaning and purpose' in their professional and personal lives" (31). Indeed, Astin and Astin make a point that could also be a lodestar for research on spirituality when they say, "…academia has for far too long encouraged us to lead fragmented and inauthentic lives, where we act either as if we are *not* spiritual beings, or as if our spiritual side is irrelevant to our vocation or work" (2). If spirituality really does have some sort of ontological status, then the unfortunate consequences of denying that status—fragmented and inauthentic lives—will cry out for wholeness and authenticity. The scholarly study of spirituality, marked by genuine inquisitiveness and a willing suspension of disbelief, will provide opportunities for the denizens of the academy to explore the value of spirituality in answering questions during the search for truth.

References

Astin, A. W., and H. S. Astin. 1999. *Meaning and spirituality in the lives of college faculty: A study of values, authenticity, and stress.* Los Angeles: Higher Education Research Institute.

Beaudoin, T. 1998. *Virtual faith: The irreverent spiritual quest of Generation X.* San Francisco: Jossey-Bass.

Fuller, R. C. 2001. *Spiritual, but not religious: Understanding unchurched America.* Oxford: Oxford University Press.

Glanzer, P. L. 2004. Taking the tournament of worldviews seriously in education: Why teaching about religion is not enough. *Religion & Education* 31(1):1–19.

Hicks, D. A. 2003. *Religion and the workplace: Pluralism, spirituality, leadership.* New York: Cambridge University Press.

Nash, R. J. 2001. *Religious pluralism in the academy: Opening the dialogue.* New York: Peter Lang.

Nord, W. A., and C. C. Haynes. 1998. *Taking religion seriously across the curriculum.* Alexandria, VA: Association for Supervision and Curriculum Development.

Roof, W. C. 1993. *A generation of seekers: The spiritual journeys of the baby boom generation.* San Francisco: HarperSanFrancisco.

Roof, W. C., and W. McKinney. 1985. Denominational America and the new religious pluralism. *Annals of the American Academy of Political and Social Science* 480(July):24–38.

Schaper, D. 2000. Me-first 'spirituality' is a sorry substitute for organized religion on campuses. *The Chronicle of Higher Education* 46(50):A56.

Speck, B. W. 1998. Relativism and the promise of tolerance. *Journal of Interdisciplinary Studies* 10(1–1):67–84. Quoting F. Beckwith, 1994 www.iclnet.org/put/resources (accessed 1997).

Speck, B. W., and S. L. Hoppe. 2004. *Service-learning: History, theory, and issues.* Westport, CT: Praeger.

Tisdell, E. J. 2001. Spirituality in adult and higher education. *ERIC Digest.* ED 459 370.

Urmson, J. O. 1988. *Aristotle's ethics.* Oxford: Blackwell.

Wakefield, D. 2002. Maintaining a Christian institutional identify while embracing religious diversity. *Religion & Education* 29(2):90–102.

Wolfe, A. 2002. The potential for pluralism: Religious responses to the triumph of theory and method in American academic culture. In *Religion, scholarship, & higher education: Perspectives, models, and future prospects*, ed. A. Sterk, 22–39. Notre Dame, IN: University of Notre Dame Press.

CONTRIBUTORS

Diane Berty has more than 25 years of experience in student affairs and currently serves as the Vice President of Student Development at East Central University in Ada, Oklahoma. She earned her Ed.D. in Educational Leadership at Tennessee State University and completed post-doctoral work in Higher Education Administration at that same institution.

DeMethra LaSha Bradley serves as Assistant Director for Academic Integrity in the Center for Student Ethics and Standards at The University of Vermont (UVM). Her research interests include religious and spiritual differences on college campuses, social class, and student ethical development. She is pursuing her doctorate in Educational Leadership and Policy Studies at UVM.

Paul Brink is Associate Professor of Political Science at Gordon College, in Wenham, Massachusetts, where he teaches political theory and comparative politics. His current research considers questions of religion and difference in contemporary political theory. He holds a Ph.D. from the University of Notre Dame.

Larry D. Burton is Professor of Teacher Education at Andrews University, Berrien Spring, Michigan, USA. His research interests include science education and the integration of faith and learning, particularly within the context of private education.

Deborah Cady is the Associate Dean of Students at Fairfield University in Fairfield, Connecticut. She received her Ph.D. in higher education administration at Boston College, her M.Ed. at the University of Vermont, and her B.A. from Saint Michael's College. Deb has worked in a variety of roles in student affairs, including residence life, student activities, new student programs, leadership development, student conduct, and religious and spiritual life.

Laurel H. Campbell, Ed.D, is an Assistant Professor of Art Education in the School of Art & Design at the University of Illinois at Urbana-Champaign. Her research interests are spirituality in education, holistic art education, teacher development, and research methodology. Current projects include qualitative research on reflective practice in teacher education. Her teaching career spans 10 years in both private and public K–20 education.

Jon Dalton is Associate Professor in Educational Leadership and Director of the Hardee Center for Leadership and Ethics <http://www.fsu.edu/~elps/hardee/>. He has been at Florida State University for 15 years and served as Vice President for Student Affairs from 1989–1999. He directs the annual Institute on College Student Values each February that focuses on moral and civic education in college student learning and development. He serves as Editor of the electronic *Journal of College and Character* <http://www.collegevalues.org/> published on the Internet at www.CollegeValues.org. He is a Past President of the National Association of Student Personnel Administrators (NASPA). His research interests are in college student development, moral and civic education, organization and management of student affairs services, ethics in higher education leadership, and international educational exchange.

Contributors

Albert DeCiccio is Academic Dean and Professor of English at Rivier College. DeCiccio is a past President of the National Writing Centers Association (now the International Writing Centers Association); he also served a five-year term as co-editor of *The Writing Center Journal*. DeCiccio regularly contributes articles and presentations about collaborative learning, writing, and writing center theory and practice. In addition, he writes about and researches the first-year experience, three times presenting for the National Resource Center's International Conference on the First-Year Experience.

Dixie Dennis is Chair and Professor in the Department of Health and Human Performance at Austin Peay State University in Clarksville, TN. She holds a B.S. and M.S. degree from Austin Peay State University and a Ph.D. in Health Education from Southern Illinois University Carbondale. Dr. Dennis engages in journal reviewing/editing and scholarly publications, particularly in the area of spirituality. Currently, she has a book, *Living, Dying, Grieving*, in press.

David Eberhardt is a doctoral student at Florida State University, currently completing his dissertation in college student spiritual development. He also serves as a Research Associate in the Hardee Center for Leadership and Ethics, where he works on various administrative and research projects and writes a monthly Ethical Issues on Campus column for the electronic *Journal of College and Character*. Prior to his doctoral studies, he spent 10 years serving in diverse Student Affairs roles at several liberal arts colleges in the southeastern United States.

Bryce E. Fox is an Associate Professor at Trevecca Nazarene University where he teaches in the School of Religion and the Department of Graduate Psychology. Bryce is an ordained minister and earned his M.A. in counseling from Asbury Theological Seminary, and his Ph.D. from Indiana University in Developmental Psychology.

Keith Garner has ten years of campus ministry experience on both secular and Christian-based campuses. He is a graduate of Texas Tech University, BS 1992 and Southwestern Baptist Theological Seminary, M. Div. 1998. Keith currently serves as the Baptist Student Ministries Director at Texas Tech University in Lubbock, Texas.

Sherry L. Hoppe has been president of Austin Peay State University since 2000. A 30-year veteran of Tennessee higher education, she previously served as president of Roane State Community College for twelve years and was also interim president of Nashville State Community College. In addition, she held several leadership positions at Chattanooga State Technical Community College. She holds an Ed.D. from the University of Tennessee. The co-author of a biography on the life and work of civil rights activist Maxine Smith, she has also co-edited two volumes on service learning as well as sourcebooks on identifying and preparing academic leaders and spirituality in higher education.

Elliott Ingersoll is a psychologist in private practice and a professor at Cleveland State University. His research interests are counseling and spirituality, psychopharmacology, and

Integral Theory. He is a founding member of Integral ReSource Group and lives in Kent, OH, with his wife and two children.

William Jenkins is a professor of literature at Crichton College, Memphis, TN. He is interested in the intersections of religion and culture in America, especially in the ways that pop culture alters expressions and practices of Christianity. His most recent article was on the aesthetic problems of Jesus films.

John Wesley Lowery is Associate Professor in the School of Educational Studies at the Oklahoma State University and Coordinator of the College Student Development Program. He previously served on the faculty at the University of South Carolina. He earned his doctorate at Bowling Green State University in Higher Education Administration. He previously held administrative positions at Adrian College and Washington University. He has a master's degree in student personnel services from the University of South Carolina and an undergraduate degree from the University of Virginia in Religious Studies.

Christina Murphy is the Dean of the College of Liberal Arts and Professor of English at Marshall University in Huntington, West Virginia. Dr. Murphy has published extensively on administrative issues in higher education and is the author of nine books and more than fifty articles and book chapters. She has won national awards for her scholarly publications and has also received national recognition for her work as the editor of the scholarly journals *Composition Studies* and *Studies in Psychoanalytic Theory*.

Robert J. Nash has been a professor in the College of Education and Social Services, University of Vermont, Burlington, for 37 years. He specializes in philosophy of education, ethics, higher education, and religion, spirituality, and education. He holds graduate degrees in English, Theology/Religious Studies, Applied Ethics and Liberal Studies, and Educational Philosophy. He holds faculty appointments in teacher education, higher education administration, and interdisciplinary studies in education. He administers the Interdisciplinary Master's Program, and he teaches ethics, religion, higher education, and philosophy of education courses, as well as scholarly personal narrative writing seminars, across four programs in the college, including the doctoral program in Educational Leadership and Policy Studies. He has supervised over 100 theses and dissertations. He has also published more than 100 articles, book chapters, monographs, and essay book reviews in many of the leading journals in education at all levels; as well as eight books in the last 10 years.

Constance C. Nwosu is Associate Professor of Education at Canadian University College, Lacombe, Alberta, Canada. Her research agenda is focused on the integration of faith and learning in Christian higher education, with particular interests on professional development of teachers, classroom implementation, and also student integration.

Rick Ostrander is Dean of Undergraduate Studies at John Brown University in Siloam Springs, Arkansas. He earned his Ph.D. in American Religious History from the University of Notre Dame. Dr. Ostrander's interest in the history of American spirituality and the history of higher education is attested by his two books, *The Life of Prayer in a World of Science: Protestants, Prayer, and American Culture, 1870~1930* (Oxford University Press, 2000) and *Head, Heart, and Hand: John Brown University and Modern Evangelical Higher Education* (University of Arkansas Press, 2003). He is also a member of the History of American Christian Practice project funded by the Lilly Endowment. In 2004, Dr. Ostrander lectured in Germany on American higher education as a Fulbright Senior Scholar at the University of Wurzburg in Wurzburg, Germany.

Moses L. Pava is the Alvin Einbender Professor of Business Ethics and Professor of Accounting at Yeshiva University's Sy Syms School of Business, where he has been taught since 1988. Pava's research interests include business ethics, financial accounting, corporate social responsibility, and the interface between religion and business. His work in these areas is frequently cited in both the academic and professional literatures. He has written numerous books and articles on these topics including *Leading with Meaning*, *Business Ethics: A Jewish Perspective*, *The Search for Meaning in Organizations*, and *Corporate Social Responsibility and Financial Performance* which was named by *Choice Magazine* as an Outstanding Business Book Selection. In addition, Pava serves as editor of the annual series *Research in Ethical Issues in Organizations* published by Elsevier. He also serves on the editorial boards of *Business Ethics Quarterly* and the *Journal of Business Ethics* and is a frequent contributor to and reviewer for these journals.

Allen L. Pelletier, M.D., FAAFP, is Assistant Professor of Family Medicine at the University of Tennessee College of Medicine in Memphis. He received his M.D. degree from the LSU School of Medicine, Shreveport. Dr. Pelletier is a board-certified family physician and a fellow of the American Academy of Family Physicians.

David K. Scott received his D.Phil. from Oxford University and has worked as a nuclear scientist and as an educator, most recently as the Chancellor of the University of Massachusetts Amherst. He is now interested in creating a Community for Integrative Learning and Action (CILA) and in exploring the role of spirituality in higher education.

Karsten Siebert is a student and graduate assistant in Cleveland State University's Community Agency Counseling program. His research interests are unconscious processes in relationships and spirituality in counseling. Karsten holds a graduate business degree from Universität Osnabrück, Germany, and is a graduate of the International Coaching Program at the Gestalt Institute of Cleveland.

Bruce W. Speck is Provost and Vice President for Academic and Student Affairs at Austin Peay State University in Tennessee. After earning a Ph.D. from the University of Nebraska, he held faculty appointments at Indiana University-Purdue University at Fort Wayne and the University of Memphis. He also served as associate vice chancellor for academic affairs and dean of the College of Arts and Sciences at the University of North Carolina at Pembroke. He has published two books on writing, six annotated bibliographies, and co-edited volumes on assessing online classes, internationalizing higher education, grading students' classroom performance, identifying and preparing academic leaders, spirituality in higher education, service-learning, and teaching nonnative English speakers, as well as authoring a book of poetry. He is the co-author of the biography of Maxine Smith, a civil rights leader in Memphis, Tennessee.

INDEX

Absolute Unitary Being, 77
academic freedom, 58, 126
acceptance, 74–75, 116, 129, 131, 132, 186, 224, 244, 259, 264, 282
Age of Reason, 13
authenticity, 11, 112, 116, 126–7, 133, 143, 262, 287

balance, 53, 90, 98, 105, 125–26, 163, 196, 219, 222, 260–61, 267
behavioral leadership, 112–13, 121, 123
being, 4, 35, 42–43, 47, 111, 115–16, 118–21, 127, 131–33, 141, 143, 204
    Absolute, 6
    divine, 35, 40
    search for, xii, 125
    study of, 3
    supernatural, 38
beingness, 41
beliefs, 35, 37, 39, 44–45, 47, 57–58, 70, 74, 90–91, 100–101, 104, 107, 114–16, 125–28, 133, 139, 144, 149–50, 158, 162–64, 169, 176–77, 182, 184, 192, 197, 214, 217, 224–25, 231–34, 239–43, 245–46, 254–55, 261, 269–70, 285
    Christian, 242
    educational, 227, 230–31
    personal, 48, 153, 158–59, 161, 243, 269
    religious, x, 24, 53–58, 61–62, 65, 169, 217–18, 242, 246
    spiritual, 121, 200, 217, 232, 234, 270
biology, 69, 76–78, 144, 202, 218, 267, 273, 286
Both and Model, 194

Christian, 7–9, 13–15, 21, 24, 60–62, 115, 127, 143, 167, 169, 172, 176, 188, 191–92, 194–95, 197–200, 239, 242, 247, 250, 252, 255, 261, 282
    college, 176, 169, 172–73, 191
    worldview, 115
Christianity, 7, 15, 23, 172, 192–95, 200, 239, 282
civic engagement, 273, 284
civil religion, 7–9
cognitive development, 97–98, 103, 107
conceptual framework(s), 36

congruence, 114, 116, 126, 129–30, 133, 261, 265
consciousness, 22, 36–38, 41–42, 47–48, 71–73, 88, 162, 177, 202, 205–06
constructivism, 16–17, 25
contextual understanding, 116, 130
contingency leadership (theory), 113, 126
Copernican revolution, 204
Cosmology, 37, 205, 252
counseling, spirituality and, 44, 106, 193, 198, 246, 249, 252–56, 272, 276
cultural identity, 99, 106
cultural validation, 44

definitions, 19, 38, 45, 48
    of leadership, 262
    of spirituality, 36, 43, 45, 71, 114, 160, 253, 279–81, 283–84
Dewey, John, 6, 9, 16, 25, 186
dialectic, 12
DNA, 69, 76, 78

empiricism, 4, 11, 210
enlightenment, 4, 5, 8, 11–14, 18–20, 41–42, 86, 203
epistemology, 3–6, 8, 10–13, 16–17, 25, 37, 39–40, 279
ethics, 91, 164, 179, 221–23, 225, 234, 245–46, 251, 255, 261, 280, 283
existentialism, 74–75, 143–44, 253–54

Fiedler, Fred E., 113
First Amendment, 53–59, 61, 63
first year seminar, 90–91
forgiveness, 114, 116, 132, 244
foundationalism, 39
fragmentation, 123, 127, 208
freedom of association, 57, 59
freedom of speech, 56–57, 59
frontal cortex, 71–72

genetics, 69, 21
god(s), 138, 149
God, 9, 18, 23, 76–77, 86, 114–15, 138, 141, 143, 191–95, 199, 205, 214, 250, 281
    appeal to, 7
    belief in, 5, 13, 48, 70
    beliefs about, 70
    essence of, 72
    existence of, 13
    Kingdom of, 142

under, 9
God-directed, 70
God Gene, 75
God's name, 55

healthcare, 17, 209, 214–17, 273
and spirituality, 17–19, 218–19, 285
Holocaust, 179
holographic theory, 207
Humanism, 143, 199
humanities, 4, 181–82, 209

individualism, 19, 26, 49, 123, 203
Integrating Model, 194
integration, 7, 117, 123–26, 133, 159, 194–95, 200, 202, 205, 210, 226, 231–33, 252
intentionality, 40–41
interconnectedness, 42, 46, 117, 124

Jefferson, Thomas, 8
Judeo-Christian, 13
cosmology, 252
faith, 14–15
religion, 13
tradition, 8–9, 282
values, 24
Jung, 72–73, 78, 119–120
junior year seminar, 91

knowledge domains, 38

law(s), 15, 54, 69, 129, 183, 209, 255
leadership trait theories, 112
learning communities, 89, 286
legal issue, 53, 55
Life Attitude Profile-Revised, 74
limbic system, 71–72, 76–77

Maslow, Abraham, 38–39, 111, 113, 131
meaning(s), 11, 19, 25, 35, 37, 40, 44, 71, 74–75, 86, 91, 97, 103, 108, 111–12, 114–15, 117, 119–21, 128, 133, 138–39, 143–45, 148, 151–52, 157, 159, 161–64, 176–77, 179, 203, 224, 249, 261, 269, 272, 274, 276
and purpose, 75, 80, 114, 144, 150, 240–41, 245, 247, 267, 287
in life, 74–75, 80, 100, 114, 117, 123, 147, 160, 245, 262, 267–68, 270–72
in work, 116, 120

-making 98, 106, 120, 264
of life, 44, 72, 98, 100–08, 119–20, 256
of spirituality, 180, 255, 268
search for, xii, 118–19, 240, 243–44, 271, 274
system, 49
to life, 71, 79, 138
mesolimbic dopamine pathway, 72
metaphysics, 3, 9, 26, 36, 283
metaphysical, 3, 4, 7, 24–25, 36, 39, 60, 137, 143–44
moral conversation, 146–53
Muslim, 172, 213, 216–217

narrative(s), 10, 138, 141, 145, 148, 150–51, 157, 159, 169–70
Activism, 142
grand, 10, 286
Mainline Believers, 140
Mysticism, 141–42
Postmodern Skeptic, 144
religious, 139–40, 146, 152–53
spiritual, 139, 144
Wounded Believer, 141
naturalism, 4, 6
neuroscience, 41, 202
neurotransmitter, 72, 76
nursing, spirituality and, 17–20, 24

objectivism, 4, 11
ontology, 3, 283
Opposition Model, 193–94
Ouchi, William, 113

pedagogical approach, 231–34
pedagogy, 11, 23, 92, 172, 279, 283
person-environment theory, 98–99
phenomenology, 41
Plato, 3–4, 94, 210
Pluralism, 8, 21, 25, 49, 101–02, 149, 183–84, 186–87, 205, 279, 281–83
positivism, 4–6, 10, 12–13, 15, 18, 24
postmodernism, 6, 10–11, 25, 205
pragmatism, 6, 9, 16, 25, 181
prayer, 23, 63–64, 90, 103, 193–94
psychoanalytic theory, 191–92

quantum mechanical theory, 205
Quintilian, 88–89

racial identity development, 99
rationality, x, 11, 280–81
reflective practice, 161
reflective teaching, 233
Relational Leadership Model, 128–29, 260–61, 263–64
religion & spirituality, xi, 4, 20–22, 35–49, 51, 53, 58, 80, 101, 114, 138, 146, 162, 164, 213, 215, 217, 219, 240, 283, 285

secularism, 8, 14, 36, 140, 173
self-discovery, 24, 104, 274
self-knowledge, 37, 164
self-transcendence, 76
servant leadership, 122, 133, 243
service learning, 9, 16, 22, 30
slavery, 175–81
social capital, 44–46
social justice, 91, 138, 142–43, 160, 177
social sciences, 4, 5, 245–46, 285
spiritual history, 18, 218
spiritual reflective practice, 158
Spirituality in Higher Education project, 268, 271–72
Supreme Court, 53–56, 59–64, 80, 185

theology, ix, 14, 55, 78, 91, 169
Theory X, 112, 115
Theory Y, 112, 115
Theory Z, 113
tolerance, 25, 116, 131, 151, 261, 279, 281–83
transcendence, 6–7, 9, 24–25, 42, 74–76, 114, 179, 203, 214, 283
transformative leadership, 91
twins' studies, 78

U.S. Supreme Court, 53–56, 59–64, 80, 185
Uncritical Integration Model, 194
ungodly, 191–92
unity, 8–9, 47, 115, 122–24, 128, 133, 159

value, 4, 20–21, 40–41, 91, 94–95, 104, 118, 128–29, 131, 148, 159, 162, 180, 186, 189, 194, 206, 243, 261, 264, 284, 287
value messages, 73
values, 4, 15, 23–24, 40–41, 71, 86, 90, 100–101, 103–105, 107, 116, 126–30, 133, 160, 164, 166, 180, 186, 216, 232, 244, 245, 246, 253, 259, 261–65, 269, 273–74, 276, 283–84
  Christian, 257
  personal, 217, 232, 270
  religious, 218
  spiritual, 181
virtues, 86, 89, 129, 132, 148, 188

well-being, 17, 20, 42, 260, 262, 272
wholeness, 17, 97, 99, 102–03, 105, 112, 115, 123–25, 127, 131–33, 163, 208, 283, 287
worldview, 6, 14, 21, 24, 115, 138, 152, 180, 182, 184, 201, 203, 205, 208–09, 250, 253, 281, 283